Praise for *Software without Borders*:

"It's only logical that the benefits large companies have reaped for so long by using offshore software development resources, would now become an imperative for small- to medium-size companies to capitalize on as well."
—STEVE JURVETSON, Managing Director, Draper Fisher Jurvetson

"This is an up-to-the-minute, common-sense summary of legal issues to be aware of when deciding how and where to do your software development. This book addresses the key ways to protect your intellectual property in offshore outsourcing relationships. It discusses the use of written agreements to protect your interests, as well as the use of other precautionary measures for protecting your intellectual property."
—FRED M. GREGURAS, Of Counsel,
Corporate Group, Fenwick & West LLP

"Outsourcing is the only way many companies can compete effectively in today's global economy—yet most companies have very limited skills and expertise in its execution. For companies willing to 'do their homework' and 'learn the ropes' for selecting and managing offshore software development resources, the potential rewards are high: quick turn time, high-quality output, and substantial cost savings. This book helps you 'learn the ropes.'"
—DAVE SOMMER, VP, E-Commerce,
CompTIA, and Publisher, SoftwareCEO

"Whether it's your first time or you just want to get it right this time, this book puts software development outsourcing success so easily within your reach."
—STEVE BENGSTON, Managing Director of
Emerging Company Services, PricewaterhouseCoopers

"The best programmers are much more productive than the average ones. And you are behind if you aren't using the best—regardless of where they are located. Once upon a time, only the largest organizations dared to split development between locations, and they were the earliest to take advantage of modern telecommunications to go offshore in search of talent. Steve shows how smaller companies—even start-ups—can effectively make use of offshore software development."
—DR. JOHN R. MASHEY, Techviser: Consultant to VCs & Tech
Companies, and former Chief Scientist of Silicon Graphics

"Lower development costs mean greater profits. Offshore outsourcing may be your answer. This book takes you by the hand and helps you get it done quickly, safely, and profitably."
—GALEN HO, Senior Vice President,
Performance Excellence, BAE Systems

"Steve Mezak spotted the merits of the outsourcing trend and understood its impact way ahead of the rest of us. He is now helping us to recognize, cope with and even take advantage of the changes and opportunities outsourcing has brought. The knowledge he shares in this book will help all software engineering organizations that are still grappling with the issues around outsourcing."

—WILLIAM GROSSO, SDForum Board of Directors

"Any company considering outsourcing its software development, needs this book. It's the first and last word on getting it done on a cost-effective, quick, professional, and safe basis."

—DR. MARSHALL J. BURAK, Dean Emeritus, College of Business, San Jose State University

"The foundation of any successful development project is appropriately identifying, tailoring, and then applying proven best practices. There are no absolute rules, but instead choices that must be made based on wisdom and context. Choosing well—and then executing—is the path to success. The challenge, then, is how to make choices when you may not have the desired wisdom, and executing when you don't have the experience. One way to overcome this challenge is to leverage the wisdom of others. This is what you're doing when you're reading this book. You're leveraging the wisdom and experience that Steve Mezak has acquired through many years of successful outsourced engagements. You'll find that it is both a great read and a valuable reference."

—LUKE HOHMANN, founder & CEO, Enthiosys, Inc. and author of Beyond Software Architecture: Creating and Sustaining Winning Solutions and Innovation Games: Creating Breakthrough Products Through Collaborative Play

"Steve has provided good insight into how to prepare a software development project for outsourcing—and he has appropriately noted there are no "silver bullets." Especially useful is the peppering of the book with real-world examples from his own successes and challenges. A great resource for companies interested in being successful with outsourcing!"

—JON KERN, Agilist

"Outsourcing and open source can be great complements—managed properly. Managed improperly, either can pose significant risks to your business. Software without Borders provides a recipe for outsourcing success. A must-read."

—BERNARD GOLDEN, CEO, Navica, Inc. and author of Succeeding with Open Source

"The Internet enables instant 24/365 communication between programmers and engineers around the world. This book shows you how to collaborate with global engineering talent and accelerate your software development."

—ANU SHUKLA, founder, President & CEO, RubiconSoft, Inc.

"Outsourcing has become ubiquitous. As an Agile software development and project management consultant, nearly all of the companies I work with use some degree of outsourcing for their software engineering. The cost savings are evident, but the results aren't always optimal. This book captures Steve's extensive experience with software outsourcing. It will help you get the most out of your outsourcing initiatives."

—KEN COLLIER, Ph.D., President, KWC Technologies, Inc.

"The chapter on offshoring is a key chapter in Steve's book. The data is accurate and the challenges of working in India and China are well-described—as are the opportunities. Some of the finer insights include an understanding of the Indian environment, such as the factors that lie behind recruitment, and issues to do with corporate governance and ramp-up rates. All in all, I am very happy to recommend that this book be read."

—RAFIQ DOSSANI, Senior Research Scholar, Stanford University

"Eliminate the dangerous learning curve for outsourcing. This step-by-step, 'how-to' guide will save you time, money, and major headaches."

—RAJESH SETTY, author of Beyond Code

"Many of the companies using outsourcing for their software development fail to realize the legal requirements for ensuring that they wind up actually owning all of the software that they pay for. *Software without Borders* explains these important requirements in language that any reader can understand."

—JOEL RIFF, GCA Law Partners LLP

"Whether you're an outsourcing veteran or are considering it for the first time, this book gives you all the information you need to hook up with worldwide software development teams, enabling you to deliver more products more quickly, in parallel, and at a reduced cost."

—TREB RYAN, CEO, OpSource

"The lessons learned by outsourcing's greatest successes and most miserable failures are clearly and concisely detailed here, making it a valuable primer for anyone farming out their software development to offshore resources."

—NAGHI PRASAD, VP of Engineering, Verity

"WPI is a pioneer in producing internationalized engineers. Talent recognizes no borders. Well-educated, technically-adept software developers around the world are available to deliver reliable software quickly and inexpensively. And this book shows you how to connect with them"

—RICHARD F. VAZ, Associate Professor,
Worcester Polytechnic Institute

"Software developers, CTO's, and CIO's everywhere are grappling with the need for inexpensive and immediate interface between programmers and engineers. Offshore outsourcing is the answer. And this book gives you the tools to help you choose your outsourcing vendors wisely and to engage in successful, long-term relationships with them."

—KEN BELANGER, CEO, Informia, LLC

"The question isn't if companies should rely on these offshore software development resources, it's rather how do they find the best vendors the fastest and optimize their relationship with them. This book answers those very critical questions."

—DR. BORIS ROUSSEV, Associate Professor of Information Systems, University of the Virgin Islands and Co-Author of the Book, Management of the Object-Oriented Development Process

"Global technology needs global leadership, and Steve Mezak's book provides a comprehensive blueprint. If your company is working across borders, you need this book."

—MARK GERZON, author of Leading Through Conflict: How Successful Leaders Transform Differences into Opportunities

"The world is shrinking when it comes to software development. There are so many possibilities to take advantage of. This book gives you the information you need to leverage that talent, enabling you to deliver value more quickly, and in a cost-effective way."

—BOB SCHATZ, Chief Development Officer, Solstice Software, Inc.

"A clear and comprehensive guide for anyone working in the software industry, both novices and seasoned veterans. This book gives a practical view of how you can use outsourcing to make your business more successful."

—BERT VERMEULEN, founder, Corp21, providing consulting, incubation, and investment services to businesses

THE RISK-FREE OUTSOURCING SERIES

SOFTWARE without BORDERS

a STEP-BY-STEP GUIDE to OURSOURCING YOUR SOFTWARE DEVELOPMENT

STEVE MEZAK

Earthrise Press
Los Altos, California

Published by
Earthrise Press, Los Altos, California, USA

First Edition, June 2006

Editing by Rebecca Pepper
Text design and formatting by Bookwrights
Cover text by Graham Van Dixhorn of Write To Your Market, Inc.
Globe art courtesy of www.Mapability.com
Screen shots of eBay website Copyright © eBay, Inc., all rights reserved, and have been used with their permission.

Printed and bound in Canada

ISBN-13: 978-0-9778268-0-3
ISBN-10: 0-9778268-0-5

Dedication

For my brother John, who taught me a long time ago that an engineer is supposed to know what the #$%^ he or she is doing.

"We must learn to live together as brothers or perish together as fools."

— Martin Luther King

"Outsource everything but your soul."

— Tom Peters, author of
In Search of Excellence and *Re-Imagine*

Contents

Preface

Did you ever get stuck in a rut, doing things in the same old way, and then heard or seen something that completely changed your perspective and you could never be satisfied with the old way again?

Can you imagine going back to using a typewriter instead of a word processor on a computer? No way!

Sometimes you go looking for a new approach out of frustration with the old. Other times a new perspective comes like a bolt out of the blue when you least expect it. You may not even know you have a limited perspective—like a fish that doesn't know it is underwater.

I had such an experience 37 years ago. It happened on Christmas Eve in 1968. A few days earlier three astronauts were blasted into space from Florida. It was the launch of Apollo 8—the first manned space mission to leave earth orbit.

I was 12 years old then, curled up on a cozy armchair in my parents' living room in New Jersey. It was a cold night, and a fresh snowfall was outside. Our Christmas tree was in one corner of the room, and our TV was in the other.

By Christmas Eve, the astronauts had entered into orbit around the moon and broadcast a televised message back to Earth. The picture was a little grainy, but it was in color. It showed the surface of the moon below and sometimes the Earth in the distance each time they came around the front side of the moon.

The astronauts read from the Book of Genesis in the Bible during the telecast. For me, this feat of human engineering, combined with the spiritual imagery of the reading, was deeply awe inspiring.

A few days later, on December 29, 1968, one of the astronauts snapped a photograph that has become an icon of manned space travel. It is the earthrise photo showing the Earth nestled in space with the surface of the moon below.

In that single photographic frame was an image that included all of humanity. Suddenly our geographic, economic, and personal differences seemed very small.

It is popular to think of the world as a small, flat place these days. But the reality is that we are all on one small, round planet in an adroit orbit around the sun. We are all in the same boat. We are all inextricably interconnected, whether you realize it or not.

How about you? Are you globally connected? Are you taking advantage of all the resources granted to you on this small planet we live on?

My wish is that this book will give you a new perspective on the global resources available and how to use them effectively. Yes, you can save a great deal of money by doing software development offshore. And you can get better-quality software in the deal as well. But there is something else.

I hope you also come to appreciate other people and places in the world, their culture, customs, and values. Low-cost offshore out-sourcing is a convenient business reason that can bring us all closer together. And that has to be good for all of us on this planet.

Steve Mezak
May 2006

Who Should Read This Book?

- CIOs or IT managers responsible for application development
- CEOs, CTOs, or VPs of engineering or product development who are responsible for creating software products
- VPs of product marketing and product managers working with customers and engineers to design and implement software products and applications
- Programmers and software developers who need to understand the forces of outsourcing and how it will affect their career
- Outsourcing executives who want to understand the business from a client's perspective

Acknowledgments

To my friends and fellow authors that gave me great inspiration, humor and support over the last year—I couldn't have finished this book without you!

Deborah Baker-Receniello	Dr. Bruce Eichelberger	John Eggen
Dr. Douglas Rice	Howard Greenfield	Robert Middleton
James R. McCarthy	Lorna McLeod	Rob Holdford

Many thanks to you all that helped me with the publishing process:

Betsy Taub	Chelise Ellis	Katie Banks
Jill Clair	Ron "Hobie" Hobart	Mayapriya Long

Thanks to my peer reviewers that suffered through my first drafts and were kind to reply with excellent criticisms and suggestions:

Alexey Selin	Alistair Cockburn	Andrew Keenan
Anu Shukla	Barry Mason Rubenstein	Bernard Golden
Bert Vermeulen	Bob Schatz	Boris Roussev
David Sommer	Dennis Elenburg	Edward A. Ipser, Jr.
Fred Greguras	Galen Ho	Joel Riff
John Lee	John R. Mashey	Jon Kern
Karl Wiegers	Ken Belanger	Ken Collier
Lance Travis	Luke Hohmann	Mark Gerzon
Marshall Burak	Marta Rodriguez	MR Rangaswami
Naghi Prasad	Paul R. Niven	Rafiq Dossani
Rajesh Setty	Richard Vaz	Sanford Rockowitz

Steve Blank	Steve Connors	Steve Jurvetson
Tom Poppendieck	Treb Ryan	Vivek Swarnakar
William Draper	William Grosso	Yair Raz

And finally my sincere thanks to all that gave their advice on the title of the book, especially my old friend Professor David Cyganski who spent hours on end with me brainstorming a long list of titles, and last, but not least, thanks to all of you that voted for your favorite title:

[Wong] Kwok Wai	Abdol Rahman Said	Abha Gupta
Achu Kamath	Aditya	Akhilesh Soni
Alexandr Tszyu	Alfio Mizzi	Allen L. Mitchell
Alphonso G Archer	Ameet Zaveri	Amit Srivastava
Andrew Wallen	Anthony Bristol	Antonio Navas
Antonio Sangermano	Anup Mathur	AP
Athanasios Pavlos	Athar Osama	B. A. Aravinda
Balasubramanian S.	Barney Pell	Ben Kennedy
Ben Woodacre	Bhavesh Garg	Bhumika Ghimire
Boris Roussev	Brook Gonsowski	Calvin Hesson
Carolyn	Carolyn J. Black	Chandima Cooray
Charles Polgrean	Charlie Destries	Charlie Mezak
Charly El-khoury	Chas. Dye	Chepuri Krishnamurthy
Christopher David	Christopher Hall	Christopher Stolk
Clay Bullwinkel	Clive Boulton	Cory Smith
Craig Maccubbin	Craig Rosenberg	Cynthia Jordan
Dana Thomas	Daniel Rutten	Daniel Ulibarri
Dave Dwyer	Dave Schultz	David Angers
David B Rainard	David Cyganski	David Dooley
David E. Douglas	David Feldmeier	David Hall
David Shirley	David Silber	David Weir
Dean Stevens	Dennis VanHorn	Dev Ramnane
Dian Schaffhauser	Dmitriy Kruglyak	Dr. Douglas Rice
Ed Oliveira	Ed Prentice	Ejaz Ahmed
Elie Asmar	Ellie Skeele	Emiliano Zulberti
Emmanuel Agu	Eric Mariacher	Ernie Baker
Evan J. Abrams	Evelyn Fong	Faisal Buafra
Fernanda Gomes Luz Braga	Frank Zhang	Fred Greguras
Gary Khan	George Parsons	Gerry D'Agostino
Gloria Bolden	Handmade Interactive	Harpreet Khurana
Harris & Moure, pllc	Hauke Daempfling	Heinz Platten

Hong Xue
Ihor Seheda
Jackie Lewis
James R. Connor
Jay Bhandari
Jeff Meister
Joe Blank
Joel Riff
John Griesing
John Nemeczky
Jose Magaña
K R Prasad
Kamaraju Sivva
Ken Landoline
Kevin Wong
Kunal Sharma
Larry Roffelsen
Lisa Anderson
M.S Sivakumar
Manjeet Singh
Mario Chaves
Marty Pine
Maurice F. Kiely
Michael Doilnitsyn
Michael Mankowski
Mike Kodumudi
Nagraj Venkataraman
Naveen Yadav
Nilesh Waghchoude
Orlando Ramirez
Pat Brooks
Patricia Wahlstrom
Paul Isham
Peter Trurnit
Philip Gust
Pradeep Ravi
Professor Carl Hewitt
Radha Krishna Mocherla
Rahul Purohit
Rajaraman Manivannan

Hugh Morgan
Inna Ashmanski
Jagdish Reddy
James Veilleux
Jay Farmer
Jie Yang
Joe Gomes
John David Quartararo
John Lee
John Pallett
Jose Dupoux
Kai Reu
Kapil Arora
Kevin C. Gormican
Koushik Kumaraswamy
Lakshma Gopidi
Larry Somrack
Loren David Liebling
Mahesh Pillai
Manuel Coronado Arreaga
Marius Panait
Marty Tenenbaum
Md. Iqbal Hasan
Michael Kustanas
Michael Prozan
Monty Swaiss
Nambi Sankaran
Neeraj Nityanand
Nimi Devaprasad
Paraiso Jerry
Patrice A. McClintock
Patrick
Paula Mezak
PG Lim
Phong Le
Prakash Kini
R. Male
Radomil Novak
Raj Gidvani
Rajesh Setty

Ian Ferguson
Jack Morre
Jagdish Reddy
Javier Cásedas
Jeff Hotz
Jim Mathios
Joel Kaplan
John Gardner
John Mashey
John Perkins
Judy Winestone
Kai Zeng
Kelly Ireland
Kevin Ryan
Krishnarao Rahalkar
Lakshmi Karthigeyan
Linc Jepson
Luke Hohmann
Manilal K M, Kerala
Manuel Gonzalez
Mark Graham
Matt Musiak
Merwin Mathew
Michael Levy
Michelle Messing
Mukali Vatapetam
Nari Kannan
Nikk Syal
Obii Obiji
Parijat Agarwal
Patricia Block
Patrick O'Malley
Peter Miller
Phil Sakakihara
PMP Mario Gonzalez
Pratik Mehta
Rabi Karmacharya
Rahul Arora
Raj Kosaraju
Randolf Kissling

Ravi Chandran C.R.	Ravi Kotti	Ravishankar Anand
Reiko Sota	Rich Mironov	Richard Berge
Richard Bullen	Richard Scheel	Rick Marshall
Rik Dryfoos	Robert A. Jones	Robert Zager
Rod Homer	Russ Aldrich	Russ Horton
Sam Farsaii	Sandeep Jain	Sandeep Pande
Sanjay Mathur	Sanjeev Mohan	Satish Chohan
Saumitra Das	Saurabh Gupta	Serge Ashmansky
Seshadri Iyengar	Shrenik	Sidarth Ambardar
Siddartha Mukerjee	Smita Yedekar	Sridhar Keppurengan
Srini R. Srinivasan	Stephen L. Johnson	Steve Bernardez
Subbu Ponnuswamy	Subramanian Raghavan	Sudipto Dey
Sumit Mishra	Sunil Daryanani	Superstar
Suresh C. Narayan	Swati Thakar	Tauqeer Bashir
Tenzing Norbu Lama	Teresa M Grant	Tim Walger
Tony Lavia	Uday Madireddy	Valdo Rojas
Venkata Chalam	Venkata Krishna Kavarthapu	Vijay Shah
Vijayakumar	Vineeta Kautuk Naik	Vinod Sood
Vinten Chai	Vivek Swarnakar	Walt Froloff
Walter Creech	Walter Tijiboy	Wayne Lin
Wayne Xie	Wing Huen	Yaary Kochavn
Yahya Mahmoud	Yair Raz	Yongnan Liu

Introduction

It was a fine spring day in Denver. The snow was melting from a late-season snowstorm, not unusual for Colorado this time of year.

The CIO was busy dealing with a networking problem. The firewall system was not letting all the traffic through for the new web services interface for the supply chain software that had just been installed.

He was interrupted by a call on his cell phone. "Jack, we have a problem." What else is new? Jack thought and almost said it.

"It's the new data warehousing project," Mary said. "It's behind schedule again."

"So what else is new?" This time he did say it.

Mary said, "Yes, I know, but we really need to do something about it. These consultants we've hired are costing us an arm and a leg, and progress has been so slow."

That's what we get for paying them by the hour, thought Jack. As the saying went, use a small brush if you are paid by the hour to paint.

Mary continued, "They are working as hard as they can, and they are even spending some extra hours they are not billing us for."

"Then what do you suggest?" Jack asked.

"It's the way the project is being managed," Mary said. "We thought having all the programmers here would reduce the need for specifications. But at the rate we are going, we are going to blow our budget for this project in the first three months."

Jack could see it coming. The pressure from the CEO to outsource this project would be inexorable now. "We are going to have to find a way to make offshore outsourcing work for this project."

"I know," Mary said reluctantly.

∾ᘯᘲᘲᘯ∾

It was a rainy Wednesday in Silicon Valley. The young entrepreneur was getting into her car to drive up to Sand Hill Road for an appointment with a venture capitalist. Kelly had made the connection through a friend who was working at another startup in which this VC had invested.

Even though this was not her first investor presentation, she was a bit nervous. "I won't need a Peet's coffee this morning," she thought. That would make her too jumpy.

She had just the right amount of information in her PowerPoint presentation covering sales, marketing, and software development. She was looking to raise $5 million in this first round.

"It's nice to know you think you can build this into a $100 million company in four years," said the VC, "but what we really want to know is how you are going to get customers to pay your first million in sales."

Another VC in the room asked, "Do you really need $5 million? You know this isn't 1999 anymore. How will you spend the money we give you?"

Kelly jumped ahead to the PowerPoint slide showing the budget. So much for her carefully planned presentation!

"Those engineering costs seem rather high. Aren't you outsourcing your software development?"

"We feel it is too risky," said Kelly.

"You'd better reconsider or at least find some way to reduce those product development costs," said the other VC.

Afterwards, Harry, the VP of engineering, asked Kelly, "How did it go?"

"I am not going back into another VC meeting until you tell me how we are going to outsource the product development."

"I thought we went over this already. It is too risky to outsource."

"Well, they say it is too expensive *not* to do it. And they are not going to fund us if they think we are throwing money away on engineers here in Mountain View. So you are going to have to find a way to make it work."

"What about programming jobs leaving the U.S.? Don't they care about that?"

"No, of course not. And frankly, I am losing interest in that argument as well. If we don't find a way to make outsourcing work, we won't get funded and none of us are going to have jobs. And I don't mean just you and me—I mean the dozens of marketing, sales, and support jobs we are creating. They will all go away. Unless you can make outsourcing work, and make it work quickly."

❦

Vijay had just hung up the phone. It was midnight in his condo in New Jersey, and he had just finished a conference call with his brother Sandeep back in Bangalore, India. It was 9:30 in the morning of the next day in India. Sandeep was having trouble with the team. Another engineer had quit.

Or more accurately, he never came to work to begin with. It is common for an engineer to accept multiple job offers and just go to the one he likes the most without letting the others know. It would be impolite to turn down a job offer in India.

But Vijay knew that Sandeep would handle it. He always did. After all, he had built up their small team of six engineers and created the software product in just eight months. They had funded it with their combined savings of just under $50,000.

Now Vijay was about to close a big deal with a client he had first met almost a year ago. Seeing the problems they had managing inventory gave him the idea for the software and caused him to start the company to begin with. The risk of using his savings to develop the software was finally about to pay off.

Thank God for Sandeep and the engineers in India! Vijay thought. There was no way they could have afforded to develop this software in New Jersey. All that uproar about jobs moving offshore, he thought. Vijay shook his head. "Some people just don't know an opportunity when they see one." He said it out loud to no one in particular.

❦

From San Jose to Boston in the United States and in many other countries as well, these scenes are played out every day. Many people know about the promise of outsourcing—lower costs and accelerated completion of programming projects and software products. And yet deciding to outsource is not an easy decision for many companies. Is outsourcing only for the foreign-born entrepreneurs and executives?

In his book *Crossing the Chasm*, Geoffrey Moore introduces the concept of innovators and early adopters, who are the first to become involved with a new trend or product. When it comes to outsourcing, it seems that we have crossed the chasm from this first stage to encourage an early majority of people and companies that now find value in outsourcing. They believe that outsourcing of software development has been tried and tested by the early adopters and now is safe for them to try.

Or is it? Studies have shown[1] that more than half of outsourced work fails to meet financial goals. So have all the problems, risks, and dangers really been eliminated? Is it safe for you to outsource your software development? Given the pressure to outsource, how can you decide whether outsourcing is even appropriate for your company?

This book will help you decide. I have faced these questions in deciding to outsource my own software development. In some cases I was told I had to outsource; in others I made the decision myself. Together we will explore the issues of outsourcing—when to do it, where to do it, and how to do it. Even when *not* to outsource.

In this book, you will discover practical solutions to the problems that arise when outsourcing. The overall goal is to make your outsourcing as risk-free as possible. Each chapter presents an outsourcing issue and shows how you can navigate past the shoals of other people's mistakes to arrive at the end goal of delivering your software on time, within scope, and on budget. And that budget will be much, much lower when you use offshore outsourcing.

Here is what you'll find in each chapter:

Chapter 1: Deciding to Outsource. What factors should you consider in making your decision? When are the risks of outsourcing too great to bear? If you do decide to outsource, how should you do

---

1. For example, see *Calling a Change in the Outsourcing Market: The Realities for the World's Largest Organizations* published by Deloitte in April 2005. A link to this in-depth study is on the book's web site: www.SoftwareWithoutBordersBook.com.

it? Should you contract with an offshore vendor or one in your home country? Or should you use more than one vendor?

Chapter 2: Where to Outsource. More than 80 percent of outsourcing is done in India. But is that the best place for you? Outsourcing to China is growing rapidly. Is that the right destination for your outsourcing? What about Eastern Europe or Latin America?

Chapter 3: How to Select Your Outsourcing Vendor. What criteria should you take into consideration when selecting your outsourcing vendor? Just having a personal referral to a vendor from a friend or relative is usually not enough. The vendor you choose should meet the business, technical, and time zone criteria that work well for your organization.

Chapter 4: Offshoring, or Creating Your Own Offshore Subsidiary. You can save even more money when you create an offshore subsidiary, because the salary you pay your offshore engineers is lower than the outsourcing rate. But what about the setup costs and management overhead? See if it would make sense for your company to use a partner to build, operate, and then transfer (BOT) your offshore engineering team into your own subsidiary later.

Chapter 5: Describing Your Software for Outsourcing. It is critical for you to have a specification for your software that explains what it should do. Yet you don't need to spend months creating a huge document that rivals the size of *War and Peace* in order to direct your outsourcing effectively. This chapter describes how big your specification should be and what it should contain.

Chapter 6: Controlling Your Outsourced Software Development. Will your internal engineers be working from the same code base as your outsourced team? How will you handle integration if they are working separately? What are agile software development methods, and when should you be using them, whether you are outsourcing or not?

How will you be able to keep in touch with your outsourcing vendor? What tools, in addition to email and instant messaging, can you use to collaborate and to control their work?

Chapter 7: Software Outsourcing Metrics. How will you measure the performance of your outsourced team? What levels of productivity should you expect? Should you measure your results differently for new development than for maintenance programming?

Chapter 8: Protecting Your Intellectual Property. Are there countries you should avoid? What needs to be in your contract to give you the legal protection you need? Besides a contract, what else do you need to protect your intellectual property?

Chapter 9: Outsourcing Your Quality Assurance. Maybe you should start outsourcing with this often neglected part of software development. Do you have a robust QA process in place? Will affordable testing and QA increase the value of your software and company?

Chapter 10: Five Situations Right for Outsourcing. Some companies outsource all software development, and others are more picky. What should you look for in a software project to make it a prime candidate for outsourcing?

Chapter 11: The Future of Global Software Development. Is outsourcing a fad, a flash in the pan? Is globalization good or bad? What can you do to protect your career and thrive if outsourcing continues to grow in popularity?

Appendix A: The Outsourcing Strategy Decision Matrix. Presents the details of a decision matrix described in Chapter 1. You can use the matrix to decide which of five outsourcing strategies is the best for you, if any, or if in-house software development is your best choice. Download the matrix from the book's web site to automatically compute your scores.

Appendix B: The Outsourcing Readiness Test. Twenty questions you can use to determine your readiness for offshore outsourcing your software development.

Appendix C: Avoiding the Seven Deadly Dangers of Outsourcing. Mastering global outsourcing and distributed software development is critical to the success of the software industry. This chapter summarizes the stumbling blocks others have encountered when offshoring their software development and recommends techniques that can help your company avoid months of frustration and could save you hundreds of thousands of dollars.

❧⤳❧

This book gives you an overview of what it takes to outsource successfully and then delves more deeply to give you the specific tools and techniques required. These include spreadsheets and documents you can use directly as well as pointers to other books and reports to give you the background, knowledge, and confidence you need to get you as close to risk-free outsourcing as possible.

Specific real-world examples are used throughout the book to show you how outsourcing is done successfully. Some examples show the pitfalls others have fallen into, and how you can avoid them.

You are welcome to visit the book's web site for updates and corrections as well as links to many useful tools.

Here is the URL:

www.SoftwareWithoutBordersBook.com

I welcome your thoughts on the book and on outsourcing of software in general. You can send me your comments via the book's web site or directly by email to:

Steve@SoftwareWithoutBordersBook.com

Chapter 1

Deciding to Outsource

Whenever you see a successful business, someone once made a courageous decision.

—Peter Drucker

I f you are familiar with Geoffrey Moore's book *Crossing the Chasm*, a veritable bible for marketing at startups in Silicon Valley, you will recognize the concepts of "early adopters" and "innovators." These individuals are the target market for products from early-stage and largely untested startup companies.

Why do early adopters buy and adopt a new software product? It is the thrill of trying something completely new with the hope of being rewarded with a significant benefit before competitors even realize things have changed.

Which side of the chasm are you on with outsourcing? Are you one of those crazy early adopters who tried outsourcing years ago, before it became a trend? Or are you one of the "early majority" who realize that it is safe to try outsourcing now that the early adopters have pioneered the way?

Outsourcing is the key to five of six software development strategies you can employ. In this chapter we look at several situations where outsourcing makes good sense, and we uncover the reasons why. Then we identify 17 criteria that you can use to decide which strategy is best for your own situation. These are delivered as part of a decision matrix that will quickly combine your scores indicating

**"We found someone overseas who can drink coffee
and talk about sports all day for a fraction
of what we're paying you."**

the importance of each criterion and then will calculate the totals for each outsourcing strategy.

Suppose the results show that you should use one of the outsourcing strategies for outsourcing your software development. The next question to consider is, "Are you ready?" For the answer, you can take the online Outsourcing Readiness Test, described in more detail in Appendix B. The 20 questions on the test give you a good idea of your strengths and weaknesses when it comes to outsourcing and where you will need help to improve your chances of success.

Finally, the end of this chapter includes a description of the kinds of help available for your outsourcing decisions. A range of consultants and experts are available to help guide you through the outsourcing process.

"Survey: Outsourcing Saves Less Than Claimed"[2]

You have probably seen reports and articles with that kind of headline. The survey reports that savings average only 15 percent, rather

---

2. This headline is from an article published on April 13, 2006, by ZDNet online at: http://news.zdnet.com/2100-9597_22-6060771.html.

than the 60 percent often claimed by outsourcing vendors. So is out-sourcing a waste of time? Why bother outsourcing to the other side of the world if you don't get the cost savings? Is there some other reason to do it?

Yes, you should be able to cut costs and improve the quality of your software development process. Although the savings vary from situation to situation, more businesses are outsourcing for other reasons than just the cost savings. But let's look at the savings issue a little more closely.

Surveys like this are accurate, but the reduced savings occur when a diverse mix of many different kinds of outsourcing is at-tempted. This survey reports on the "outsourcing of information technology *and* business services," which is much more than just software development. The weaker savings are a reflection of out-sourcing multiple business processes that are not well-defined to begin with.

For example, a company wanted to outsource software develop-ment from their IT department. They had a year's backlog of planned software development projects. At the same time, they decided to also outsource all the accounting and tax preparation from the rest of the company. At the time, the tax returns and accounting were being done in separate business units. They wanted to consolidate these activities and then outsource them. And they wanted to deal with a single vendor for all of it—tax prep, accounting, and software development.

Accounting and software development? That is a strange mix. And the client first needed to figure out what their business process was for tax prep and accounting and then outsource it. This engage-ment had the smell of a disaster about to happen, and it is situations like these that often have less savings than expected.

Also, the size of the companies, engagements, and dollars men-tioned in these surveys are huge. These big deals get the headlines because they are so large, difficult to implement, and then difficult to manage. Decision makers in these situations often have very little sense for the technology used or even the day-to-day operations of their businesses. Decisions are made based purely on a financial analysis, which may not correspond to what is really going on in a multi-hundred-person organization.

But Wait: There Is Still Hope!

In contrast, the outsourcing of a single software development project is a different, simpler story. Suppose you have 12 engineers at various skill levels working for 18 months. Do you think you will save only 15 percent over that time by doing the work in India vs. the U.S.? It's a good bet that the savings will be much, much greater, even when you factor in the extra time needed occasionally for delays in communication. Such delays can be minimized by having the U.S.-based team members participate in frequent meetings by phone.

Let's look at the numbers. Suppose your vendor is one of the more expensive offshore outsourcing vendors and their rates average $5,000 per engineer per month. You will likely pay double that for the equivalent U.S.-based engineers doing the same work. So that is a savings of $5,000 × 12 engineers × 18 months, for a total savings of over $1 million during the life of the project.

The savings are from a combination of lower rates and the offshore team having professional software engineers who really know how to develop a product. Is it perfect? No. Is it easy for you to get up and participate in conference calls every day, even late at night or early every morning at the beginning of the engagement? Probably not. But the results—the cost savings and the high-quality software that is delivered, speak for themselves.

Using these studies as an excuse for not outsourcing is like whistling past a graveyard. There is no question that outsourcing with smaller teams of 5 to 25 software engineers has tremendous cost benefits. Next we look at five situations in which outsourcing of software development offshore is a tremendous benefit.

Four Weddings and Avoiding a Funeral

There are four happy situations in which outsourcing is an excellent and valuable strategy to enhance your success. And there is one situation in which outsourcing can be used to avoid disaster. See if any of these situations fit your company:

1. You are creating your first software product (version 1.0).
2. You need to create a new or an additional software application.

3. You want to augment your internal development team.
4. You need to do maintenance programming on an existing product.
5. You must cut the burn rate to enable your company to survive.

Let's look at each of these situations in more detail.

Creating Your First Software Product

Skepticism from venture capitalists is still prevalent when the use of outsourcing for creating the first software product at a startup is discussed. It is true that outsourcing is not a viable strategy for every startup.

For example, a technical entrepreneur creating a new online game product will want to experiment and try out different ideas. Until the entrepreneur is finished inventing and innovating in source code, he or she is just not ready for outsourcing.

The lesson here is that it is difficult to specify a product when you have not finished innovating how and what the product will do Outsourcing your version 1.0 will require some amount of specification. That is the challenge.

But the advisability of outsourcing also depends on the nature of your innovation. An online game requires technical and artistic innovation that can be difficult or impossible to specify ahead of time. In contrast, an enterprise software application typically uses standard software technology and delivers a business innovation in the way that the software is used. In such cases it is easier to create a specification that in turn enables effective use of outsourcing.

Outsourcing your version 1.0 will also give you an instant development team and accelerate your time to market, or to the users of an internal application at your company.

Creating a New or an Additional Software Application

You can use outsourcing to avoid distracting your existing development team from other important work. Perhaps your new product is an add-on or extension to your main product. You can keep your internal developers working on your main product while the outsourced team completes the add-on. It is usually easy to specify an add-on product by making use of existing product documentation and other "artifacts" from the development process of your main product.

For example, you might use outsourcing to create a version of your software product to address a new market at a low cost. The starting point can be the source code of your main product. Your existing product is then a major component of the "specification" for the new product. You need only add a short description of the changes required in the new user interface.

Augmenting Your Existing Team

You can use an outsourced team to augment the work of your existing development team. This approach gives you the raw manpower required to develop your software, as well as needed technical expertise your internal team may not possess. In addition, you can get round-the-clock development when the outsourced team is offshore and multiple time zones ahead, which will help you get your software developed quickly.

In the past it was common to outsource to a U.S.-based company to acquire special technical expertise, and this is still true today. Face-to-face communication with such a team is very valuable in the early product definition phase. You then have the choice of using your internal team or the outsourced team to do the coding.

Testing and quality assurance (QA) of your software is a terrific way to get started with outsourcing and can provide a critical function that is often understaffed in many software development organizations. Final integration testing that is manually intensive is a good fit for outsourcing. Outsourcing of QA does not mean your own engineers can just toss the code over the wall (or ocean) without doing any of their own testing. Engineers should still perform unit tests of their own code.

Outsourcing of QA often does not require divulging your source code to the offshore team. It lets you try outsourcing while limiting the exposure of your intellectual property. (See Chapter 9)

Handling Maintenance Programming

Maintenance programming for supporting an existing software application or product is a very popular use of outsourcing. Some outsourcing teams specialize in this kind of programming. After an initial ramp-up period, it is easy for them to make incremental changes to your existing code.

At one of my software companies, we used an Indian operation to support version 1.0 after a new version 2.0 had been developed and had become the main product. We still had a few customers who did not want to pay to upgrade, and we were contractually committed to support them with version 1.0. Outsourcing of this non-strategic activity made a lot of sense.

Some people believe that maintenance programming is the only "safe" use of outsourcing. This is not true. There are outsourcing companies that will never aspire to do more than this type of programming. But there are also many outsourced teams of professional programmers that are experts at creating brand new software applications and products.

Cutting the Burn Rate

The need to cut the rate at which you're burning through capital can lead to difficult choices. Highly paid programmers may need to be sacked to extend the life of your company.

In the typical scenario, a software company or IT department starts out by hiring a full engineering team to create a software application. Then software development takes longer than expected. Or the target market was misjudged and it takes longer to close business. Or both. The use of outsourcing in this case can mean the difference between corporate life and death.

Using outsourcing to replace employees can be tricky. You need to keep key employees as a core technical team capable of managing the new outsourced programming team, and to do product management if you are a software product company.

Of course, a better approach is to use outsourcing to minimize costs right from the start.

Outsourcing has definitely matured beyond the early adopters and is now being embraced by the early majority of software companies. It has become an integral part of the product development process at American software companies.

Using outsourcing is like a marriage. It takes commitment from both sides to make the relationship work. Good communication is required. Success factors like these are the lifeblood of thriving companies making effective use of outsourcing.

The Outsourcing Dilemma

Do you have an outsourcing dilemma? Are you being pressured by your CEO, your board of directors, your investors, or your own budget to cut your software development costs? Meanwhile, are you concerned about media reports of public outrage over the trend of vanishing U.S. jobs? Both the real and imagined risks of outsourcing may appear so overwhelming that it seems best to chuck the idea altogether. Is it possible to make a rational and dispassionate decision about whether to use outsourcing at your company?

In 2004 you could tune into any Lou Dobbs show on CNN and hear about Lou's latest entry onto his "Exporting America" list of American companies. These are the companies that are "either sending American jobs overseas, or choosing to employ cheap overseas labor, instead of American workers." It would be easier for Lou to list companies *not* using offshore outsourcing. Nevertheless, his point strikes an emotional chord with many Americans.

Yet your corporation has an obligation to provide attractive pricing to your customers. You must also be responsible to shareholders by accelerating the process of getting new products to market, cutting costs, and increasing profits. What is the "right" thing to do?

Thou Shalt Outsource

I was first exposed to outsourcing at one of my software startup companies in 1991. I was the third person in the company and the first technical hire. I thought my job was to hire a team and develop the software product from scratch. But on the first day, the CEO said he wanted me to manage the outsourcing of the software development.

"Out what?" I asked. He asked me to manage a small custom software development firm in Oregon as they created version 1.0 of our software.

"But I want to write code!" I told the CEO.

He said, "Do you want to write code, or do you want to be a millionaire?"

At first it seemed like a tough choice. But this little company in Oregon had developed a software application for another client that was almost exactly what we needed. They had retained the rights to sell the software to others, and the CEO had negotiated a terrific deal that gave us the software along with the custom changes we needed.

Actually, the choice wasn't so tough after all. I worked well with the team, and my role ended up being one of product manager rather than software engineer. I helped with some technical decisions, but my main responsibility was defining and directing the activities of the outsourced engineers to make sure they kept on track.

Like my situation in 1991, your decision to outsource may come as a directive from someone in charge. The decision to outsource can come from one of two directions. The first is from the top down—from the board of directors and management of the company when they realize that the benefits and cost savings of outsourcing must be obtained for the company. When the top-down directive to outsource is given, managers and engineers are often thrown into a tizzy as they try to decide how and where outsourcing makes sense for their business. Of course, the directive is often given without specific direction, along the lines of, "Just go do it—you figure it out."

The second direction is from the bottom up, when employees are given more work than they can accomplish within the budget they are given. If you are a proactive employee or manager within a company in this situation, you can explore the option of outsourcing as a way to stretch your budget and be more productive. Your task is then to convince management that outsourcing is a safe and productive way to improve your business results.

The good news is that there is now a process and procedure to help you decide the best way to outsource. We will look at 17 criteria to help you make the best choice for your situation. But first I will introduce a useful technique to help you make a more objective decision.

By the way, the company I worked for in 1991 that outsourced to Oregon had a successful public offering of its stock in 1996 and then got acquired at the height of the stock market in 2000 for $9 billion.

An Outsourcing Decision Matrix

Is offshore outsourcing the most economical and reliable way to develop your software? In many cases, the answer is yes. But getting to that answer may be difficult.

Even getting to a defensible answer of no may be difficult. It is one thing to ignore outsourcing and simply continue on your present course. It is another thing to say, "We have looked at outsourcing and decided that it is inappropriate for our company. And here are the three main reasons . . ."

There are many criteria you can use to evaluate your outsourcing decision. Let's look at three—budget, project length, and your need for technical expertise.

I used to think that budget was an overwhelming driver for outsourcing, trumping most other considerations. However, although budget is usually the main reason people have for wanting to outsource, it is just one factor to consider. You may have other factors that weigh more heavily in your decision.

For example, a well-funded financial services software company in San Francisco was hiring Java programmers. Because they have a big budget, outsourcing was not being considered. They wanted to build a team in San Francisco and did not see outsourcing as a desirable option. For them, the cost savings of outsourcing were not as important as other factors they might be considering. Of course, because there is no financial pressure, they may simply be able to continue to ignore outsourcing.

A second criterion for making a decision about outsourcing is project length. Projects lasting less than one year are excellent candidates for outsourcing on a contract basis. The quick ramp-up and relatively low cost of contract outsourcing also make it attractive for many projects lasting longer than a year. Once you've established a satisfactory relationship with an offshore company, outsourcing of multiple projects can occur over a period of many years.

If you do plan to outsource for more than one year, you may want to consider creating a subsidiary to increase your savings. However, taking this route involves more startup expenses and a longer ramp-up time. Contract outsourcing is still a good choice.

The third criterion is your need for technical expertise. Technical expertise may seem like an obvious requirement for an outsourced firm. What I mean here is acquiring expertise your internal team does not possess.

Is it important to quickly bring in particular technical expertise to your company? For example, you may need to create a .NET version of a Borland C++ product that you have now. Do you have time to train the existing team or to hire employees to bring in this new expertise?

You can put these three criteria into a matrix to evaluate multiple software development approaches. For each approach you are considering, you assign each criterion a rating on a scale from 1 to 5, where 1 is a low rating and 5 is high. For example, you can score budget as a 1 for in-house development because it is expensive to hire employees. In comparison, offshore outsourcing can be given a high score of 5 because of low cost.

Let's put these criteria together for a hypothetical company that is evaluating several outsourcing options and in-house development. The company is planning a long-term software development project (longer than one year) but with a limited budget. Another challenge is that the existing engineers employed by the company do not have experience with the new software technology to be used. The decision matrix would look like Table 1-1.

Table 1-1. Simple Decision Matrix for a Hypothetical Company

	Budget	Long-Term Need	Need for New Expertise	Total Score
In-house	1 Low ranking *because hiring employees is expensive*	4 High ranking *because they prefer to keep expertise in-house for long-term projects*	2 Low ranking *because employees will to be trained or replaced*	7
Onshore Outsourcing	2 Low ranking *because onshore outsourcing has about the same cost as in-house development*	2 Low ranking *because they prefer not to use contractors for long-term projects*	5 High ranking *because they can select a team with the needed expertise*	9
Offshore Outsourcing	5 High ranking *because this choice is about one third the cost of employees*	2 Low ranking *because they prefer not to use contractors for long-term projects*	5 High ranking *Because they can select a team with the needed expertise*	12

The numbers entered into the cells rate the software development approach for each of the criteria. For example, in-house development with well-paid engineers, office space, and computers rates only a 1 in the Budget column. In this example, offshore outsourcing receives the highest score and is the best choice for this project when considering only these three criteria.

A decision matrix is a quantitative tool to help you make an objective decision. In the next section we will use a decision matrix with many more criteria. We also use relative weights for the criteria so that their impact is either emphasized or reduced.

You may not need a tool like a decision matrix if you have specific, overriding requirements that quickly lead you to decide to use outsourcing or to avoid it. The sooner you review the issues and make the decision, the sooner you can either cut costs and take advantage of the benefits of outsourcing or eliminate the distracting specter of outsourcing and stay focused on your internal software development efforts.

Six Strategies for Software Development

You have several options for developing your software. Offshore outsourcing is not your only choice.

In-House Employee Engineers

Building a staff of software engineering employees is the classic approach. However, it is also the most expensive one, requiring cash for salaries, office space, and equipment. Filling out the team can take months, and you must also have strong technical management to lead the team, implement an effective software development process, and meet your critical deadlines. This is not always easy, even if you already have some technical talent on your team.

One way to cut costs is to offer stock instead of salary to employee engineers. I have seen several startup companies in Silicon Valley use this approach. It can work well for several months. After that, financial pressures on individual team members and discouragement due to lack of income can lead to attrition and turnover. In other words, paying engineers only with stock is just not a long-term strategy. Although it allows you to reduce salary expenses, you must still pay for office space and equipment.

If you do not have offices and everyone is working from home, you lose the advantages of informal interaction among the individual team members in a company office. Employing a team of widely distributed individual engineers also poses a significant management challenge. You must make sure the results of their work will be useful to the company. It may be better to have these early founding engineers write specifications and create a demonstration prototype for an outsourced project rather than having them write a significant amount of source code that is likely to be thrown away later.

Table 1-2. Pros and Cons of Using In-House Engineers versus Outsourced Engineers

Type of Team	Pros	Cons
Build staff of expert engineers	• Direct access	• High cost of salaries and overhead • Takes months to find, hire, and ramp up • Requires daily management
Hire engineers for stock (free)	• Direct access • Low cost	• Takes months to find, hire, and ramp up • Office and equipment overhead required • Less credibility with customers if you don't have cash to pay employees • Requires daily management • Engineers may be less committed to success with no salary
Use outsourced engineers	• Shorter ramp-up • Low to very low cost • Potential instant team • Built-in project management • True 24-hour development and QA cycle with offshore team • Better financial control	• Potential security issues • Potential communication issues

Table 1-2 lists the advantages and disadvantages of the approaches I've just discussed. As the table shows, using outsourced engineering talent to develop your software has many key benefits and fewer risks compared to the other approaches. The first key benefit is low cost—critical for most projects these days with limited funding. Second, you can hire an instant team, fully staffed with engineers who have worked well together on previous projects. Existing teams are more stable and have a good sense of the strengths and weaknesses of individual members. This leads to more accurate schedules and completion of critical product milestones.

Onshore Contract Outsourcing

Onshore contract outsourcing involves hiring a company in your own country to handle your software development. They may in turn use offshore engineers for some of the work on a large project, but all of your interaction and communication will be with engineers in your country, possibly within your own offices.

This type of outsourcing has several benefits:

- Quick access to technical and/or business expertise
- Fast ramp-up on your project
- Direct, in-person communication and management
- Variable cost rather than the fixed cost of employees

If you have no specifications or time to create any, and you need to communicate your requirements directly, onshore contract outsourcing can be a good alternative.

From a financial perspective, there are two reasons to take advantage of onshore outsourcing. First, you may not be concerned about its higher cost, compared to going offshore. Or other reasons, like those listed above, may be more important to you than cost.

But if lower cost, or at least cash, is a major factor, there is a second financial reason to choose onshore outsourcing. You may be able to negotiate a deal that requires less cash by offering royalties, stock, or some other incentives and bonuses to an onshore company.

Remember my first experience with outsourcing in 1991? In that deal, the outsourcing company in Oregon received royalties from future software sales. They viewed the royalties as a way to make "real money" in the transaction. My company was thrilled to obtain valuable software and programming services for less cash up front.

However, outsourcing in general is a cash-based business. The programming services are delivered and payment is expected promptly thereafter to cover the salary and expenses incurred during delivery of the service. It is unusual for an outsourcing company to accept noncash compensation, but some will for the right opportunity. Even some offshore outsourcing companies will accept stock, but all parties will likely feel safer when they are in the same country under the same legal system governing contracts and stock transactions.

Offshore Contract Outsourcing

The most common form of outsourcing is to contract with a company that is "offshore" or in another country where the labor rates are lower. Some countries like India made science and engineering education a high priority many years ago. The result is a large supply of smart engineers available to write your software.

In addition, many of these engineers have spent time in the U.S. and European countries and are familiar with our language, customs, and business practices. In moving back home, they are able to provide sophisticated software development services that meet our needs extremely well and at a lower cost.

Of course, the Internet is a great enabler of offshore outsourcing and is an instantaneous communication medium for source code, messaging, and voice.

Nearshore outsourcing is outsourcing to a firm in a nearby country. In the U.S., this is outsourcing to Canada, Mexico, or the countries of Central America.

Finally, for any type of outsourcing, the work can either be performed on a time and materials basis (sometimes called time and effort), where you pay for the work performed on an hourly, weekly, or monthly basis, or your agreement can specify milestones at which well-defined features and functions are to be delivered. Payment is then made as each of these milestones is met.

In-House and Offshore Blend

Some companies seek 24-hour software development by using engineers here and an offshore team many time zones away. The idea is that engineers in your company do their programming and check in their work at the end of their day. At about that time, the day of the offshore team on the other side of the world begins, and work can pick up where your engineers have left off.

As a practical matter, this type of blended development, in which two sets of engineers are working on exactly the same code base, is difficult to coordinate. A better approach is to clearly define areas of responsibility in the source code, usually with some independence between the areas so that each team can make uninterrupted progress.

The better the definition of the interface between the two teams, the more independently each team can work productively. Individual engineers on both teams can be given the responsibility to integrate the work of the teams on a regular, if not daily (and nightly), basis.

Offshore Subsidiary

If you are building a large team of software engineers, creating an offshore subsidiary may be the right strategy for you. This approach usually does not make financial sense unless you need fifty engineers or more.

You also need to have tremendous confidence in the strategic value of creating a subsidiary in the selected country. Will you be selling into the market in that country? Do you need to take advantage of low-cost talent there?

Having a subsidiary also gives you the most savings over time because you are paying the lower salaries directly to your engineering employees. However, creating a subsidiary requires some costs up front that the other strategies do not require.

Build, Operate, and Transfer

Rather than creating a subsidiary from the start, an intermediate step is to use a technique known as build, operate, and transfer, or BOT, that is popular in India. You hire an offshore company and they provide engineers on a contract basis. In other words, they build your offshore engineering team and then operate it for you, taking care of human resources and management duties.

In addition, you have the option of transferring these engineers into your own offshore subsidiary after a year or two of contract work. The transfer is just an option—you can continue on with contract outsourcing indefinitely.

BOT is popular with software companies that do not want to start by creating a subsidiary, but that want the option of doing so at a later time. They also want to keep software development as a variable cost, with the flexibility to add engineers and remove them as needed, and even to completely end their outsourcing of software development without financial penalty. Shutting down a subsidiary is not as easy.

Subsidiary creation and BOT are described in more detail in Chapter 4.

Seventeen Criteria to Consider

Now let's put it all together and use a decision matrix with a full set of criteria to determine not only whether outsourcing is right for you, but which of the five outsourcing strategies, if any, is best. There are 17 different criteria to help you compare these options.

These criteria are divided into three categories: political (criteria 1 through 3), business (criteria 4 through 11), and technical (criteria 12 through 17). Each criterion is described briefly here. Appendix A provides a more detailed discussion and helps you rate each criterion on a scale of 1 to 5. The full decision matrix is online and available for you to download at the book's web site, www.SoftwareWithout BordersBook.com.

1. **Concerns about employee morale.** If outsourcing is used, will it have a significant impact on existing employees or cause major upheaval?
2. **Customer concerns about your outsourcing.** Will your customers care if you use outsourced software development to create and test your products?
3. **Cultural affinity.** How comfortable are you working with engineers from another culture?
4. **Export restrictions.** How important are export restrictions on your product?
5. **Other reasons for going offshore.** Your company may need to open an office in another country for sales and support or to maintain a special relationship with a large customer or a partner in that country.

6. **Budget.** Of course, cost is always an issue, but is it a major driver in your outsourcing decision?

7. **Concerns about risk to intellectual property.** Outsourcing will expose the intellectual property of your product to people outside of your company, potentially in other countries. What is your tolerance for this risk?

8. **Speed of ramp-up.** Do you need to start developing your software right away?

9. **Leeway in schedule.** Can your product release schedule tolerate slippages?

10. **Length of project.** Are you planning to continue development with outsourcing over the long term, or are you just filling in to make a deadline?

11. **Impact on value of company.** Are you looking to use outsourcing to enhance the valuation of your company?

12. **Need for domain expertise.** Are you looking to address a new market in areas where your present development team lacks domain expertise?

13. **Need for technical expertise.** Do you need specific technical expertise quickly or for a short-term project?

14. **Status of requirements and specifications.** How well have you captured the requirements of what your software will do?

15. **Need for process compliance and ceremony.** How well defined is your methodology? Do you expect to have a formal process (high ceremony) for document, code, and product reviews?

16. **Team size.** How many engineers do you need to hire to develop your software?

17. **Project type.** The type of software development project you have can influence your outsourcing strategy.

The decision matrix converts your responses to each of these 17 criteria and computes a score for each of the 6 outsourcing strategies.

For example, if you indicate in the decision matrix that you need a small team of engineers to create your software (criterion #16), the matrix adds more points to the score for the offshore contract outsourcing strategy than it does for offshore subsidiary creation, because it is not practical to create an entirely new subsidiary business entity when hiring a few engineers on a contract will suffice. Similarly, if you face export restrictions (criterion #4), in-house development and onshore outsourcing will get more points.

You should not just automatically go with the strategy that has the highest score. The decision matrix is only a tool to explore which is the best outsourcing strategy for you. Sometimes just considering the criteria is valuable in helping you reach a conclusion.

The Outsourcing Readiness Test

Some companies are jumping into software outsourcing before they are ready. They hire a team, maybe the wrong one, and then expect them to start producing software right away. In their rush, they skip the planning, goal setting and careful evaluation of how outsourcing fits into their organization.

What does it mean to be ready for outsourcing? Is there a way to measure your readiness? You can answer a series of 20 questions on the Software without Borders book web site to get an idea of where you stand. The results will tell you if you are ready to go, should proceed cautiously, or should seek immediate help.

One company I met with recently is already outsourcing software development from its engineering group. "How is it going?" I asked. "It depends on who you talk to," I was told. The executives of the company thought it was going great. The company was paying less for engineering talent. Board members seemed satisfied.

But after further conversation, I learned that the engineering department had never really bought into the concept of outsourcing. They resisted working with the outsourced team. Their results were actually less than spectacular. Clearly, this was a company not completely ready for outsourcing.

Another example is this email I received the other day:

> We are looking to get started soon. I would like to get a quote from your firm for its services. I need an auction style site to be built that could withstand up to 10 million hits per day. I need to know how fast it can be built and how much it will cost.
>
> I look forward to hearing from you . . .

In my reply I asked for more information about what was needed. At least a few additional details or some sort of specification is required to give any meaningful answer. If you do not have these details, you are not ready to outsource, especially on a fixed-cost basis.

And if you proceed with outsourcing despite not being ready, you face the risks of extra costs, huge delays, and the complete failure of your outsourced software development.

Why do people start outsourcing without planning? There are different reasons. Sometimes it is ignorance. Other times it is an intense desire to get the software developed as quickly as possible.

Even if you are not completely ready for outsourcing, you can get help to compensate for areas of weakness. That is the other benefit of the readiness test: just by answering the questions honestly, you can focus on the areas where you need help to minimize your outsourcing risks.

The help you need in these areas can come from several different sources. It might be books and articles that describe proven methods for outsourcing. It might be software tools to help you manage outsourcing. Or it might mean hiring additional people that have outsourcing experience.

Whatever your source of help, make sure the people involved have real and proven outsourcing experience.

A good outsourcing team can provide much of the help you need. For example, the team can collaborate with you when you are lacking a complete specification. You can describe the basics of what you need and a series of email conversations can add clarification and detail.

Before you jump into outsourcing, make sure you are ready. Take the test and think about your answers. Be honest. Don't get discouraged if you get a low score on the readiness test. As you'll learn in Appendix C, one of the seven deadly dangers of outsourcing is not taking advantage of outsourcing at all. Learn from your test results and make the changes needed to make your outsourcing as risk-free as possible. Seek out advice and other resources to help with areas where you need improvement.

The 20 questions used in the Software without Borders outsourcing readiness test are in Appendix B. Or take the test on the book's web site.

Reassigning and Repurposing an Existing Team

One of the challenges you may face in considering whether outsourcing is right for your company is what to do with an existing engineering team. I've met many VPs of engineering who are concerned about this problem. They have 10, 20, or 50 engineers, but they realize that they have to embrace outsourcing as a way to save money and increase their productivity.

What do you do with those engineers? We've all heard horror stories about how engineers are used to train the outsourcing team and then are fired. But nobody really wants to do that. There has to be a better way

There are two clear choices. You can either use your existing engineering team for new software development and outsource the maintenance of the old software, or use the existing engineering team, which by now has years of experience with your existing software, for maintenance and have the outsourcing team develop the new software. The latter isn't always an attractive choice because like all engineers, your engineering team will want to work on the new, fun stuff.

Perhaps the best choice is a blend of the two, in which some of your engineers maintain the old software along with the outsourced team. In this scenario, your engineers would often not be writing code themselves. Instead they would direct the activities of the offshore team. Other outsourced engineers would become developers on the new architecture, also directed by your engineering team.

Your existing engineering team would then become more of a management organization—writing specifications, tracking projects, and helping to solve the difficult technical problems that arise. This compromise is the best long-term solution, enabling engineers to transition their careers in a world where outsourcing will continue to become more commonplace.

Getting Help with Outsourcing

If your experience with outsourcing is limited, you should consider getting help with this important decision. There are four types of advisors to consider:

- **Outsourcing strategists** specialize in outsourcing specific business processes like accounting, call centers, or software development. Others are generalists, offering advice on outsourcing in general. Some will help you assess which business processes should be outsourced and which should remain in-house, or whether you should outsource at all. Most will help you locate and evaluate outsourcing vendors and generally will work with you at your site. Some will travel to investigate vendors and help you with the final selection.

Outsourcing strategists are most useful when you have a diverse set of projects or processes that need to be outsourced. If you have just a single programming project, then obviously you don't need a strategist to tell you what to outsource.

These strategists generally charge on an hourly basis and can be engaged for six months or more, depending on your needs. The fees add up, and it is common to spend $50,000 to $100,000 for these advisory services.

- **Brokers** are individuals with connections to more than one outsourcing vendor. They are compensated by a referral fee paid by the vendors they represent. Brokers can help you select a vendor more quickly, as long as it is one of the vendors they represent. They usually do not offer advice on what you should outsource. Brokers are focused on closing business, and you will not have much interaction with them after you select your vendor.

- **Single-country experts** are individuals from a specific offshore country who will help you with vendor selection in that country and can also deal with government, tax, and cultural issues that may affect your outsourcing. Single-country experts will usually offer some strategic advice about what you should and should not outsource, but they are most useful once you have selected a specific country for the location of your offshore subsidiary. They can be invaluable at cutting the red tape and bureaucracy you will encounter in setting up a business in a foreign country.

- **Prime contractors** are companies that have relationships with multiple prequalified outsourcing vendors. A prime contractor is similar to a general contractor in the construction industry who brings in qualified independent tradesmen like electricians and plumbers when you need them to complete construction in your home or business. The outsourcing prime contractor subcontracts to, and manages the services of, the outsourcing vendors of your choice.

Although a general contractor will usually be the one to select and manage the subcontractors, you will help your outsourcing prime contractor select the best outsourcing vendor to meet your needs. You will then work directly with the outsourcing vendor as software development proceeds. The prime contractor will take responsibility for managing your outsourcing to a successful conclusion.

In addition to these four types of outsourcing advisors, some outsourcing vendors offer advisory services themselves. However, you should be aware that their goal will be to maximize their own business and billable hours, not necessarily to provide the most objective and impartial advice.

Unlike outsourcing strategists, single-country advisors, brokers or outsourcing vendors with captive programming teams, a prime contractor delivers both impartial and objective global outsourcing advice *and* services. The use of a prime contractor to facilitate your outsourcing is covered in Appendix C, "Avoiding the Seven Deadly Dangers of Outsourcing."

What's Your Decision?

Will you offshore your software development or not? It's an important question, and this chapter has given you some tools to help make your decision. You must consider business, political, and technical criteria in selecting the best outsourcing strategy for your company.

Which of the six strategies for software development is the best fit for your company? The decision matrix will help you compare the use of engineer employees with offshore and onshore outsourcing and the creation of an offshore subsidiary.

Take the outsourcing readiness test to see if you are prepared. Then consider your options for getting help to make your outsourcing decisions and offshoring a success.

Actually, I am expecting that for many of you the offshoring decision has already been made. Your CEO, board of directors, or bank account has dictated that software development costs need to be cut to the bone. Offshore outsourcing has become a necessity.

If your software development strategy decision is to outsource, then your next step is to consider the various locations of the world that are popular outsourcing destinations. That's what we cover in the next chapter.

Chapter 2

Where to Outsource

*We have learned that we cannot live alone, at peace; that
our own well-being is dependent on the well-being of other
nations, far away. We have learned that we must live as
men, not as ostriches, or as dogs in the manger. We have
learned to be citizens of the world, members of the human
community.*

—Franklin D. Roosevelt

A large number of detailed studies and overviews of the global
outsourcing market are available. Some cost thousands of dollars, and some are available for free on the Internet. I don't feel
compelled to duplicate their contents here.

Many of the details in these studies are interesting, but many are
not. After all, if you are interested in outsourcing to India or Brazil,
do you really care to know the population of Minsk or even that it is
the capital of Belarus?

The world stage is constantly changing. Much of the information
here is destined to become out of date as soon as it is printed.
Therefore, updated information for these countries and regions of the
world will be delivered on the book's web site.

Another problem with much of the information about outsourcing countries is that it covers many different kinds of outsourcing,
such as call centers, business process automation, database administration, data entry, etc. The rankings of these countries as outsourcing

destinations are not specific to the type of outsourcing you need. You may not want to outsource your call center or the processing of medical records to Bucharest, but it could be an excellent place to develop your .NET application.

Furthermore, rankings of outsourcing vendors focus on the largest ones. Who is biggest? The surveys, studies, and reports show which vendors have the most people, the biggest revenue, the fastest growth rate, and the most locations around the world. But should you just hire the biggest outsourcing vendor you can find in any country? Probably not.

The goal of this chapter is to give you an overview of the various locations of the world where outsourcing services are provided, and to help you understand why some software development organizations choose to use the services in those locations. It will not help you become a champion on the *Jeopardy* TV show or an ace at Trivial Pursuit.

Therefore, this chapter does not

- Give you an encyclopedia of detailed information, such as the total bandwidth available to Bangalore or the average rainfall in Russia
- Describe my personal experiences flying around the world
- Compute an abstract index or numeric rating to compare each country or region at a glance
- Tell you that Chile is better than China or that Bulgaria is better than Brazil. In your case, one or the other statement, or their opposites, could be true. You will have to decide for yourself.

In fact, where you outsource is probably less important than the people and vendor you choose to work with. If you already have a preference or affinity for outsourcing to one country or another, you might just skip this chapter. Country preference is only one of the vendor selection criteria presented in Chapter 3.

If, however, you do not have a preference, or you assume that India is the only outsourcing destination to consider, read on. You might be surprised to learn about the diverse destinations available for your outsourcing. You will get a good sense of these countries and regions of the world, and you'll learn enough to decide whether you should consider them for your outsourcing and why. And who knows, you might just win a million dollars on *Jeopardy* some day and be able to visit all these places!

 **India**

Everyone outsources to India! Or at least it seems that way. Actually, about 80 percent of all IT outsourcing is done there.

But "IT outsourcing" is a broad category that includes call centers for customer and internal help desk support as well as business process outsourcing (BPO) for data entry and processing of forms and applications. This is the outsourcing we hear about in the news when people complain about American jobs being replaced by poor service with unusual accents from India.

But the real reason for outsourcing to India is not that they have a lot of people who can talk to Americans on the phone. It is that decades ago the Indian government made it a priority to educate scientists and engineers, and the language chosen for that education was English. Today India produces more than 100,000 IT graduates per year[3].

American colleges and universities have also contributed to India's outsourcing success over the years by accepting many students from India (and elsewhere) that were trained in the U.S. and, in some cases, also stayed and worked here for a while.

Now many have returned to India, where their understanding of Western culture and business practices has eased many of the cultural and communication problems we experienced when outsourcing to India started in the mid-1990s.

All of the software engineers you encounter from India will speak English. Although their spoken accents may present a challenge from time to time, written English in emails and instant messages should not be an issue.

There are other reasons why outsourcing is now a large and active part of the Indian economy. India is the largest democracy in the world, and it has the tenth largest economy.

India has a good legal system due to the nature of India's democracy and British influence. Laws exist to offer protection of your intellectual property and enforce contracts. However, there is much inefficiency in the courts, and getting to trial can take a long time.

---

3. "Knowledge Professionals", NASSCOM, nasscom.org

Government support of outsourcing goes well beyond the education of workers. The Indian government created special software technology parks (STPs) in most of the major cities of India in the early 1990s. These STPs have reliable electrical power, high bandwidth, and reduced bureaucratic red tape. They have become a haven where software outsourcing vendors can thrive and prosper.

Bangalore: The Silicon Valley of India

Bangalore is the most widely known city in India for outsourcing software development from the United States. The problem with Bangalore is that it has become *too* popular. Like Silicon Valley in the late 1990s, there are too many job opportunities and not enough qualified engineers to fill them. Employee attrition and salary inflation are serious problems in Bangalore and a few other Indian cities.

Make sure your prospective vendors are taking sufficient steps to maintain or improve retention of skilled engineers. Some vendors provide corporate housing, transportation, and meals for employees.

You don't want to be in the position of the VP of engineering whose Indian outsourcing rates were raised unexpectedly. The vendor notified the VP that rates were going up by 20 percent, with only two months' notice. This was not in the VP's budget, and she had to cut back on the number of engineers working on her software. Build price protection into your agreement to avoid this problem.

The outsourcing news about India is dominated by stories about large American companies that have set up their own operations in India to take advantage of the large number of high-quality engineers. You don't have to create your own subsidiary, however. There are many vendors providing services.

The outsourcing vendor market in India is dominated by the large outsourcing vendors. They may get your initial mindshare, but there are literally thousands of smaller companies there too, and many are excellent. They are probably already trying to get your attention by calling and emailing!

Rock Around the Clock

Many people who outsource to India want 24-hour development. For others, the time difference is a big challenge. The time difference between the West Coast of the U.S. and India is 13½ hours (12½ during

U.S. daylight saving time). It is a little better for the East Coast, where there is overlap between the East Coast morning (8 A.M. EDT) and late afternoon in India (5:30 P.M.).

The time difference is not a showstopper for outsourcing to India, but it is a factor you should take into consideration. In general, you should expect to have regular direct communication with your offshore team. If you don't mind the occasional late night or early morning conference call or IM chat, there is no problem.

In fact, some companies prefer to work with India because it enables full 24-hour software development. This takes careful coordination if engineers you have in the U.S. are working on the same source code as your outsourced engineers in India. In most cases, however, the outsourced team is working independently of the daily programming work performed in your office.

Besides the challenge of coordinating the workday, the distance to India makes travel difficult and time-consuming. It can take 24 hours and at least two stops to get to your destination city in India. Frequent travel is not usually required, but most companies that are developing software in India are sending people in one direction or the other every three to six months.

Finally, there is some political risk because of the ongoing dispute with Pakistan over Kashmir, but this seems to have calmed down as of this writing.

Who Should Go?

There are many success stories of software development organizations getting excellent results from outsourcing to India. Indian vendors have broad experience with all of the standard software technologies, such as .NET, Java, and LAMP[4] for web and desktop applications. More firms are also creating embedded software for devices using Linux and embedded XP as well as mobile applications using Palm OS, J2ME, and Windows Mobile.

It is easy to find Indian vendors and engineers experienced with the more standard technologies. Your chances of finding expertise decrease as the sophistication of your chosen technology and need

---

4. LAMP stands for **L**inux, **A**pache, **M**ySQL, and either **P**HP, **P**erl, or **P**ython. See the O'Reilly web site www.OnLamp.com for more details.

for innovation increase. Vendors working on the cutting edge of software technologies are not impossible to find—just more difficult.

One reason for this is that many of the best Indian engineers aspire to and make the move into management as soon as they can. Culturally, they find much more prestige in managing a group of engineers than in focusing their career on mastering one particular technology in depth or dedicating themselves to innovate the latest advance of a software technology or its application.

Projects requiring the discipline of a well-defined process are also good candidates for success. Some Indian firms specialize in defining these processes and applying them to both software development and data processing. Many Indian vendors are CMMI certified (CMMI, or Capability Maturity Model Integration, is discussed in Chapter 6. Briefly, it indicates how structured a firm's software development process is.)

For example, American companies are using Indian vendors to capture data from multiple sources, and they are achieving a very high level of accuracy. Some data are copied from electronic sources like web sites and CD-ROM, and other data are entered manually. All are subject to strict quality control standards enforced by software custom-developed by the Indian vendors for data validation.

Who Should Hesitate?

If you are creating scientific applications with complex algorithms that need to be invented by your outsourcing vendor, India may not be the place for you. Vendors with engineers who are expert at complex math implemented in FORTRAN or C and C++ are not as common in India as in other parts of the world.

Many Indian vendors take pride in their ability to collaborate with clients and apply good software design to application areas that are well understood. This covers many common applications in business, finance, and engineering.

But if you have an innovative new software application for which little or no spec is written, you are likely to struggle when collaborating with a vendor in India. Imagine if you were creating a social networking web application like Friendster and did not have the user interface and the rest of your application completely specified. Remember that Friendster enables its users to meet friends of friends for dating. Could you rely on a vendor to successfully collaborate with you to complete the design in India, where dating is frowned upon and most marriages are still arranged? Probably not!

Also, if you work a strict 9 to 5 weekday schedule, you will have difficulty finding the time required to collaborate in real time with your Indian vendors. Vendors in India know that they have to be flexible, coming in early and staying late in order to work with their clients on the other side of the globe. But it is unrealistic to expect the flexibility to be only on their side and not yours. If you cannot handle some early morning and late night conference calls or chat sessions of your own, then India is not the place for your software outsourcing.

China

Made in China. Should that label be applied to your software? The costs are low, and there are literally hundreds of thousands of Chinese engineers. You just need to find the handful of engineers that you can communicate with and that will develop your software with quality and integrity.

China is a fascinating and wonderful place. It does have one of the few communist governments left in the world, but it has been adapting well to doing business with the rest of the world since 1978. The government keeps tight political control and is relatively stable.

There is some potential risk over China's conflict with Taiwan, which has stayed politically separate from the People's Republic of China (PRC) on the mainland. The PRC still considers Taiwan to be part of China.

Even though the two governments do not see eye to eye, the people are peacefully coexisting and even cooperating at the business and personal levels. Many Taiwanese companies have offices in China and have software and manufacturing operations on the mainland.

There are reports that corruption is rampant, especially in provinces far from Beijing. On the other hand, personal relationships are traditionally very important in Chinese business, and this is sometimes misinterpreted as unwarranted and suspicious favorable treatment. Personal introductions through trusted business associates were a requirement in the past and are still very helpful today for making progress in the Chinese business world.

Think Bigger Than Texas

China is the most populous country on the planet, with an estimated 1.3 billion people, many of whom are relatively poor and live as peasants in the countryside.

However, Chinese universities graduate a lot of very competent engineers. The total labor force is estimated at 790 million people. There is a large pool of more than 200,000 IT workers, with a whopping 50,000 new IT graduates per year[5].

Major cities have a good infrastructure of electricity and communications that is steadily improving. Furthermore, the Chinese government offers strong support to the developing outsourcing industry and has encouraged recent increases in the number of IT university graduates. The return of IT professionals from the U.S. and Europe, along with recently graduated talent from its own universities, promise to combine into an effective work force. Some vendors are even recruiting experienced software development managers from India to help run their operations.

There are more than 50 government-sponsored science and technology industry parks that are incubators for outsourcing vendors. Several initiatives encourage Chinese vendors to become certified as part of their efforts to market to the U.S., Japan, and Europe.

Who's There?

Many Chinese vendors have offshore operations in the U.S. and other countries where they offer their services. In fact, these Chinese companies are often wholly owned foreign entities (WOFE) or subsidiaries of American parent companies.

In addition, many Western companies have set up their own R&D facilities in China to tap the huge Chinese professional labor force that is available. They have a saying at Microsoft about the ability to hire top engineers there: "Remember, in China, when you are one in a million, there are 1,300 other people just like you."

---

5. Global Outsourcing Report 2005, produced by Mark Minevich, Going Global Ventures Inc. and Dr. Frank-Jürgen Richter, HORASIS, March 2005

What Will It Cost?

The outsourcing rates in China are generally 10 to 20 percent lower than many vendors in India. Since the number one reason companies outsource their software development is to save money, you would think everyone would simply outsource to China.

However, English language proficiency and cultural differences are still issues. On the bright side, most recent IT graduates speak English reasonably well, and their written English is even better. The government encourages mastery of written English, not only for IT outsourcing but also to attract overseas investments.

Meanwhile, China is hosting the 2008 Olympics in Beijing. The government knows that the push to communicate in English will enhance China's stature in the world.

The lack of technical and business management experience on many domestic Chinese teams can lead to ineffective project management. Consequently, writing custom code to your detailed specification has been an effective use of Chinese talent, especially if you spend the time to manage their efforts yourself. This type of outsourcing is called "body-shopping" and does not fit outsourcing situations in which you need local management as well as "bodies" to do the programming.

The core competencies of Chinese outsourcing vendors are in implementing basic functionality for software applications and in maintaining applications. They also have strength in embedded systems and mobile computing, due to the large amount of electronics manufacturing in China and the widespread use of cell phones.

Security Concerns

Stories involving weak intellectual property (IP) rights and protections in China are legion. China's weak points continue to be bad IP protection, lack of enforcement, and a copycat mentality. But this is deeply embedded in China's collectivist culture, and only slowly changing. The government knows that it must adopt Western standards for IP rights if is to have any chance of competing in the world.

Ultimately, it comes down to the level of trust you have with your vendor. Like the government, vendors know they must adopt Western values with regard to IP rights, or no one will hire them.

Who Should Go?

If you are looking for low-cost software development, China should be on your list of countries to consider. However, you may want to make sure your software will be of limited use in the Chinese market. For example, a U.S. company is using a vendor in China to help create mortgage processing software sold in the U.S. The risk of someone being able to make use of such software in China is slim.

A presence in the Chinese market is usually required if you plan on selling your software or other products there. If you set up your own operation with your own Chinese staff, you can then also hire your own engineers for software development. Partnering with a vendor to set up your own operation is not usually done, as it is in India. Joint ventures in China are more risky.

As I mentioned before, if you have a well-defined specification, Chinese vendors can provide the programmers you need. Other Chinese vendors are investing in training for CMMI certification. Many vendors tout their CMMI 4 or 5 level of certification as a way to compensate for the fact that they are less proficient in English than vendors in other countries. If you want a high CMMI certification, Chinese vendors should be on your list.

Who Should Hesitate?

If you need to collaborate frequently in spoken English, it will be a challenge to find a Chinese vendor that is easy to work with. Or you will pay more for an American-based vendor with its own operation in China and wipe out the cost savings of making China your outsourcing destination.

If your software has value in the Chinese market, and if the idea is easy to duplicate, be very careful in approaching outsourcing to China. Ultimately, the safety of your software comes down to the integrity of your vendor. Unless there are other compelling reasons to outsource to China, most people will go elsewhere.

Finally, there is the time zone challenge. Like India, China is many time zones away. There is overlap with the late afternoon and early evening on the West Coast of the U.S. From the East Coast you are 13 time zones away (12 when the U.S. is on daylight saving time). Be prepared for flexible working hours when you need to communicate with your Chinese vendor in real time.

Russia

Russia has fantastic programming resources, and my personal experience in outsourcing to Russia has been excellent.

As you probably know, the economy of Russia has undergone a transformation from communism to a free-market economy. The government is now starting to put support behind promotion of IT and software development outsourcing with the creation of "technoparks" for locating modern R&D facilities and special economic zones with reduced tax rates. In early 2005, President Putin announced the start of a special program to set up, develop, and support IT technoparks in four regions of Russia.

But individuals and companies have not been waiting for the Russian government. There is a ready supply of excellent technical talent that is already completing software applications for clients around the world.

Russia has one of the world's best educational systems and a large pool of highly qualified software engineers and researchers. The World Bank estimates that Russia has the third highest number of scientists and engineers per capita in the world.

Russia has more than 20,000 professional IT personnel[6], and this labor force is growing. Most Russian programmers have a formal science degree and have worked in complex defense programs and industry. This practical and real-world experience is very valuable compared to book-learned programming skills. Many Russian programmers have left their industry jobs and now work as freelancers from home.

Think Bigger Than China

Russia is a huge country covering the full width of Asia, but it has only four locations where software outsourcing has become popular. Not surprisingly, these are the locations of the first technoparks:

---

6. Global Outsourcing Report 2005, produced by Mark Minevich, Going Global Ventures Inc. and Dr. Frank-Jürgen Richter, HORASIS, March 2005

- Moscow area: The capital of Russia and a major population center.
- St Petersburg: Named Leningrad during the communist days, this northern city is very cosmopolitan and full of European art, architecture, and culture.
- Nizhny Novgorod region: Between Moscow and the Ural Mountains on the Volga River: An industrial center now growing as a center for IT outsourcing.
- Novosibirsk: In central Siberia, three time zones east of Moscow. It is the third largest city in Russia and the location of a major science academy built by the Soviet Union in 1957.

The labor costs in Russia are comparable to those in India, and like India they are starting to increase in the major cities, such as Moscow and St. Petersburg. Costs are still low in the more rural areas.

Russia Is in Europe, Isn't It?

Russia has an Eastern European culture, but it is still in an early stage of capitalism. Thus, there is limited understanding of foreign markets, customer service, and culture.

English is recognized as a required language for technical work, but most programmers have a heavy accent when speaking in English. Written English is usually very good and very effective for communication by email and instant messages.

There is a significant time zone difference between Russia and the U.S. However, there can be some overlap between the end of the day in Russia and morning in the U.S. Novosibirsk is farther east in Siberia and is only a half hour different than India

Programming for Extra Credit

As I mentioned earlier, Russia has highly skilled IT workers who take pride in their excellent technical experience. They are creative, smart, and imaginative and a good choice for R&D and innovative expansion. They will do more than you asked for in some cases.

Formal management experience is limited but growing. Most intelligent programmers work well in groups and small teams, especially following a team technical lead. And the quality of the software development work is high, probably because most programmers have had real-world experience in industry.

You should exercise some caution with regard to the reuse of your software in other projects. Russia's IP laws are not fully enforced and not always respected. Russia has been making progress in revising its IP laws, but ultimately you will need to rely on the integrity of the vendor you choose.

Who Should Go?

In general, Russian programmers have expertise in large, complex systems requiring careful engineering and sophisticated algorithms. Scientific applications involving hardware and software and complex mathematics are well implemented.

Software built with open-source technology, like Linux, C++, and Java, is a strong candidate for implementation in Russia. The experience with C and C++ goes beyond your usual Windows application into C++ software written for Linux using the C++ standard template library (STL) and other related open-source tools.

Who Should Hesitate?

Simple applications, automation of straightforward business processes, and basic data entry are projects that can be performed more cost-effectively elsewhere.

In addition, applications requiring a deep understanding of Western business concepts that are less familiar to Russians may take some ramp-up time compared to other locations more experienced with capitalistic practices. For example, a basic brokerage account management system will require a detailed specification. However, a sophisticated options trading system using advanced math to implement a trading strategy would be a good fit.

Also be careful if you are developing highly proprietary software, because of weak IP rights in Russia.

 **Canada**

Canada is not the first place most people think of when they look at options for outsourcing. Yet in some situations it deserves serious consideration. If you are in the U.S., you'll find Canada very similar culturally, and there are few time zone issues.

Outsourcing is provided from most provinces but seems to have more strength in the maritime provinces of New Brunswick, Nova Scotia, and Prince Edward Island. Toronto, Calgary, and Montreal are other common outsourcing destinations.

Cost savings are usually the motivator for outsourcing, and Canada's hourly rates are only a little lower than those in the U.S. However, the total cost can compare well to other distant outsourcing destinations such as India when you factor in the extra cost of travel and of the on-site engineers sometimes required for more distant outsourcing to be successful.

Open Door Policy

Canada has a very stable democratic government and a solid political system. In addition, both the federal government and most provincial governments offer very lucrative tax breaks for IT-related exports and operations within Canada.

In fact, some American companies use the strategy of creating a subsidiary in Canada that performs all their programming work. The overall impact of the tax credits and other financial incentives is to lower the cost of the engineering team in the Canadian subsidiary to that of outsourcing to India.

But you do need to create a subsidiary as a fixed cost asset, and you need to decide whether it fits your overall outsourcing and business strategy.

Also, NAFTA enables easy movement of engineers to and from the U.S. You can use a Canadian outsourcing vendor to bring engineers to your location in the U.S. to work on-site for a rate lower than domestic contractors would charge.

The door is open to Canada—to go there and create a subsidiary and to bring engineers in the opposite direction to work in your office.

They Speak American

Legally and culturally, Canada has strong IP protection and privacy laws. Its culture is very similar to that of the U.S. English and French are both spoken, and programming in Canada is a good option if you need these two languages in your software.

Canadians also have a good grasp of both U.S. and European ways of thinking and culture. There is no need for cross-cultural training.

Canada has an excellent educational system, and the government actively promotes job creation. There is a flow of professionals who are lured south to the U.S. by higher pay and lower taxes, but many eventually return home.

Who Should Go?

If your software development requires good communication, unencumbered by cultural differences, Canada should be on your list. If you have limited specifications and need to collaborate closely with your outsourcing team, a Canadian team will be available during normal working hours.

Creating a subsidiary in Canada for employing your engineering team can save you cash if you don't mind having a foreign business entity and your company split across multiple locations.

Who Should Hesitate?

You get good project management and highly skilled employees in Canada, comparable to those in the U.S. and Europe. It's too bad the rates aren't lower! If you have a tight budget and need to keep costs down, Canada is likely to be just too expensive.

Philippines

To some, the Philippines is the ideal outsourcing destination in Asia because of the large base of highly educated English-speaking workers.

The Philippines has a good educational system, with one of the highest rates of graduation in the world. The university system graduates more than 15,000 students focused on technology each year.

The government is relatively stable, but there are frequent political disputes and disruptions. Some threat exists from both Muslim separatist groups and communist insurgents, but this rarely affects the capital city of Manila on the northern island of Luzon, where almost all IT outsourcing activity takes place.

I'm Ready for My Close-up, Mr. DeMille

Perhaps the biggest problem faced by the Philippines is the need to improve its image. The government is now starting to promote itself as an ideal outsourcing location that is able to compete successfully with India and China.

And compete it can, with outsourcing rates that are low and competitive with other, better-known outsourcing destinations. Flights to and from North America are generally easier than to other Asian locations as well. Federal Express operates its hub for all of Asia out of Subic Bay, just west of Manila.

Although not a member of the Anglosphere,[7] the Philippines is culturally very compatible with the U.S. English is widely spoken and is essentially the second national language of the country. The Philippines was a U.S. commonwealth in the early 20th century and became an independent nation on July 4, 1946, about a year after the end of World War II.

The Philippines has a good legal system, and IP protection is increasing. Of course, you will need to rely on the integrity of your vendor for complete protection.

If there is a weakness with outsourcing to the Philippines, it is the lack of skilled project management and experience with large software development projects. It is easier to find body shops offering programmers than vendors with well-structured and well-managed teams of programmers. So far, the more successful outsourcing engagements in the Philippines have been for call centers and outsourcing of other business processes.

---

7. A word coined by Neal Stephenson in his 1995 novel *The Diamond Age* to mean the U.S., Canada, U.K., Ireland, New Zealand, Australia, and South Africa—countries that all share a common language, culture, and legal traditions. See also *The Anglosphere Challenge: Why the English-Speaking Nations Will Lead the Way in the Twenty-First Century* by James C. Bennett.

The time zone difference can also be a challenge. Like China, which is in the same time zone, there is some workday overlap with the late afternoon and early evening of the western U.S. The East Coast must deal with a 12 to 13-hour difference.

Who Should Go?

Straightforward software development projects that are well specified are a safe choice for outsourcing to the Philippines. Standard technologies like Java and .NET are well understood and commonly used for both desktop and web applications.

Even if your application is not completely specified, you can collaborate in English with Filipino engineers. And flying to Manila to ramp up your Philippine outsourcing team is relatively easy to do

Embedded software development is also done in the Philippines, especially in support of the large electronics manufacturing industry in the country.

Who Should Hesitate?

If you require a crack team of programmers to innovate a software solution to your problem or to help you win an opportunity, the Philippines may be too relaxed and carefree a place for your outsourcing. Also, the time zone difference is difficult to overcome if you need overlap with your workday.

 ## Vietnam

"Vietnam!? I never thought of outsourcing there!" That is what one client said about the small, distant country whose conflicts became such a flashpoint in the 1960s. Indeed, as your fathers, uncles, and brothers, and maybe even you, went off to fight more than 30 years ago, nobody knew we would be sending software projects to Vietnam so many years later instead of soldiers.

After some key economic reforms by the communist government, Vietnam today is a stable and secure environment, and is now a good destination for IT outsourcing. The Vietnamese IT market is growing rapidly, and the government has set aggressive goals for training IT workers and increasing software exports. In fact, taxes for software exports are minimal, and the government considers IT and the software industry to be a critical part of the Vietnamese economy.

The government has created several new technoparks around the country to support IT and software outsourcing. These are modern facilities with a good telecom and electrical infrastructure. This infrastructure is weak elsewhere in the country.

Many large companies from the U.S. and Japan are outsourcing software development projects to Vietnam, and some are creating captive software development operations or subsidiaries there.

Young at Heart

Half the population of Vietnam is under 30 years of age, born after the war. They are optimistic, intelligent, and well educated. The education system is excellent, with good programs of study in mathematics and technologies that support the IT industry.

Many Vietnamese expatriates have returned after working as programmers and engineers in the U.S. and Europe. Now they facilitate the use of Vietnamese talent by customers in other parts of the world and help overcome cultural and language barriers.

In fact, the English-language skills of the Vietnamese are generally weak, but they are improving, especially among the young. Engineers can usually read and write English, and email and instant messaging are effective tools of collaboration. But they often speak with a heavy accent, making it especially hard to understand them over a noisy VOIP connection. Vietnamese expatriates who have moved back from English-speaking countries play a critical role as managers who can communicate effectively with clients offshore.

There is little or no attrition, and so it is relatively easy to keep a team together for an extended period of time. Vietnamese firms have a good understanding of the software development process, and they embrace the use of formal methods such as CMMI and ISO-9001. The effect is to overcome language issues quickly. In other words, it may take a couple of conversations, by phone or email, to explain exactly what you want, but there is never any doubt about where you are in the process and what needs to be done to create high-quality software.

On average, costs are very low, certainly below the costs in India and often below the costs of outsourcing to the more expensive urban centers in China. In fact, I have heard that some Indian companies are outsourcing to Vietnam to reduce their own costs!

As in China, respect for IPR has a relatively short history and is only now being promoted as a requirement for doing business with Western countries. Illegal copying and selling of digital media, including software, is common in Vietnam.

Who Should Go?

If you are Vietnamese and your family history with the country was not overly traumatic, then outsourcing software development to Vietnam seems like a no-brainer. High-quality and enthusiastic engineering talent is easily available and ready to implement your software. You will have no communication issues.

If you do not speak Vietnamese, you can still make effective use of talent there if you have a good definition of what you need. Quality assurance work is well suited for Vietnam when you have documented test cases that can be entered into a good testing process.

The same is true for software you need to have written. Given reasonable specifications, Vietnamese engineers will accurately estimate the amount of effort needed and then execute well to deliver your software.

Who Should Hesitate?

Cultural differences make collaboration and innovation for Western markets more challenging. You will probably not want to rely on Vietnamese engineers to design the user interface for your software.

Consumer and mobile phone applications that have a market in Vietnam and elsewhere in Asia may be more risky because of traditional lack of respect for IP.

Other Southeast Asian Countries

 *Malaysia*

Besides the Philippines and Vietnam, several other countries in Southeast Asia are sometimes mentioned as outsourcing destinations. At the top of the list is Malaysia. IT outsourcing services are available in Malaysia at competitive rates. However, the focus seems to be on BPO and on smaller projects, such as web site design, graphics, and animation.

 *Singapore*

Singapore is another country that is often mentioned for outsourcing, but the focus there is on manufacturing. For IT, it is more likely that the large financial institutions and other businesses of Singapore will send outsourcing projects to nearby countries, such as India and Vietnam. However, there are now several IT outsourcing vendors serving the Singapore market and the Western world.

Australia and   New Zealand

In the same neighborhood as the Southeast Asian countries are Australia and New Zealand, for which North Americans have a great cultural affinity. Alas, the cost savings are not high enough to justify the challenges of time zone and distance. Most of the software development relationships I have heard about are joint ventures that enable engineering talent to enter the U.S. market as a joint venture with an American company. The company focuses on sales and marketing in the U.S., where the company is based, and then does all of the software development with its own captive operation Down Under, where the special skills of the engineering team are not as amply rewarded in their own relatively small market.

Central Europe

Outsourcing of software development to Poland, Hungary, and the Czech Republic has now become more expensive than in other locations a little farther east or in other parts of the world. The focus of these countries is to be a "nearshore" outsourcing option for Germany, Switzerland, and the rest of Western Europe. All three are members of the European Union.

For North American companies, there are less expensive alternatives for outsourcing of software development. However, if you have other strategic reasons to be in Central Europe, then creating a subsidiary in any of these countries is a good choice. English and German are the most popular foreign languages spoken, with German taking the lead.

 *Poland*

Poland has a good relationship with and respect for Western countries, including the U.S. Large U.S. companies such as Intel and Motorola have set up operations in Poland. Generally, these operations are for research and development of both hardware and software. Several special economic zones (SEZ), in which companies enjoy tax incentives, have been defined by the Polish government.

Poland has also become a manufacturing center for many European companies. Therefore, embedded software and other software that is closely related to hardware is often outsourced to Poland.

 Czech Republic

The Czech Republic has made a very successful transition from communism to capitalism and has become well integrated economically with the rest of the European Union. The government strongly supports IT and technology business in the country. Tax subsidies are offered to service centers doing software development.

The Czech Republic has a well-educated work force of programmers and engineers. But because of its closeness to Germany, Austria, and Switzerland, both geographically and culturally, most outsourcing business is focused on providing software and web site development services for these and other Western European countries.

Hungary

Hungary has also made a smooth transition from communist rule and was quick to modernize its telecom infrastructure. There is a high level of education in Hungary but a limited number of engineers for large operations. It has the same cultural affinity to Western Europe and focuses on the German, Austrian, and Swiss markets.

Who Should Go?

The bottom line is that in these countries of Central Europe you can easily find excellent programming talent that understands how to develop software. The professionals there are familiar with business practices and are easy to work with. If you need to set up a subsidiary to develop software and service your European customer base, you should seriously consider one of these countries as your offshore location.

Who Should Hesitate?

Outsourcing to these countries is relatively expensive compared to other areas of the world, and even when compared to the countries next door in Eastern Europe. If you don't need close proximity to markets in Western Europe, you will find a better outsourcing value elsewhere.

Belarus

Tucked away just north of Ukraine is the country of Belarus. Like Ukraine, Belarus was formerly part of the Soviet Union. In fact, it used to manufacture most of the computers and computer components in the former USSR.

Every year the technical universities and colleges graduate about 2,000 highly qualified IT programmers and engineers. It is one of the most technologically advanced countries in Eastern Europe, and its competitive advantages make it an attractive outsourcing area.

The main advantage of outsourcing to Belarus is the low cost compared to India and the urban areas of other Eastern European locations. However, a major issue is the country's political image. President Lukashenko came to power in 1994, and won a third term in 2006. He has an authoritarian style of rule and intolerance for opposition.

Nevertheless, the Belarusian government actively supports IT outsourcing and has created a high-tech park where offshore programming services can be offered with reduced taxes and bureaucratic red tape.

Belarus has several large and well-established IT outsourcing vendors employing more than a thousand people and sporting CMMI certification. Naturally, the focus of the large vendors is on big clients in the West. Other, smaller vendors are also in Belarus and are very capable of delivering well-managed and effective programming teams for clients.

Who Should Go?

If you are looking for a low-cost destination for your outsourcing in Eastern Europe, Belarus might be for you. Well-educated engineers in Belarus are more than capable of executing your software development in all the standard technology stacks.

Who Should Hesitate?

If you plan to visit your outsourcing team frequently, traveling to Belarus will be time-consuming from the U.S. There are no direct flights to Minsk, the capital, and you will need to make one or two stops along the way in Europe.

Also, if political turmoil concerns you, Belarus may be too exciting a place for your outsourcing. On the other hand, working closely with people in Belarus will support their continued effort to achieve fairness and uphold democratic ideals.

 Bulgaria

If you are thinking of outsourcing to Bulgaria, you will be in good company. Large companies like IBM, SAP, HP, and Cisco have had operations there for many years. SAP in particular developed its Java-based NetWeaver software there.

Bulgaria has a terrific educational system for engineering and computer science at universities in many locations around the country. One interesting statistic I discovered online is that Bulgaria ranks second[8] in the world in its citizens' score on IQ tests! Bulgaria also ranks high in terms of its number of IT graduates who have strengths in research and creative skills.

Once dominated by the Soviet Union, Bulgaria has turned around its economy and is planning to join the European Union. Bulgarians have a good understanding of Western European culture.

Who Should Go?

Bulgarian outsourcing vendors excel in the more challenging programming technologies. Development of a complex application using C++ is a great fit. Java programming is also well understood.

---

8. Radio Bulgaria reports Bulgaria is just behind first-place Israel.

Who Should Hesitate?

Software development using more standard programming technologies like .NET and LAMP may be more cost-effective elsewhere. Rates are increasing in Bulgaria as other European countries discover the skills and value available. Entry into the European Union may accelerate this rise in rates.

 **Romania**

Romania has another very attractive Eastern European software outsourcing story to tell. Rates are low and the workforce is well educated. The country is also on track to join the European Union.

Romania's population of IT professionals is one of the largest in Europe, and no wonder, since IT professionals are exempt from income tax payment. Several Western companies, such as Alcatel, IBM, Oracle, and Siemens are creating R&D operations in Romania.

Wages are low and will take some time to catch up with the rest of the European Union, but otherwise the business culture is very European. A very high percentage of the Romanian workforce speaks English, French, German, or Italian.

Like the rest of Eastern Europe, Romania has very little time overlap with the U.S., although early morning in the U.S. does overlap with the end of the workday in Romania. Outsourcing to Romania is very attractive for the rest of Europe, since Romania is only one hour ahead of Western Europe and two hours ahead of the U.K.

There has been a lack of IP protection and enforcement in Romania in the past, but this is changing as the government is committed to creating new laws and compatibility with other European Union nations.

Who Should Go?

It is hard to find a reason not to go. Romania has a highly skilled and creative workforce focused on creating custom software. There is more experience with standard technology platforms like .NET and LAMP. If you are creating a sophisticated Java application or one in C++, make sure your potential Romanian vendor has the level of experience you need.

Who Should Hesitate?

Only a requirement for a significant amount of travel or the desire for more overlap with your workday in the U.S. should keep you from considering Romania as your outsourcing destination.

Ukraine

There was great respect and admiration for Ukraine when its illegitimate presidential election was peacefully overturned in 2004. In addition, many Ukrainians believed that the Orange Revolution and the election of Victor Yushchenko would open up the country to the West, which would improve the economy. And indeed, Western companies are now opening up shop in Ukraine to take advantage of its large, experienced pool of technical talent.

Ukraine has more than 300 outsourcing companies that export IT outsourcing services. Unlike the IT outsourcing companies in Belarus, which are some of the largest in Eastern Europe, the Ukrainian IT companies tend to be smaller.

The capital, Kiev, is just a two-hour flight from major European cities such as London, Amsterdam, and Paris. To make the trip to Ukraine even simpler, its government has introduced visa-free travel for visitors from the European Union, the U.S., and several other countries.

Kiev is Ukraine's major outsourcing location. Companies are now looking to other Ukrainian cities, such as Kharkiv, Donetsk, Dnipropetrovsk, Lviv,[9] and Odessa, each the location of excellent technical universities.

Ukraine has one of the highest levels of education in Eastern Europe. It is strong in education and science, with almost a thousand colleges. The National Academy of Sciences supports more than 100

---

9. Lviv or Lvov—what is the correct spelling and pronunciation? Ukrainians prefer Lviv, thank you very much. Lvov is the Russian spelling.

scientific research institutes and 8 technoparks, which focus on the commercialization of high-technology research.

Fly Me to the Moon

The number of engineers, the quality of their education, and the relatively low cost are the main reasons for outsourcing to Ukraine. Many top computer programmers worked in the former Soviet Union's space and military efforts. Now the country is producing complex systems such as rockets, satellites, and space research equipment. Ukrainians like to point out that their country has launched more satellites than NASA.

Ukraine is hungry to catch up with its neighbors. Since the Orange Revolution, the new government has demonstrated its intent to transform the country and eventually gain membership in the European Union.

Ukrainians have a great affinity for the U.S. and the European Union, and there is a large Ukrainian population in the northern U.S. and Canada.[10] The English skills of engineers in Ukraine are adequate but not as good as in some other outsourcing destinations. You will have to trade off intelligence and programming experience for a possible heavy accent in spoken English in some cases. It's best to rely on written English, which is usually sufficient for most outsourcing projects.

Ukrainian and other Eastern European programmers take pride in their technical abilities. A significant number will advance to become technical leads on programming teams rather than administrative project managers. In effect, they lead by example and force of knowledge rather than officious authority. They are best used to collaborate with you to deliver an innovative solution, rather than just to serve as body-shop programmers coding to your detailed specifications.

---

10. Indeed, my own maternal grandparents immigrated to the U.S. separately, from Lviv, in the early 20th century. They met in New Jersey, married, and raised a family. My mother was the oldest of their five children, all of whom attended an ethnic Ukrainian school in New Jersey. Our family lost touch with relatives back in Ukraine just before World War II.

Sanctions Lifted

Ukraine has been a major source of pirated CD-ROMs, DVDs, and software in Europe. In 2001, sanctions were levied against Ukraine by the U.S. government for failing to protect U.S. patents, copyrights, and other intellectual property. Ukraine was the only country designated a "priority foreign country" in the U.S. Trade Representative's annual Special 301 Report, the ranking reserved for the worst situations.

In 2005 Ukraine passed laws to protect IP rights, and the U.S. government lifted its sanctions against Ukraine in January 2006.

Who Should Go?

It will be possible for you to find a Ukrainian programming team that has mastered the particular software technology you need. Anyone with sophisticated software that will benefit from collaborating with a well-educated programming team should seriously consider Ukraine. Software applications requiring scientific knowledge are particularly well suited, as are projects for embedded systems or those using languages like C and C++.

Who Should Hesitate?

The recent change in government and the passage of IP laws have removed the most serious concerns for outsourcing to Ukraine. Still, you may prefer a country with a more established history of IP respect and enforcement.

Software used to automate business processes or more mundane data processing tasks will not make use of the advanced skills of most Ukrainian programming teams and could be tackled with a level of enthusiasm below what you need.

 **Mexico**

Outsourcing to Mexico seems like a perfect idea—it is close to the U.S. and shares the same time zones. Programmers in Mexico are experienced with the latest technologies, especially if they are used by businesses for programming projects in Mexico. And rates are low enough to be competitive with India. So what's holding things back?

There are cultural differences that are small but noticeable. Mexicans are sometimes ambivalent about dealing with American clients and seem to feel overwhelmed and neglected by their larger neighbor to the north.

For example, after the passage of the North American Free Trade Agreement (NAFTA) there was an upsurge in manufacturing done in Mexico. Now this has largely moved further offshore to China, leaving Mexico in the lurch. Will the same thing happen with software outsourcing?

But being so close to a large trading partner like the United States is hard to ignore. With good humor, Mexicans see both the opportunity and the risk of their situation. Perhaps the attitude of Mexican businesses toward the U.S. is best expressed in this Mexican saying: *"Pobrecito Mexico—tan lejos de Dios y tan cercas de los Estados Unidos!"* or "Poor little Mexico—so far from God and so near the United States!"

Recently the Mexican government has invested in an initiative to help Mexican companies enter the U.S. market. This includes outsourcing vendors and also Mexican software and high-tech companies offering their own products. An incubator/accelerator named TechBA was created, with offices in Silicon Valley, to help Mexican companies do business in the U.S.

English proficiency is low within the general Spanish-speaking population of Mexico. However, English is spoken widely by IT professionals and engineers.

Who Should Go?

Standard business software development in .NET, Java, and other common technology platforms is easily done in Mexico. Development of software applications that are multilingual for both English and Spanish are an obvious fit.

If you need to closely collaborate with your software development team, then having one in Mexico is very convenient. Because of NAFTA, engineers are able to come to the U.S. for an extended period of time to work at your facilities. This approach is useful for staff augmentation, or for adding engineers to your own team or for handling short-term projects like custom software development for your customers. Bringing Mexican engineers to the U.S. and paying their living expenses can be less expensive than hiring local contractors.

Who Should Hesitate?

Less scientific and software research is done in Mexico compared to other countries. If you need advanced software innovations, you are more likely to find advanced expertise in other countries.

Costa Rica

Costa Rica is sometimes called the Switzerland of Central America. It is small and politically stable, and it has no army, since the U.S. has promised protection. Money normally earmarked for military expenditure is spent instead on an excellent university system.

Costa Rica is best known for coffee and tourism. The increasing popularity of Costa Rica as a U.S. tourist destination is no mystery. It is similar to Hawaii but closer and less expensive.

In 2005 the government declared its intention of making Costa Rica the high-technology center of Central America by 2010. This little country does have some great things going for it that make this goal achievable. For example, it takes less than a day's travel to get there from almost anyplace in the U.S. The workforce is highly educated because of an excellent school and university system. The literacy rate of the population is 98 percent, and the universities graduate about 3,000 engineers each year.

Intel is already there, with a 3,000-person facility focused on chip manufacturing. Microsoft and Oracle are also well established.

Costa Rica is technologically strong now and is committed to future growth. It will nurture its own software development industry to take on even more outsourced projects from the U.S. Innovation within the Costa Rican software industry will enable it to serve the rest of the world in many ways over the Internet.

Because of the country's geographic and cultural proximity to the U.S., Costa Rican engineers are familiar with Western business practices and standards. Spanish is the primary language, but most engineers speak English reasonably well. All read and write English.

Outsourcing rates in Costa Rica are competitive with India, especially if you factor in travel costs.

Who Should Go?

If you are thinking about outsourcing but do not want to outsource many time zones away, you should seriously consider Costa Rica. It is a beautiful country. Everyone is friendly, and almost everyone can speak English. And Costa Rica is serious about being a leader in high technology.

There is good experience with standard web and desktop application technologies, especially .NET, Java, and Oracle.

Who Should Hesitate?

The savings may not be as great for your outsourcing to Costa Rica as in other, more distant locations. You will have to balance your need for programming resources in a nearby time zone with the overall cost of your outsourcing.

Experience with open-source technologies like LAMP exist but is limited, for some reason. You are more likely to find experience with programming languages and tools that have enjoyed commercial success in Costa Rica rather than those that have earned the admiration of the international open-source community as a whole.

Other Central American Countries

Theoretically, the other Central American countries of El Salvador, Guatemala, Honduras, Nicaragua, and Panama are also possible outsourcing destinations for software development. Like Costa Rica, they are close to the U.S. in time zone and distance. However, there do not seem to be many vendors in these countries. Of these countries, Nicaragua and Panama show the most promise.

Nicaragua

Very recently the government of Nicaragua has expressed interest in attracting outsourcing service providers to the country. A large percentage of the population is young, and the government naturally wants them to have good job opportunities.

The government has created aggressive incentives to encourage the outsourcing business, including no taxes on earnings for outsourcing vendors whose clients are outside Central America

So far, only a few outsourcing vendors have responded, although several corporations are creating their own operations in Nicaragua.

Costs should be low because of low salaries and taxes and the desire to get started in the outsourcing business. Nicaragua is in the Central time zone and is just a few hours away by air from several major American cities.

English proficiency is presently an issue but should become less of a problem over time as more technical professionals are trained to work in the outsourcing industry. The government has created an English-language registry so that outsourcing vendors can find workers in Nicaragua.

Panama

Meanwhile, farther south, the country of Panama aims to be the preferred destination for American companies that want to create an operation based in Latin America. In 1999, the U.S. government turned over the former Canal Zone properties to the government of Panama, including several former U.S. military bases. Now the Panamanian government is leasing out those facilities to any interested companies, including U.S. companies that want to have a presence in Central America.

Because of the decades-long U.S. presence in Panama after the building of the Panama Canal, the Panamanian culture is very focused on the U.S., especially within the former Canal Zone. American popular music and baseball are well known. In addition, many ATM machines will dispense dollars rather than Panamanian balboas. All in all, it is a very easy place for American companies to set up shop.

Who Should Go?

If you want to blaze new trails in outsourcing, these other Central American countries are a huge opportunity for reducing costs and receiving services from an outsourcing vendor that is relatively close to the U.S. If you can speak Spanish and can provide the guidance and management needed to bring a relatively young company up to speed, outsourcing to one of these countries will give you very good cost savings over other outsourcing destinations.

Who Should Hesitate?

There are many other regions of the world that have a more established outsourcing business and vendors with diverse skills. Outsourcing to these up-and-coming Central American countries offers opportunities but will give you challenges in English language ability and software development experience. But stay tuned. The outsourcing business could give these countries a chance to successfully compete in the world market in a few short years.

 **Brazil**

In October of 2003 the investment banking firm Goldman Sachs published a report projecting that four emerging countries will dominate the world economy by 2050. The four countries are Brazil, Russia, India, and China, whose names conveniently form the memorable acronym BRIC. The report elevates the stature of these four countries because of the size of their nascent markets for goods rather than the fact that they are present-day destinations for outsourcing.

In fact, if the acronym were to indicate the top outsourcing destinations for software development today, the "B" would more accurately be representing Bulgaria, not Brazil. Several large outsourcing vendors operate in Brazil, and there is no doubt that much programming work is performed in Brazil for other Brazilian compa-nies. But not very many small and medium-sized outsourcing vendors exist there that focus on providing software development services for the U.S. and other Western countries.

Brazil is the largest and most populous country in South Amer-ica. Portuguese is the official language, and English proficiency on the whole is low.

Brazil is physically closer to the U.S. than many other outsourc-ing destinations. The time zone is two hours ahead of Eastern Stan-dard time in the U.S.

The costs in Brazil are competitive with India. Rates are lower in the less well-known cities and higher in Sao Paulo and Rio de Janeiro. Most Brazilian IT outsourcing vendors focus on BPO and on provid-ing body-shop software development resources.

IP rights in Brazil have been under review by the U.S. Trade Representative for several years. Recent progress in Brazil has caused the U.S. government to continue its review of IP rights in Brazil and to resist lobbying efforts to remove its General System of Preferences (GSP) benefits. The GSP is a U.S. trade policy that enables countries like Brazil with developing economies to export products duty-free to the United States.

Who Should Go?

Lower costs and time zone proximity are attractive factors for select-ing Brazil. Experience with open-source technologies seems good. Brazil promises to be a good bargain for outsourcing if you can find a qualified vendor. Vendors tend to be large body shops or very small firms with limited ability to market their services to the U.S. and other Western countries.

Who Should Hesitate?

Programming for scientific applications seems limited. Mastery of English may be difficult to find.

Other South American Countries

Besides Brazil, Argentina and Chile are the two South American countries that are most often mentioned as outsourcing destinations.

Neither one has made a strong effort to market to U.S. clients so far. This is primarily due to limited English skills and distance. At least the distance is to the south, which makes these countries attractive because of their workday overlap with the U.S. Columbia and Peru are also possibilities, but the political turmoil in those countries makes them less desirable.

Argentina

Argentina has a very talented pool of technically savvy and well-educated resources ready for work. During the dot-com boom, the country was home to approximately 65 percent of the design and implementation work of most regional Internet startups. A large population of highly trained programmers and designers helped the country stand out among its Latin American neighbors in the technology domain. Unemployment during Argentina's 2001 currency crash was a boon to outsourcing vendors within Argentina. They are making their services available to the rest of Latin America and are starting to look at the U.S.

Chile

Chile is the most politically stable country in South America. Its sound economic policies have contributed to steady growth and have helped secure the country's commitment to democratic and representative government.

The government is encouraging training for outsourcing services, but the number of well-educated IT workers is presently small. Chile lacks well-known top universities.

Rates in Chile are a little more expensive than in other Latin American countries. There is an affinity for outsourcing to Spanish-speaking countries. English proficiency is low.

Who Should Go?

Vendors from Chile and Argentina are available for your outsourcing. Confirm that they do good work by checking references with other clients in the U.S., or if you speak Spanish, verify their work in Latin America. You are likely to find a bargain with vendors in Argentina that are looking to expand beyond their limited domestic market.

Who Should Hesitate?

These are new outsourcing destinations, and unless you are ready to be a pioneer, other outsourcing countries will be more experienced and easier to deal with.

 **Pakistan**

Outsourcing to Lahore or Karachi? These Pakistani cities may not be at the top of your list. But the government and several trade associations in Pakistan are trying to change that. Unfortunately, travel advisories from the U.S. State Department confirm that it is still somewhat unsafe for Americans to travel there.

Pakistan shares India's British colonial history and has a large number of English-speaking workers. As in India, many workers have returned home after working in Western countries.

Pakistan is playing catch-up with India in offering various outsourcing services. Expert software development with smart, English-speaking programmers is one of them. The Pakistani government is offering a 15-year tax exemption on software exports, and is encouraging investment in IT. They are looking to attract multinational corporations to set up operations in Pakistan and to encourage software outsourcing vendors to offer services offshore.

The Pakistani government has set up four IT parks in Karachi, Lahore, and Islamabad with good working conditions, Internet connectivity, reliable electricity, and minimal bureaucratic red tape.

Since it is more dangerous for Americans to travel to Pakistan compared to other outsourcing destinations, Pakistani companies have opened sales offices within Western countries like the U.S. and Canada. Several major American companies are outsourcing to Pakistan to take advantage of the excellent labor pool. Outsourcing rates are comparable to those in India and should actually be a bit less because of lower demand.

Who Should Go?

If you can tolerate the risk of political disruption and can outsource without visiting your programming team, Pakistan offers excellent talent and rates lower than India next door because of the lack of demand at this point in time. Pakistani engineers can handle most programming projects, especially those that use the standard technology stacks of .NET, Java, and LAMP.

Who Should Hesitate?

Even though doing business with smart Pakistanis who understand Western countries and culture will help both countries in the long run, any American company should think twice about outsourcing to Pakistan. Outsourcing is a business decision, and if you need rock-solid stability and the ability to meet your programming team as needed, there are definitely safer places to outsource your software development.

 **Israel**

Smart and tenacious engineers who can solve just about any problem would be a fair characterization of the talent available in Israel. However, the cost of this talent is high, and so Israel is usually not an option for outsourcing your software development if saving money is your main goal.

The country has several excellent research facilities and universities. Multinational corporations like IBM, Microsoft, Motorola, and Intel have operations there.

The recent immigration of Russian Jews to Israel has provided a somewhat lower-cost labor force. Some Israeli companies have also set up operations or partnered with companies in less expensive countries like Jordan and Russia to reduce costs.

English is spoken widely in Israel, and the country shares many values with the West. Israel has an exceptionally innovative culture, and there are strong IP laws and enforcement. It has a very skilled programming workforce and excellent technical and business management.

Who Should Go?

Israel is the country in the Middle East that is closest to the West culturally and also in cost. It is more common for Western companies to create an operation in Israel for research and development, with major portions of the actual development outsourced elsewhere.

Who Should Hesitate?

If you need a world-class research facility, Israel should be on your list. However, if you just need economical programming resources, there are other countries with excellent talent and much lower costs.

Other Middle Eastern Countries

Egypt

Egypt is an outsourcing destination in the Middle East offering good English language proficiency and low cost. Direct government support of outsourcing is limited, however.

Much of the press about outsourcing to Egypt involves call centers that service Europe, which is close in time zone. But there are also vendors offering application development and maintenance services.

Turkey

It is an age-old question: Is Turkey in the Middle East, Asia, or Europe? In fact, it has applied to join the European Union, and in business terms it is more focused on Europe than the Middle East or Asia.

Low rates are possible from vendors in Turkey, but most of the focus has been on general IT outsourcing, including call centers and business process outsourcing, rather than software development.

United States

No kidding. You can outsource to vendors in the U.S. for situations in which you need to do a great deal of direct, in-person communication. If you have limited time or experience to specify your software, working with a local vendor can be a good choice.

Doing so will be more expensive than offshore outsourcing, but you can consider outsourcing the creation of your specification to a U.S. firm and then using offshore outsourcing after that. Some American vendors have partnerships with offshore firms and can manage the offshore part for you as well, for a fee.

Other American vendors are locating operations in rural and less costly areas of the country. Even so, the rates are about twice what you would pay in India and other offshore locations.

Where in the World Will Your Software Be Developed?

By now, I imagine you are either happy to go with the flow and outsource to India or pleasantly surprised by your options for outsourcing destinations around the world. Did this chapter reinforce your preferences or challenge them?

You may still have no particular preference for a country or region. That's okay. In the beginning of the chapter I said that the quality of the vendor you select is the most important success factor for your outsourcing. An objective process for selecting your vendor carefully is covered next, in Chapter 3.

Chapter 3

How to Select Your Outsourcing Vendor

It is our choices . . . that show what we truly are, far more than our abilities.

—J. K. Rowling, in *Harry Potter and The Chamber of Secrets*, 1999

I n his 2004 presidential campaign, John Kerry criticized George W. Bush for the failure to capture Osama bin Laden. According to the *New York Times*,[11] Kerry asserted that Bush had "outsourced" the job of capturing the terrorist leader to "Afghan warlords who let Osama bin Laden slip away.'"

Whether you agree with Kerry or not, his remarks emphasize the importance of picking a good team if you do outsource. By far, the largest success factor in outsourcing is selecting a good team to begin with.

How do you do it? This chapter will show you an objective three-step process along with several tools and a list of selection criteria you can use to make sure you pick the right vendor for your software development.

---

11. New York Times, September 24, 2004.

A Vendor Selection Nightmare

A VP of engineering at a software company told me that it took him more than five months to select an outsourcing vendor. On his own, he carried out a careful search for an outsourcing vendor in India, China, and South America. He sought a low price point to give him a specific cost savings over hiring engineers in the U.S.

He evaluated 22 vendors in these three countries. Then he made nine site visits. Site visits are not always necessary, but in his case the company was interested in a build, operate, and transfer (BOT) arrangement giving it the option of transferring the team to its own subsidiary.

After all this work, time, and money, he still got less than satisfactory results. He selected a U.S.-owned outsourcing vendor with an operation in China. The vendor was in the process of acquiring a second team of programmers in China. The VP found this second Chinese team to be excellent, and they quickly sketched out an architecture and design for the software that was needed. He then worked out the financial terms with the U.S.-based vendor and signed the agreement.

But the acquisition of the second Chinese team by the U.S. outsourcing vendor fell through. A junior team from the existing operation in China was assigned to the VP's project instead.

Then the nightmare began.

The English skills of the junior programmers were limited, making communication very difficult and inefficient. And their programming skills seemed even worse. Their day-to-day activities had to be closely directed by the U.S.-based VP and his staff. The source code developed in China was reviewed daily.

Because of the 16-hour time difference with China, managers in the U.S. spent many late nights emailing detailed instructions (even pseudocode) and answering questions by phone when it was daytime in China. This led to severe morale problems within the U.S. staff, made worse by the fact that the U.S. staff never thought outsourcing was a good idea to begin with. Missed deadlines and vociferous employee frustration eventually elevated the issue to the board level.

But the damage was done. Within two months, the VP was gone. The outsourcing engagement he so carefully arranged went bad and caused such an awful ruckus that he was forced to leave the company.

Will this happen to you?

Not necessarily. You certainly could spend five months of your own time and come up with a good vendor. But if your software development project is small or your time line is short, it is hard to justify expending this kind of effort, even if you end up finding the perfect team.

Or you might get a lucky referral from a friend to a good vendor and start outsourcing more quickly. But will it be the best vendor? Is there a better vendor out there that is more experienced, works faster, and costs less? You'll probably never know.

Is there a way to find a team quickly that will also give you reliable results? Yes, there is. But it is not a simple purchasing process.

Did You Ever Purchase an Employee?

Hiring an outsourcing vendor is like hiring the employees on your internal software engineering team. Yet many companies go about the process of selecting an outsourcing vendor as if it were a purchasing process, seeking the lowest price for a service that will satisfy all the "requirements."

Did you ever purchase an employee for your engineering team? Of course not. Hiring an employee takes a careful evaluation of candidates through interviews and reference checks, followed by a reasonable negotiation over salary.

Sometimes you have a choice between two or more employee candidates. Do you negotiate hard so you can hire one of them at the cheapest salary? Probably not. If you do, you risk hiring an employee who will stay only until a better job comes along elsewhere. And then you'll have to start the long hiring process all over again.

It is the same for an outsourcing team. Negotiate too hard and there is little incentive for them to perform well. You frequently hear stories about people who have gotten bad results with their outsourcing. Oftentimes these stories involve a small outsourcing team that took a project at a low bid out of desperation for new business. Do you really want to work with an outsourcing team that is desperate? If you negotiate a deal that is too good for you, you will get the results you deserve.

In the mid-1990s, a friend of mine—let's call him Romeo—was the first employee at a Silicon Valley startup. Romeo was negotiating with the founding CEO for his starting salary and stock before coming on board. The CEO had raised a small seed round of initial funding and offered a very low salary.

"But I have five kids," Romeo said.

The CEO said, "Yes, I know, but what does that have to do with how much I pay you?"

The CEO had a point. After all, the salary should be commensurate with the value the employee brings to the company. But as any smart negotiator knows, you have to take the other person's perspective into consideration.

Romeo accepted the salary and stayed at the company for a while. But he was completely discouraged during his last six months there, before he left to start his own company.

The same can happen with your offshore vendor if you squeeze too hard. As morale declines, your programmers will leave your project or the outsourcing vendor entirely to work on more interesting and lucrative software development opportunities elsewhere.

But let's assume you will be practical and fair. You will negotiate in good faith with your prospective outsourcing vendors. Here is a process to find the best outsourcing team for you.

A Three-Step Process

Are you overwhelmed with the number of software outsourcing vendors? It is amazing how many there are—and they all seem to have come out of the woodwork in just the last couple of years.

One Accelerance client put it this way: "It's like we are walking down the shampoo aisle at Wal-Mart and we don't know what to buy. There are just too many choices!"

You want to take advantage of the real and substantial savings of global software development, but you don't want to waste time and money learning how to do it. In today's fast-paced and cost-constrained world of software development, no one can afford a long learning curve and the expense, in both time and money, of making a mistake.

Therefore, you need outsourced engineers who work together as a cohesive, professional software development team, following a well-defined software development process. Not a bunch of programmers thrown together in a room, working on the cheap in some exotic foreign country.

Your team needs to be expert in the technology you need. You want to find a team that can quickly execute your software development projects, not one that will be learning on the job and on your nickel.

But how do you do it? There are so many vendors just begging to develop your software. You could hire an outsourcing advisor to help you with the process, but they charge a high hourly rate and are therefore motivated to take as long as possible using a "complete and thorough" (and that means expensive!) process to evaluate your outsourcing choices.

Most of us cannot afford that luxury, and so you probably feel left on your own to sort through your choices.

Here is a straightforward three-step process you can follow to select the best outsourcing vendor for your software development. The three basic steps you should follow are:

1. **Source:** Find vendors you want to consider.
2. **Screen:** Apply an objective set of criteria to narrow down your choices.
3. **Select:** Look in more detail at your finalists and select the best one.

Pretty straightforward, right? So why don't others just follow these simple steps and achieve success with outsourcing? Some do. But most get distracted by the details, especially if they are already running a company or software development organization.

Probably the biggest obstacle to selecting a vendor is a lack of clarity about what the process should be. People often combine these three steps, and so they are unconsciously sourcing, screening, and selecting all at once.

Let's look at each step in more detail to see how you can choose your outsourcing vendor quickly and safely.

Step 1: Source—Create Your List of Outsourcing Vendors

Most people find their outsourcing vendor in one of three ways—by personal reference, Internet search, or solicitation by the vendor. You may already have several vendors on your list but would like a few more choices.

Personal references are the most common way for outsourcing vendors to find new business. Selecting a vendor is an important decision. Vendors know that relationships give you the confidence to proceed and even overlook some of their deficiencies.

It's What You Know AND Who You Know

Without established relationships, it can take months to find, evaluate, and select the best outsourced software team to meet your needs. How do you objectively select the best outsourcing team for you? How can you get beyond the strong influence of relationships, or lack thereof, to select the team that will guide and travel with you on the road to success?

When I was a teenager, my mother told me, "To be successful in life, it's not what you know, it's who you know." Naturally, as a teenager, I decided to fight against this parental pearl of wisdom, and I fought to increase "*what* I know" to become successful. "Wouldn't it be better to learn as much as possible and not have to rely on other people?" I thought.

As I grew older, I discovered that just being intelligent does not always lead to success. First of all, there are multiple ways to define intelligence.[12] And intelligence is more than what you know.

For example, a CEO was introduced to a Russian outsourcing company by one of the angel investors in his company. All of the investors wanted the CEO's company to start using offshore outsourcing to conserve cash as they developed their product.

The CEO thought outsourcing was a good idea too, but there was something about the Russian team that rubbed him the wrong way. He had a feeling in his gut that this was not the right team for his software development. After some reflection, he realized that their presentation lacked a consistent story about software quality. Somehow his gut "knew" this, and he was uncomfortable moving forward.

He also did not like making a major decision about outsourcing his software development with a choice of only one vendor. Even though the vendor came recommended by a trusted friend, the CEO wanted more choices.

Let's face it: relationships play a big role in hiring decisions. But although relationships are important, you cannot rely on them alone. When hiring both employees and your outsourcing team, you need

---

12. For discussions of the different types of intelligence, see *7 Kinds of Smart* by Thomas Armstrong and *Emotional Intelligence* by Daniel Goleman.

to use a combination of both *what* and *who* you know to make good decisions about who to hire to develop your software.

Googling for Global Vendors

If you move beyond referrals, the majority of the vendors on your list will likely be the result of late nights you spend Googling for vendors around the globe.

Outsourcing vendors pay thousands of dollars to search-engine optimization experts to use whatever tricks are required to improve their ranking on the popular search engines. And many vendors spend thousands more on search-engine ads to lead you to their web sites. Of course, once you get to the site it is hard to judge objectively whether they are the right vendor for you.

Here's how a typical online vendor search goes. You do a search using technical keywords like ".NET" and "outsourcing" and you get back a list of a few vendors. Are they good at .NET or just at the search engine optimization that puts their URL high in the results? It's hard to tell, so you just add them to the list.

Maybe you should be more specific, so you use the keywords ".NET," "C#," and "outsourcing." More vendors. But there's also an ad: "C# Outsourcing—cheap, cheap, cheap!" You add them to the list.

But you can't resist and you click on the ad. The web page says, "Experts at Windows and Linux". C# on Linux? Not likely, but for now they're on the list.

You persevere and eventually you create a long list. But then what? That's covered in step 2. But first there is one more source of vendors to consider for your list.

Don't Call Us, We'll Call You

Being contacted by an outsourcing vendor shows a level of ambition on their part, which is a good thing. You can use your first impression of this contact to help you decide whether the vendor should be placed on your list. Did they visit your web site and know about your business? Do they have other clients similar to you? Or is their first call a fascinating (to them) monologue covering every detail of their past achievements?

In summary, it is actually pretty easy to come up with a list of outsourcing vendors. The trick is to use an objective process to quickly shorten the list, so that it contains only the candidates you should seriously consider. We cover that next in step 2.

Step 2: Screen—Use Key Criteria to Shorten Your List

Next you should think about all the important characteristics you want to look for in your outsourcing vendor. Here are the top three criteria I recommend that you use to select your outsourced team:

1. **Technical competence**
2. **Experience working on your size project**
3. **Overlap with your workday**

Actually, there are more than 12 criteria I recommend for screening your outsourcing vendors, and they are divided into two categories: technical and business.

Technical criteria include expertise with the specific technology "stack" you need for your product. Examples are Java, Microsoft .NET, and LAMP. Can the team adapt to your software development methodology, such as RUP, agile, and test-driven development? (See Chapter 6 for details on these software development methodologies.)

Business criteria include cost, of course, but also the number and size of projects performed for other clients. Is this firm big enough (or small enough) to handle your projects with the importance they deserve? To you, a project needing a team of 10 engineers may not be small, but try getting even the time of day from a large outsourcing company that has taken on your project but usually bags projects needing a hundred engineers or more.

The outsourced team must show respect for your intellectual property by using appropriate technical, legal, and personnel procedures. Ask if they have had situations in which a client's intellectual property was at risk, what actions they took, and what the final results were.

Let's look at these top three vendor selection criteria in more detail. As you might expect, the highest priority is the technical ability of the outsourcing vendor.

Checking for Technical Competence

You need to go deep into particular details to confirm that the outsourcing vendor has the experience you need. Make sure they have successfully completed projects for other clients using your target technology.

It is pretty easy to find outsourcing vendors that specialize in one or more of the five common technology stacks—Microsoft .NET,

Java, LAMP, C/C++, and COBOL. Some will specialize in just one of these, but it is also common for vendors to have a track record with two or three.

For example, a vendor can focus on just Microsoft technologies and also provide special services for clients using specific Microsoft languages, tools, and server products like SharePoint or BizTalk.

The outsourcing vendor team members may have received their experience on other technology platforms. And of course, your project may require multiplatform experience too. This can be an important requirement for you to begin with.

Generally, the use of .NET and Java requires a more sophisticated engineering team. C# and Java can support the creation of complex programs developed by a team of engineers.

The scripting languages used in the LAMP stack can be used to create sophisticated programs too. However, many projects using scripts written in Perl, PHP, or Python are relatively small and developed by individual engineers and freelancers.

Programming in C and C++ is a relatively specialized skill reserved for device drivers and programs that run on specialized hardware. Software that supports millions of users on a web site like Google or Yahoo is often written in C++. This is a different environment than the older Microsoft Visual C++. Visual C++ was used to create smaller programs for use on individual PCs running Windows.

When you ask about technical competence, do not settle for an answer of "No problem, we can do that!" The vendor should describe projects completed for other clients in which your required technical skills were used. They need to convince you that they really understand the technology and will not be learning on the job.

Determine the top three most important technical skills that you want the outsourcing vendor to have. If you focus on more than three, you may get caught up in the minutia of technical detail that is just not as important as some of the additional criteria and "soft skills" of the team, which we will cover shortly.

Pattern Recognition

Another useful technical ability is the use of design patterns[13] to reduce programming time. Most professional software development

---

13. For references on design patterns, see the bibliography and the Software without Borders web site.

teams now regularly take advantage of their experience with design patterns as they begin new projects.

Following well-known patterns enables programmers to write code more quickly, while reducing the chance of errors when compared with creating software completely from scratch. You will want your offshore vendor to be familiar with design patterns if you rely on them to make professional technical decisions about your software architecture.

Too Big, Too Small, or Just Right?

You should consider the overall size of the vendor in terms of the number of engineers they employ as a factor in your decision. Too small, and the vendor may not have enough engineers to keep your project staffed at the level you need. Will the vendor have additional resources "on the bench" if you need to grow or to quickly overcome a sudden loss of talent due to normal attrition?

However, if you choose one of the large outsourcing firms in India, you may not get the attention you deserve. You may experience the swapping of people on and off your project, poor communication, and lack of responsiveness to your questions. These large firms are looking to bag the big deals requiring hundreds of engineers. Will you be an important client to your vendor or be ignored like a gnat on an elephant's rear?

Consider the number of engineers you need to develop your software and whether the vendor has experience dealing with the same size project. Most software is developed by small, agile teams of between 5 and 25 engineers. Fewer than 5 and your success will depend heavily on the qualifications, skill, and experience of the individual engineers. With more than 25 engineers, the management and communication structure of the group becomes the dominant success factor.

Regardless of the number of engineers on a team, it should have a combination of senior and junior engineers. This keeps costs in line and enables you to focus your communications on the senior members of the team.

If you need only one or two engineers, consider using individual freelance programmers. Individual programmers can be found on web sites like Elance Marketplace and RentACoder.[14] Your results

---

14. Links to these and other freelancer web sites are on the Software without Borders web site.

on these sites will depend on the skill and ethics of the individuals you select from those that bid on your project.

One entrepreneur tells me that he gets satisfactory results for about 80 percent of the projects he outsources with these sites. For the other 20 percent, the programmers never finish the work or stop responding to his emails and, of course, are not paid. The bottom line is that he is able to get most of his small programming projects completed for a few hundred dollars each, but with a great deal of monitoring and communication to ensure that he gets what he needs.

If you need more than a couple of programmers, you should hire a team that is capable of working together. You can check the resumés of the members, as is recommended in step 3, before you make your final selection. The dynamics of the team and the management provided by the technical leads are more important than the quality of each individual engineer's resumé.

You should be aware that most vendors will prefer a long-term relationship in which their programmers become your trusted offshore development team. Remember, you should think of the process of selecting an outsourcing vendor as being like hiring employees. Selecting an offshore software development vendor is not a simple purchasing exercise.

Rock Around the Clock

Many people who outsource think they want 24-hour development in India. Of course, India is an excellent outsourcing destination, and a majority of outsourced software development from the United States is performed by Indian companies.

There is one catch, and it is the time difference. The time difference between the West Coast of the U.S. and India is 13½ hours (12½ during U.S. daylight saving time). It is a little better for the East Coast, enabling overlap between the East Coast morning and late afternoon in India (8 A.M. EDT is 5:30 P.M. in India).

However, if you prefer an overlap with conventional workday hours, you may favor another location. For example, countries in Central America and much of South America are close, to and even share, U.S. time zones. This provides you complete overlap with the workday in most parts of the U.S. Meanwhile, countries in Eastern Europe can have some overlap with the U.S. morning and significant overlap with the Western Europe workday.

Even if you don't have a preference for one country or another, consider the overlap with your workday as a factor in making your decision.

Fourteen Criteria in a Vendor Screening Matrix

By now you should have the idea that you will use multiple criteria to eliminate all but the vendors you should be seriously considering. We have already looked at three of these criteria; now let's include a few more.

You can use a *decision matrix* to keep things organized and objective. The matrix can automatically compute a total score for the vendors you evaluate. The vendor with the highest score isn't necessarily the one you should select. The matrix will give you a good understanding of what is important for making your decision and an indication of which vendors merit your serious attention.

As I discussed above, the most important criteria are usually technical. There are five major technology stacks: J2EE, .NET, LAMP, C++, and COBOL. Your project may need a combination of two or more of these. Or you may need to go deep in a particular stack and require expertise with specific details, such as EJBs using JBoss and MySQL, or Delphi on Windows.

Expertise with your specific technical skills is usually a strict requirement for selecting a team. Table 3-1 lists some others.

You then add a column to the matrix for each vendor you want to evaluate. You rank their ability to meet each criterion on a scale, typically from 1 to 10. Then each ranking is multiplied by the weight and totaled for each vendor. You will quickly and objectively see which vendors are more likely to be the best fit for your situation.

You can download this matrix as an Excel file from the book's web site[15] as an example and an excellent starting point to create your own decision matrix to help you select your outsourcing vendor.

Indicate how important each criterion is to your decision by entering a numerical weight value in the third column. In the matrix in Table 3-1, technical skill is weighted heavily at 5 and workday overlap and relative cost are given weights of 3, meaning they are 3 times more important than the other criteria.

---

15. The URL of the vendor screening decision matrix is: www.SoftwareWithout BordersBook.com/VendorScreeningMatrix.xls

Table 3-1. Criteria for Selecting a Contract Outsourcing Vendor

	Team Selection Criteria	Team Capabilities	Weight
1	Technical expertise	Around 100 skills, from ActiveX to Zope	5
2	Domain expertise	Financial, healthcare, elearning, consumer, EDA, digital media, etc.	1
3	Software development methodology	Agile, rational, QA-only	1
4	Size of team needed	1, 2, 5, 10, 15, 20, 25, 30, 35, 40, 50+	3
5	Education requirements	Ph.D., MS, BS	1
6	Certifications and awards	MS-certified, CMM3, CMM4, CMM5, CMMI, ISO-9001, Scrum	1
7	Country	Argentina, Belarus, Brazil, Bulgaria, Chile, China, Costa Rica, Czech Republic, Hungary, India, Mexico, Panama, Philippines, Poland, Romania, Russia, Slovakia, Turkey, Ukraine, USA	1
8	Region	South Asia, Southeast Asia, Eastern Europe, Central America, North America, South America	1
9	Workday overlap	All day, all night, morning, afternoon, either A.M. or P.M.	3
10	Local staff	Yes or no	1
11	English skill	Excellent or good	1
12	Relative cost	Low, lower, lowest	3
13	BOT support	Yes or no	1
14	Subsidiary creation	Yes or no	1

Each vendor has strengths and weaknesses and may or may not satisfy the specific criteria that are important to you. Consequently, the number of vendors that can satisfy your needs will quickly be narrowed to the top two or three.

Here are examples of how the matrix helped in the vendor searches carried out by three U.S. companies:

Goal: Strong requirements for supporting J2EE and specific XML tools. In addition, they wanted a significant workday overlap with employees working for their company in Europe.

Result: Narrowed search down to three vendors in Russia, the Czech Republic, and India.

Goal: Specific requirements for an offshore team that could grow rapidly when needed. In addition, they had a strong requirement for BOT (see Chapter 4).
Result: Selection narrowed to one vendor in Panama and two in India.

Goal: The U.S. company is pushing the envelope with low-level Microsoft Windows programming. They have a limited number of employees to deal with the technical details and the management of the software development.
Result: Although several offshore vendors could handle the technical details, the client decided that a vendor in the U.S. was the absolute best choice. The higher cost compared to an offshore solution was far outweighed by the combination of local management and technical expertise provided by the American vendor.

Step 3: Select—By Checking the Three Rs

By now, you have gotten down to a short list of vendors to consider further. Vendors on the list should be able to satisfy your most important criteria for technical skill, team size, and ability to work and collaborate with you during acceptable hours in your day.

This third step is making your final decision. It involves looking in detail at each vendor to discover which is the right one for you. The key is to look at the three R's of references, resumés, and rates. Here are all the tasks, including two optional things you can do to investigate further:

1. Check references
2. Examine resumés
3. Negotiate rates and terms
4. Visit them (optional)
5. Do a pilot project (optional)

What Do Others Say?

You should select only an outsourcing vendor that has positive references. The best references are with clients in your own country. But some outsourcing teams have done great work and have references only in other parts of the world. They could still be a good choice.

The questions you ask should confirm technical ability. What creativity do they exhibit in finding solutions to problems? What is their ability to collaborate? What kind of specification and ongoing direction is needed? Were there any problems or issues?

I See Your Hobbies Are Science Fiction and Basket Weaving . . .

Some people start out asking for resumés and rates immediately. It is usually a sign that they need only a single programmer for a short period of time. That is what some companies need, especially when they have a short-term programming resource crisis.

But other times it is a symptom of a sloppy vendor evaluation process that starts out asking the wrong questions. Sure, a vendor can show you resumés at the beginning, but there is little chance those engineers will still be available to work on your software by the time you make your decision. There are more important questions to consider than checking the skills of engineers (and their hobbies) if they will never be available to work on your software anyway.

If you are truly at step 3, and you have gone through steps 1 and 2 for sourcing and screening, you are ready to look at the resumés of the engineers that could actually be working on your software. You have confirmed through reference checks that the vendor has indeed worked on projects with your target technology. Now you can look at resumés to determine whether the engineers that will be assigned to your project actually have the skills you need.

This is also a time when you can perform a phone interview of the engineers that will be assigned to your project. I have carried out "interviews" by instant messenger if the engineer does not speak fluent English but can read and write it.

The purpose of the interview is to confirm the engineer's technical skills and ability to communicate.

You can probe for problems they have run into on other projects to get a sense of their creativity and problem-solving skills. After all, they are engineers, and engineers should love to solve problems. But be aware that in most Asian cultures, it is difficult for engineers to talk about problems or issues. If you feel as though you are not getting a complete response to your questions, it may just be a cultural issue. But it could also be a sign of future communication problems.

Everything Is Negotiable (Almost)

Everyone wants a good deal, and many outsourcing vendors will negotiate with you to win your business. However, there is a limit to how deeply the good vendors will discount. After all, they are in business to make a profit, and they have overhead of offices, salaries, and equipment to pay for. These costs are much lower than what you would pay in the U.S., and that is why offshore outsourcing rates are lower to begin with.

It is also unfair to compare the rates of a reputable outsourcing vendor with those of freelance programmers. "But I can get a programmer in the Ukraine for $8 an hour!" I have been told.

"Yes, I am sure you can," I replied. And that is absolutely fine if you just need one programmer for a non-critical project. You can get inexpensive programmers, not just from Ukraine, but all other countries as well.

But if you need an outsourced team, you will also need to pay for the infrastructure and management necessary to support them. And remember, to employ the equivalent team in the U.S. will easily cost you $50 to $60 an hour or more per engineer. Offshore outsourcing gives you significant savings even without negotiating.

Remember too that some things should not be negotiable. You should retain ownership of all the source code and intellectual property. The copyrights for the source should all be assigned to you or your company. And the programming work should be completed under a nondisclosure agreement to protect your trade secrets.

The bottom line is that hiring an outsourced team is like hiring employees. You need to do the necessary work up front to determine the kind of team you need. Out of the dozens of technical and business criteria you may come up with, you must select the key factors that will winnow down the choices. Then verify the truth by careful reference checking.

Using a Pilot Project

Using outsourcing to develop a major part of your software may feel risky to you. It can be a big commitment. That's why some companies run a pilot project with the vendor they are considering before embarking on a long-term outsourcing relationship.

Outsourcing software development is often thought of as a major project, utilizing tens to hundreds of engineers, in order to gain huge cost savings. Are you ready to select an outsourced team and have a large number of programmers you have never met start writing your software? Probably not.

You should first learn how to handle the potential risks, and budget for the extra time and overhead required for managing an outsourced team.

Experienced businesspeople know that, when embarking upon any new business process, it is often prudent to start with a small (isolated) pilot to decrease the overall risk and the impact on the overall project. This allows a safe trial and a chance to move up the learning curve over a reasonable time period, while minimizing risk—making small mistakes rather than large ones, and learning from them.

There are three goals for running a pilot project. First, you can test the outsourced team's communication abilities. You can find out how well they create software from your specifications. You can also leave specific information out of your specification to see if the outsourced team comes back to you for clarification.

Similarly, you can make changes to your specification in the middle of the pilot to see how well they handle it. An outsourced team should embrace change as a natural part of the software development process.

The second goal of running a pilot is to test the team's technical skill. You want to confirm that the outsourced team has experience with your software technology. For example, one vendor did a study of several Java database persistence techniques before beginning paid work for a client. This relatively small exercise demonstrated that the vendor had the required experience with Java and inspired complete confidence in the team's technical abilities.

A third goal can be implementing a small set of non-critical features that you need in your software. At the end of the pilot, you will have your new features, and you will also have gotten a good sense of how well the outsourced team works.

For Free or a Fee?

Sometimes, in a highly competitive situation, a vendor will carry out a short pilot for free. This kind of pilot is better characterized as a benchmark to judge specific capabilities of the outsourced team. It usually lasts no longer than a week.

For example, one company created a 20-page spec[16] for a pilot to be carried out with a new offshore vendor. The pilot was originally estimated to take three weeks, but the vendor finished it in two and a half weeks. In addition, the vendor contributed improvements to the user interface based on experience with projects with similar functionality.

The client saved about $8,000 during the pilot alone, compared to what they would have paid to the onshore programmers they were using.

When it comes to outsourcing vendor selection, the up-front time and effort required to find outsourcing vendors, develop your project specifications, and communicate and manage the outsourcing vendor can seem like too much trouble. In reality, outsourcing a small project can be a very cost-effective way to confirm your offshore vendor selection. You probably have the beginnings of a specification anyway. Even if you don't, a small pilot project will help you test the ability of your selected vendor to collaborate with you to develop the software you need.

Once your pilot project is completed successfully, you'll be ready to outsource larger projects with the confidence that you will get on-time, on-scope, and on-budget performance.

Price Negotiations

Do you remember the character Wimpy from the old Popeye cartoons? In every cartoon in which he appeared, he would say, "I will gladly pay you on Tuesday for a hamburger today!" It seemed as though he was always trying to get something for nothing. His request for a hamburger with a promise to pay later was never a very believable proposition.

---

16. A link to the spec for this pilot is at the book's web site: www.SoftwareWithout BordersBook.com

Similarly, paying your outsourced software development vendor in some risky and unfair way—paying Tuesday for software today, or some other dubious financial agreement—will diminish your results. What is the best way to structure a deal so that you can get your software developed on time and on budget?

You need an outsourcing vendor that not only will deliver what you need but also has a vested interest in your success. They need to have some skin in the game. And you can accomplish this without harsh financial incentives.

Outsourced software development is paid for in three different ways: fixed price, time and materials (T&M), or a hybrid approach that combines the two.

Fixed Price

In a fixed-price project, you clearly define the software you need, and the outsourced team charges you a fixed total amount for delivering the software. You can make some changes during development, but you have to know pretty much what you want before work is started.

Variations of the fixed-price approach can include milestone payments rather than one large payment at the end of the project. You can offer incentives for early completion and/or specify a penalty for late delivery if being on time is a critical issue for you.

A fixed-price arrangement is a great way to budget your money when you know exactly what you need. However, you don't always know what you need at the beginning of a project. In fact, when you are developing a completely new software product, you *never* know.

As the project proceeds and changes are required, you will spend a good chunk of time respecifying and negotiating with your outsourcing vendor (and perhaps your legal department) to get the changes implemented. Oftentimes dealing with change orders becomes a big hassle, and moving to a T&M arrangement begins to sound tempting.

However, a consultant with experience at a larger outsourcing firm told me they loved to charge clients on a T&M basis. It can enable the outsourcing company to talk their clients into additional services and expand the scope of the original project. With these risks, naturally his clients preferred a fixed price. Even so, it is unfair to demand a fixed-price deal from an outsourcing team unless you can clearly define what you need.

The other problem with a fixed price is that the outsourced team will likely pad their bid to cover any unexpected changes or misunderstandings. You can actually pay more for a fixed-price project than you would if you worked with an outsourced team you can trust on a T&M basis.

Time and Materials or Creating Your Offshore Development Center (ODC)

T&M means you pay only for the time spent by the outsourced team to develop your software. There is usually no charge for "materials," although sometimes you may have to provide or pay for special software or hardware required for your project.

T&M is the approach used when you want to hire outsourced engineers to augment your internal team. You want the engineers to be available full-time, and you plan to direct their activities as needed. This stable environment, where the engineers come to work every day and work only on your software, is usually referred to as an offshore development center, or ODC. It's good for you because you have a team of engineers dedicated to developing your software, and the vendor likes it because they want a long-term, beneficial relationship with a stable client.

Developing software is a creative process, and creating an ODC is best when you want the outsourced team members to contribute to the design as well as to the development of your software.

However, problems can arise with T&M when too much freedom is granted to the outsourced team. You do not want to pay for engineers to go off and create software not needed by your customers, or to be "on the job" but not creating any software at all. You can outsource the work but not the responsibility.

Your ODC must have effective project management to get the best results. It needs a good blend of senior and junior engineers, along with a team lead and/or project manager. Frequent status reports and constant communication will help ensure that your engineers are working on the most important tasks.

Or the engineers in your ODC can use an agile software development process that is highly collaborative with you and has frequent iterations. If you prefer agile methods, an ODC is the way to go.

Over my career, I have worked on both fixed-price and T&M projects, and I have gotten both good and bad results with each.

What I find works best for many clients is a hybrid approach that combines features of both fixed price and T&M.

The Hybrid Approach

The hybrid approach reduces the risk of your paying too much. It also reduces the risk of the outsourced team doing too much to complete a project whose scope was not well understood initially.

Here's how it works. A large project, requiring six months or more to complete, is divided into smaller pieces with well-defined milestones. By "well-defined," I mean that specific features of your software are clearly specified and the outsourced team has made a firm commitment to deliver them by a specific date. The definition of these features can be in the form of a written specification, a software prototype, and/or a set of "use cases" that show how your customers will use the software to solve their problem.

In the hybrid approach, instead of agreeing on a price for your entire project, only the completion of the next milestone has a fixed price. As each milestone is completed, the next one is defined, and a similar commitment to its completion and price is made. Changes based on information discovered during work on achieving the previous milestone are incorporated into the next or some future milestone.

Thus, in your initial specification, the definition of the first milestone is the most important. Later milestones can be defined in general terms, along with target dates for completion. But only the next milestone is defined in enough detail to enable a commitment for a completion date and cost.

There is a similarity between agile software development techniques and the hybrid method of payment. Agile development and extreme programming are discussed in more detail in Chapters 5 and 6. Among other things, agile methods include frequent builds and product release milestones.

The phrase "time box" is used in agile development to describe the fixed and usually short periods of time during which you will use the agile development of your software. You and your ODC team members put the features you want implemented into each box, with high-priority features in the time boxes to be completed sooner than the others. If a feature is too big to fit in a time box, it must be broken down into smaller features.

You collaborate with the ODC team to determine how many features will fit in each box. It is important to obtain a commitment from your outsourced team by having them involved in the decision regarding what will be completed in each time box or milestone.

Choose your outsourcing team and payment approach carefully. Use a fixed price when you can communicate a clear description of what you need. Use the T&M approach when you have a high degree of trust in your outsourced team and you need them to work on various tasks that are difficult to predict ahead of time. Finally, the hybrid approach of splitting your product development into smaller amounts of time and functionality gives you the benefit of tracking both costs and software development progress to give you close to risk-free outsourcing.

Elements of Good Contracts and Agreements

I agreed to outsource some work to another company, and we had several discussions about what needed to be done as well as how and when it should be carried out. We also discussed the cost and payment terms, which were acceptable to both of us.

The vendor said, "Great; I'll send over a copy of our agreement." The agreement that arrived attached to an email was absolutely shocking! It had so many one-sided terms and conditions, and not on my side, of course, that I almost refused to do business with the vendor.

The agreement I received said that I had to give the vendor stock in my company, as well as pay cash. The only problem was that we had never discussed stock as compensation. The agreement also said that I had to pay $100,000 in "damages" if I ever "breached any of the covenants of the agreement," yet the agreement involved only a couple of thousand dollars per month for the services being offered.

"Oh, that's just our standard agreement" the vendor said when I called him.

Make sure your vendor has higher standards than that!

An Unfair Advantage

Some people focus entirely on the agreement and just its words as the entirety of the business relationship. It is as if they think they can look up a section in the agreement and have it tell them how to treat the other party. Yes, the agreement may be between their corporation and yours, but ultimately, it is people making these agreements. And it does not matter where people are from. My experience is that people have a universal sense of fairness that you should not betray if you plan to have a long-term business relationship with them.

Neither side should seek an unfair advantage through the outsourcing agreement. The agreement should document what you have already agreed to in principle through your discussions about the work to be performed and how and when it will be paid for. It should be a clear statement of what is *already* agreed and should protect each party from misinterpretations.

The Spirit of the Agreement

The spirit of your agreement is the ultimate purpose or reason for having the agreement to begin with. It is a real and tangible thing. If you seek out some undeserved benefit allowed by the words of your agreement, you are violating the spirit of that agreement.

And besides it probably won't work.

For example, I once hired a former friend to do some part-time database administration work for my company. He already had a full-time job, so he couldn't commit to a specific number of hours in the agreement, but he said he should be able to spend about 20 hours per month.

Twenty hours was fine. I needed someone part-time to get a few projects done and to handle problems and crises when they arose. I was able to pay him cash for work performed as well as an amount of stock that was proportional to the amount of time he promised to spend.

But he didn't spend 20 hours in a month or even in two months. He was busy at his full-time job. Imagine my surprise when he demanded the stock, especially after it became obvious that he was not able to do any of the work. Clearly he did not understand the spirit of the agreement—he was to receive money and stock for work performed, and my company was to receive his valuable database services.

He asked for his stock and I said no. Getting something not in keeping with spirit of the agreement rarely occurs.

In this case, there was limited damage in violating the spirit of the agreement, except for the end of a friendship. The impact is much larger if each party represents teams of people who either do not get paid or are unable to get the software they need.

The Power of the Purse Strings

The buyer has the ultimate power in an outsourcing relationship because the buyer can withhold payment from the seller. If the outsourcing vendor does not perform—don't pay them!

Is a company in another country going to sue you over a final payment that is less than $25,000? Probably not, because it is not worth the time, travel, and legal fees required to make it happen. Therefore, an offshore vendor (or any vendor that is smart) will go the extra mile to make you happy with their services to ensure that you pay them.

Should you take advantage of them and not pay them even if they do a good job? Of course not! If that is how you run your business, then please give this book away to someone else.

The Party of the First Part

Most outsourcing agreements have two parts—a main agreement and then exhibits for each project or programming engagement. The main agreement covers basic legal terms and definitions. It is the contract that governs the relationship between your company and the outsourcing vendor.

Your main agreement should include these elements:

- **Independent contractor relationship.** The outsourcing company is an independent contractor, and its engineers are not your employees. This distinction has important tax consequences in the U.S., especially when you are hiring individual contractors.
- **Intellectual property rights.** You own all intellectual property that is produced, including source code, inventions, etc. More about this in Chapter 8.
- **Assignment of copyright.** This is usually a separate part of the agreement that specifically assigns the copyrights of the software source code to your company.

- **Nondisclosure obligations.** These contain the definition of your proprietary and confidential information and an agreement not to disclose it.
- **Term and termination.** State the length of the agreement and the rights of each side to end it. Terms of one or two years with the ability for either side to terminate with 30 days' notice are common.
- **No conflict of interest.** Both sides agree not to enter into other agreements that conflict with this one. Sometimes this means that the vendor is restricted from performing work with competitors of the buyer company.
- **Noninterference with business.** This clause specifies that neither party will interfere with the sales and other business activities of the other's company or hire away employees of the other for some period of time.
- **Force majeure.** This limits the liability of both parties if work is interrupted by major natural disasters, like fire, flood, and hurricane, or by man-made causes such as war, terrorism, and government regulation or restriction.
- **Assignment.** The outsourcing vendor should be restricted from contracting out (or outsourcing your work) to another vendor without your written permission.
- **Governing law, jurisdiction, and venue.** If there is an issue, you will want the laws of your own state and country to apply.

These are many of the important elements of an outsourcing agreement. There may be several other clauses and details that you want to include. This book does not offer complete legal advice, and you should use an attorney if you have any concerns and questions about the meaning and wording of your agreement.

Now, where in the agreement do we talk about price? What about quality and responsiveness to bugs and problems? These details can vary from project to project. They are specified in separate exhibits added to the agreement.

The Second Part: An Exhibit with Work Details

You will usually add at least one exhibit to your agreement to cover the details of your outsourcing engagement. Additional exhibits are used for each separate project you outsource with the vendor.

The exhibit will include as much detail as you need to describe the engagement or project. A *statement of work*, usually copied from the proposal, is included. If a specification or statement of requirements is available, it will also be included.

The pricing and payment terms are also included in the exhibit, as is provision for expenses such as travel. In T&M or ODC engagements, there can be a rate schedule for the kinds of engineers that will be assigned to your project team. For example, there can be different rates for technical architects, project managers, junior and senior software developers, test engineers, and so on.

To keep things simple when there is a small team of engineers in an ODC, a single "blended" or average rate is used for all engineers developing your software, independent of their level of skill.

Your agreement should give you price protection. That is, it should not allow the vendor to raise rates during the term of the agreement. If the term is two years, you should be able to add resources to your team at the same rate as your original engineers over that two-year period.

As a practical matter, either you or the vendor can terminate the agreement within a reasonable period of time—typically 30 or 60 days. It is possible but highly unlikely that the vendor will threaten to terminate the agreement unless rates are raised, leaving you to pay more or search for a new vendor on short notice.

On a happier note, the rate schedule in your agreement exhibit can include a reduction in rates as the size of your offshore team grows. Vendors should be willing to offer you a "quantity discount" as your need for more engineers grows over time.

We have come a long way in this chapter—from dreaming about the cost savings and fast ramp-up of outsourcing to the evaluation and selection of your vendor and the signing of an agreement to get your software developed. Contract outsourcing gives you the flexibility to increase and shrink your development team as your requirements and business change over time. It is perfect for fixed-price projects and an ODC with a team of 5 to 50 engineers.

For more than 50 engineers, you can consider creating your own offshore subsidiary but it is a big commitment that not every company should make. We discuss the details of this in the next chapter, so you can discover for yourself whether creating a subsidiary is right for you.

Chapter 4

Offshoring, or Creating Your Own Offshore Subsidiary

Globalization has changed us into a company that searches the world, not just to sell or to source, but to find intellectual capital—the world's best talents and greatest ideas.

—Jack Welch, former chairman and CEO of GE

U nless you plan to hire 50 offshore software engineers or more, this chapter is probably not for you. Fifty engineers seems to be the minimum number of employees needed before creating a subsidiary makes economic sense.

And it may never make sense for your company. Offshoring is different from offshore outsourcing. Offshore outsourcing is contracting with an offshore vendor to develop your software on a fixed-price or time and materials basis. The relationship is governed by a contract and can last for a long or short time period.

Offshoring is intended to be a more permanent arrangement. It is often associated with the idea of "moving" jobs offshore. This is because you are hiring full-time employees, not here but offshore, in another country.

These jobs are moved, or created to begin with, because the salary difference is dramatic. If you are going to save money with offshore outsourcing, why not save even more money by hiring your engineers as employees offshore and cutting out the overhead of having an outsourcing vendor?

One reason is that you have to replace that overhead with your own. You have to hire your own people in a foreign country to deal with local laws, taxes, and authorities to make sure you do the right things when setting up your office and hiring your employees.

Unless you are from that country, and even from the city where your subsidiary will be located, you will need a local advisor or partner to help you with the process.

There are two ways to offshore. You can directly create your own subsidiary in another country, or you can partner with an offshore vendor to build, operate, and then transfer your engineering team into a subsidiary you create later. The second technique is usually referred to as BOT.

This is not a how-to book on creating a subsidiary. However, I want to share in this chapter some basic information about the options involved in offshoring, so that you can consider whether it is right for your situation. If you do decide to create a subsidiary and hire engineers, directly or using the BOT option, all of the other chapters on describing your software, managing your offshore software development, and measuring your productivity will still apply.

First Order T-Shirts, Then Create a Subsidiary in India

We used to joke that the first step in starting a software business is to order the company T-shirts. The second is to start coding. (Writing the specifications is a distant third!) Offshore outsourcing is now reformulating this time-tested formula. Now the joke is that you first order T-shirts and then create a subsidiary in India.

You may think you need to create a subsidiary in a foreign country in order to take maximum advantage of offshore resources to develop your software. Although the savings may appear to be greatest by taking this approach, it makes business and financial sense only when you are building a large engineering team.

It is often better to get started by contracting with an established outsourcing vendor. This approach will give you flexible use of software development resources that are still much less expensive than building a complete internal engineering team of employees.

If you are creating a subsidiary to house a large engineering team, you need to be prepared for an up-front investment of time and money. You must acquire office space and fit it out for use by the team. You need to create a legal entity that has the proper relationship with your company, to avoid issues related to taxes and ownership of intellectual property.

In short, creating a subsidiary in a foreign country is complex and time-consuming. The savings you gain by creating a subsidiary may not be worth the up-front cash required and the distraction it causes your management team when they should be focused on increasing sales and running your company domestically. Table 4-1 summarizes the trade-offs involved.

Some companies wait to use outsourcing as a last resort, to reduce their burn rate and extend their "runway"—the amount of time the company can survive without a significant increase in revenue. Making a major strategic move to outsource in a time of crisis (when money is running out) often leads to snap decisions and limited planning.

If you are running out of cash, it can be an easy decision to outsource for survival. Creating a subsidiary for even greater long-term savings may seem like the best approach. However, creating a

Table 4-1. Quick Comparison Between Offshore Outsourcing and Subsidiary Creation

	Offshore Outsourcing	Offshore Subsidiary
Set-up costs	Low	High
Ongoing costs of salary, facilities, and expenses compared to the U.S.	50%	33%
Ramp-up time	2 to 4 weeks	6 months
Direct control over organization culture, processes, and operations	Some	Complete
Contribution to company valuation	Small	Large
Control of intellectual property	Good	Better
Exposure to foreign politics and economic factors	Some	Direct*

*Currency fluctuations are a potential problem. Also, there are limits to the amount of money you can repatriate or bring back out of India or China. You will want to transfer only what you need to your subsidiary in India or China, since you cannot bring back any excess.

subsidiary at this point of crisis is unwise, because of the up-front time and costs[17].

On the other hand, if your technical team leaders are originally from the foreign country, having them move back home to Bangalore or Moscow (or wherever) and create a subsidiary there may be a viable strategy. It is certainly less challenging than it would be for an outsider unfamiliar with the local culture.

Other companies can end up with a subsidiary "back in the old country" when a key employee moves back. One company I know found themselves in this situation. Rather than lose the employee completely, they agreed to let him set up an office in India. This enabled the company to enjoy the lower cost of labor while continuing to use his services, which they value and trust.

This less formal, "friends and family" approach to creating a subsidiary costs less than usual. In addition, having employees who move back home where they are already familiar with the cultural landscape helps you avoid many problems and delays.

For example, an accountant I know has a client that created a subsidiary offshore. An employee who was originally from India went there to set up the operation. The accountant was amazed to see several expenses required to get things done quickly that were actually bribes.

Similarly, in 1992, one of my companies set up an offshore facility in India. The American VP who was responsible for the group traveled there several times a year. He had many stories to tell that show how different things can be in another country. At the end of one trip, he was ready to return home after being in Bangalore for about a week. He was at the airport boarding gate, ready to go—luggage checked and boarding pass in hand. They began loading the plane but would not allow him to get on. After making several requests to board the plane, it finally dawned on him what was required. A crisp ten-dollar bill (or the equivalent in rupees) and he was politely allowed on board and was on his way home to the good old USA. That was just the way it was in India at that time.

But if you have a company to run and software to get written, do you really want to take on the challenging details of starting a subsidiary in another culture completely on your own?

---

17. Wall St. Journal, March 3, 2004, "Lesson in India: Not Every Job Translates Overseas."

For some innovators and early adopters, the answer is yes. You can do it yourself or you can find and hire an offshore partner that is familiar with the country and culture, to set up your subsidiary in India, or some other country you prefer. Then you spend the time and money required to hire the engineering team.

The partner helps you eliminate the red tape associated with creating a new business entity, complying with local laws, accounting and tax rules. They also help you with recruiting and the human resources issues you may not be aware of that govern hiring in the local culture.

In creating an offshore subsidiary, you are converting what could be a variable-cost expense using contract outsourcing into a fixed cost. It is your subsidiary and you own it. That fixed cost will be lower on an ongoing basis than contract outsourcing. But there are startup costs required to find an office, make improvements, hire and manage the team, etc. Above all, you are making a long-term commitment to a single country.

What are the startup costs? They run from $25,000 to $100,000, depending on the location, the size of the team, and who you partner with in the foreign country. These costs should cover the incorporation of your foreign entity, accounting costs, legal advice for entering into agreements with any service providers, and recruiting of employees.[18]

As I stated at the beginning of this chapter, you should think about creating an offshore subsidiary only if you know your engineering team will grow to more than 50 engineers. Otherwise, the risks and cost savings are often not justified.

For example, a large public software company in Silicon Valley has a 350-engineer operation in Bangalore, India. Three years earlier, they found a partner in Bangalore and began building their team using the build, operate and transfer (BOT) model described in the next section.

Now, three years later, they have the option of doing the transfer—taking these engineers and making them employees of their own newly created subsidiary. Everything remains the same, but the costs will go down because the partner is then out of the picture.

Did they do it?

---

18. See "Guide to Establishing a Subsidiary in India" from Fenwick and West, and other articles listed on the Software without Borders web site.

"No, because the risks would go up," said the American executive I spoke to. Suddenly they would be completely responsible for an entire operation in a foreign country.

Don't the savings of having their own subsidiary justify it?

Here is how the executive described it. "A third of the money they spend for each engineer goes to salary and benefits. Another third goes for the infrastructure of office, computers, utilities, etc. That leaves no more than a 30 percent profit margin for the partner in India, and probably less."

Theoretically the American company can immediately save about 30 percent if they do the transfer.

But will they?

The executive thinks not. "We will still have to hire and pay for our own people to manage the business operation in India and handle human resources issues, etc. We will be lucky to save 15 percent, and those savings do not justify the extra risk and responsibility."

The moral of the story is this. Here is a large company with an option to easily create a subsidiary containing 350 engineers, and they decide not to do it because of the extra responsibility. Look at the numbers carefully for your own situation. The theoretical savings you will get may not be enough to justify creation of an offshore subsidiary immediately, if ever.

How to Build a Subsidiary in 24 Months

Rather than immediately creating an offshore subsidiary to use high-quality engineers at a low cost, many companies contract with outsourcing providers first. Part of the contract is an option to transfer the outsourced team into their own subsidiary that is created later. In India, this is known as build, operate, and transfer, or BOT.

There are two purposes in creating a subsidiary. First, it gives the owning company ostensibly greater control compared to contracting with another company. Greater control and ownership enhance the value of your company—an important issue for a young company seeking to be acquired or to complete a successful IPO. Second, the costs are lower.

However, as we saw in the previous section, creating a subsidiary is a major commitment. There are setup costs for establishing an office, finding legal and accounting services, and so on. Then you must hire one or more experienced managers to run the operation and to hire and manage the engineering team. The entire process of setting up a subsidiary takes four to six months.

Also, you may have a few individuals experienced with outsourcing but no organizational competence within your company. If that is the case, creating a subsidiary could take you even longer than normal, and you could end up making costly mistakes.

If you are not ready to invest the time and money required to create your own subsidiary, but you still want one, contract outsourcing with a BOT option is for you.

BOT gives you the advantages of having a subsidiary in the future without the long ramp-up and high initial costs required for subsidiary creation. You will gain valuable outsourcing experience by working with a contract outsourcing partner, so you will be completely ready to take on the management of your subsidiary later, if you choose to do so. Transfer to the subsidiary is an option; you can continue contract outsourcing indefinitely.

If and when you decide to exercise your option to create a subsidiary, your outsourcing team is transferred over to a new subsidiary created for you by the offshore company, and the team members become your employees. This form of BOT is similar to a contract-to-hire arrangement that companies use to fill some full-time positions.

The benefit to the U.S. company is that it gets a subsidiary at little or no additional cost with an offshore team it has worked with, knows, and trusts. The benefit to the offshore company is a business relationship that lasts two to three years before the transfer is made, building and operating a team at a profit that grows as the number of engineers increases.

BOT is a good choice if you want to start with a handful of engineers, grow a team over time, and build them into a valuable subsidiary asset. For example, you can start with 5 engineers and grow to a team of 30 or 40 or more. You also have the flexibility to grow and shrink the team as needed over time. Then, after an agreed-upon amount of time, usually two to three years, you have the option of transferring the team to a new subsidiary that will be created for you at little or no additional cost.

If you have bigger plans to build a large engineering team more quickly than two years, there is a second BOT approach. It is similar to creating a subsidiary at the beginning but lets you get started programming right away.

Here is how it works. Your offshore partner hires and/or assigns an engineering team to develop your software. They get started immediately and charge typical offshore contract software development rates (see Table 4-2). Then, for a fee, your offshore partner sets up a facility and handles the legal and accounting tasks needed to create your subsidiary.

At transfer time, you may have to pay additional fees to move the existing team over to be employees of your subsidiary. These fees are paid to the offshore firm for the original interviewing and hiring process. The employee transfer fees are completely negotiable and typically range from a flat fee per employee to 50 percent of each engineer's annual salary.

Rather than setting up a subsidiary first and then starting the programming, this second BOT approach allows you to start producing software right away. You can then have your offshore engineering team operating as a subsidiary within six months to a year, depending on the speed you require.

Which BOT approach is better? It depends on how large an offshore team you want and how involved you need to be in interviewing and hiring the team. It also depends on how quickly you want to be operating as a subsidiary and how much you want to spend up front versus over time.

Table 4-2. Cost Comparison of Two BOT Approaches

	Year 1		Year 2		Year 3
	H1	H2	H3	H4	H5
Engineers	10	15	20	25	25
BOT 1: Subsidiary in Year 2	Contract	Contract	Contract	Contract + setup	Subsidiary + transfer
Half-Year Cost	$240K	$360K	$480K	$600K + $0	$300K + $0
Cumulative Cost	$240K	$600K	$1,080K	$1,680K	$1,980K
BOT 2: Subsidiary in Year 1	Contract	Contract + setup	Subsidiary + transfer	Subsidiary	Subsidiary
Half-Year Cost	$240K	$360K + $150K	$240K + $48K	$300K	$300K
Cumulative Cost	$240K	$750K	$1,038K	$1,338K	$1,638K

Let's look at an example. Suppose you need to build an engineering team of 25-five engineers over a two-year period. Table 4-2 shows the estimated costs of each BOT approach at six-month intervals during a 2½-year period. Both offshore teams grow at the same rate and have the same number of engineers employed during each time period. Both use 10 engineers during the first six months as a contract programming team.

The cost assumptions used in the table are as follows:

- The contract rate for each offshore engineer is $4,000 per month ($\times$ 6 months = $24,000 per half year).
- The salary and overhead for each engineer as an offshore employee is $2,000 per month ($\times$ 6 months = $12,000 per half year).
- The offshore partner in BOT 1 assumes the setup and transfer costs because the two-year commitment to contract outsourcing gives them enough profit to do so.
- The six-month setup cost to create a subsidiary in BOT 2 are $25,000 per month ($\times$ 6 months = $150,000).
- The transfer costs in BOT 2 are 10 percent of the annual offshore salary, which is $2,400 per engineer ($\times$ 20 engineers = $48,000).

As you can see in this model, using BOT 2 and paying to create a subsidiary in year 1 saves money ($342,000) over time. The downside is the lack of flexibility and the distractions that setting up a subsidiary brings. Having to shrink the team halfway through year 2 would be a major problem requiring a disruptive layoff of workers.

BOT 1 costs more over time but provides the most flexibility and does not require a relatively large investment to create the subsidiary in year 1, when you may not have the cash.

Table 4-2 presents just one scenario of many that can be modeled. The number of engineers can vary over time, and costs will vary from one company and country to another. However, it is interesting to note that over the same period of time the cost of a U.S.-based engineering team of the same increasing size would be $5,700,000 (at an estimated cost of $10,000 per engineer per month). That is more than double the cost of contract offshore outsourcing.

Again, the decision to create a subsidiary must be made with a careful analysis of your situation. If you have the funds, creating a subsidiary may be the correct move for you. If you are not sure of the quality of the team and are worried about cultural differences, a BOT approach can give you the time and flexibility you need to gain confidence. If you would rather focus on the creation of your software and not think about the political, legal, and business issues of creating a subsidiary, the use of contract outsourcing is a time-tested approach.

BOT Opens the Kimono

Earlier I mentioned that a company estimated its BOT partner in India was earning about a 30 percent profit margin. That is actually rather high for a BOT. A profit of 30 percent is more typical in a short-term engagement in which engineers may be dropped from a project at any time. When they are dropped, the vendor has to continue to pay their salaries while they sit on the bench waiting for another project to arrive for them to work on. A high 30 percent margin helps the vendor afford the bench-time salaries for engineers who were hired previously for your project.

But BOT is different. As in the offshore development center (ODC) model, the intention is to have a stable team of engineers hired for the long term. Cutbacks may occur, but they will be rare. Therefore, a high profit margin is not justified.

What is your vendor's profit margin? Normally it's hard to know. You can ask, but unless you are familiar with the going rate for salaries of engineers in the offshore location, it will be hard for you to know if the answer is accurate.

With BOT it is a different story. The vendor—your partner in the BOT—has to honestly tell you what the engineers' salaries are so you can make your plans for eventual transfer of the team into your own subsidiary.

The conclusion here is that you probably should always pursue the BOT option when you are outsourcing to a large team of engineers of 20 or more. Even if you have no intention of exercising the transfer option, you will want the insight into the cost of the engineers so that you can realize maximum savings. Of course, this idea will not work if you are outsourcing to a smaller team of 5 to 10 engineers. That is too small for a subsidiary, and reputable vendors will not play along.

Go East, Young Man—To Eastern Europe, *That Is*

Horace Greeley, a 19th-century American newspaper editor and politician, once advised Americans to "Go West," encouraging them to take advantage of the opportunities in the largely untapped American western frontier. Now Eastern Europe offers similar opportunities and advantages to Americans looking for low-cost but high-quality software development resources. In the 21st century, the advice is "Go East!"

If you are looking at offshore outsourcing or creating a subsidiary offshore, you are probably thinking about India or maybe China. But what about Eastern Europe? Are there advantages to developing your software in this region of the world?

Each country and city has its differences. Someone from Poland will face difficulties dealing with the language and culture in Ukraine. Someone from Kiev will have trouble knowing what to do even in Odessa. You need to leave behind cultural assumptions and proceed in step with the local values and ways of behaving. Learn about the history and current events of the region, to help in your understanding of the culture and to create rapport.

IT design and engineering talent exists everywhere. India and China certainly deserve attention, but although they are attractive for some needs, they are less attractive for others. India has attracted a mass of activity in Bangalore and Hyderabad, and many executives feel comfortable "going with the flow" and outsourcing to those areas.

India has developed a leading mass of talent for software coding to spec. Higher-end, innovation-driven capabilities are not nearly as abundant. The same goes for China.

In India, wage levels have accelerated to the point that many kinds of work cost more than half of what the same work would cost in the U.S. Then there is the challenge of remote management, including a two-day plane trip each way. Employee retention has also become a problem. Indian employees tend to jump ship when a competing employer offers a marginal wage increase.

On the other hand, the quality of the technical talent pool in Eastern Europe is very high. From Copernicus to the nuclear scientists of the Soviet Union, Eastern Europe has a deep tradition in the most challenging of the sciences.

Most people are not aware that the Nazi "Enigma" coding machine was actually broken first by three Polish algorithm professors in 1939, when French and British teams were getting nowhere[19]. The experts reverse-engineered and smuggled working units to England, where the teams at Bletchley Park were then able to keep up with further versions. Many historians agree that breaking Enigma was crucial to the Allied victory.

Today, Eastern Europeans always place well in worldwide IT problem-solving contests, especially considering that so few of their individual participants and university teams have the money to enter and travel to the events. One such contest is Top Coder,[20] sponsored by Microsoft, Intel, Yahoo, and Nvidia. Another is the ACM-ICPC contest sponsored by IBM,[21] in which St. Petersburg and Warsaw won the global university team title in 2003 and 2004 respectively.

Eastern Europe not only has top-notch educational programs but also a high level of commercial activity. The most demanding parts for one of the two most valuable IT platforms in the world—Intel's Centrino—are being designed in Nizhny Novgorod, Russia, where they have more than 1,000 people, and in Gdansk, Poland, where they have 200 people. The Gdansk team is creating the integrated communications interface circuitry and software, including the next versions of Ethernet, WiFi, and WiMax. Intel's EVP praises their productivity to no end. Some of the most advanced base station and cell phone–embedded software from Motorola is designed and built in Krakow, Poland.

Tata, one of India's leading offshoring companies, has a center in Budapest employing hundreds of people, to better serve Europe. Microsoft's Passport security technology came from Poland via an acquisition. Nokia developed several of its mobility servers in Poland. You can regularly see the likes of Intel, IBM, Microsoft, SAP, Siemens, Alcatel, Ericsson, and Nokia covering the interviewing bulletin boards in computer science and electrical engineering departments of Eastern Europe universities.

Don't expect any of these companies to publicly praise their resources there. The last thing they want is competition for a goose that is laying golden eggs!

---

19. *Enigma: How the Poles Broke the Nazi Code* by Wladyslaw Kozaczuk, Jerzy Straszak, Hippocrene Books, 2004

20. See http://www.topcoder.com/tc.

21. See http://icpc.baylor.edu/past/default.htm.

But the secret of Eastern Europe is getting out now. Some companies are diversifying from primary resources in India or China. Some are setting up field engineering closer to their European customers. Some are just learning of this talent and going for new higher-end, innovation-oriented resources. In each case they are surprised at how fast they can establish the new resource and bring it up to speed.

Outsourcing or offshoring in Eastern Europe will give you access to a well-educated work force and experienced professionals. You will be following in the footsteps of many other large companies that have found Eastern Europe to be an excellent location for technical resources and support of their business in the rest of Europe.

Ten Steps to Select Your Offshoring Partner

Chapter 3 presented a simple three-step process for selecting a contract outsourcing vendor. That process can also be used to select a partner to help you create a subsidiary. But you may want to use a more thorough process, because creating a subsidiary is such a big commitment.

These 10 steps are a way for you to structure a more detailed process to select an offshore partner that will help you create a subsidiary. A key is to define your objectives carefully and include them in a request for proposal (RFP) that you give to prospective offshore partners.

1. **Set your outsourcing goals.** Define and review your outsourcing goals and objectives.

    What is the timing of your decision and then implementation? What is the budget for your subsidiary creation process, in terms of time and cost? Will your offshore team coexist with your internal software development team?

2. **Define your partner selection criteria.** Create an evaluation matrix with your important criteria. There are dozens of criteria you can include in these eight major categories:

    Business: time in business, how many clients, plans for future growth, rates, payment terms, profitability, etc.

    Location: easy to reach, safety issues, language, culture, etc.

    Infrastructure: power, Internet connection, office attractiveness, physical security

Technical: experience with your industry, computer languages, operating systems, databases, software development tools, etc.

Communication: telecom connections for voice and video, language and cultural compatibility

Process: quality assurance, software development methodologies, tools to support process, coding and documentation standards, certifications like CMMI, ISO, etc.

Manpower: local talent pool availability, ability to recruit new technical employees, retention track record, management experience, positive corporate culture, ability to travel to your location, etc.

Risks: stability of government and political issues, censorship, terrorism, conflicts of interest, loss of communication links, resource competition with other projects, respect for intellectual property, etc.

You can interview your internal employees and discover what criteria are important to them as you build this matrix. Experienced consultants are another resource you can tap.

3. **Define your evaluation process.** How will you go about finding outsourcing vendors and applying the criteria defined in step 2?

Will you first consider countries and regions of the world where you are willing to outsource? You may have strong feelings about where your potential outsourcing destination should be. India is where the majority of American companies outsource. You might focus on Mexico because of the closeness in distance and time zone. Or you may be open to outsourcing anywhere as long as you get good quality and service at a reasonable price.

Next, define how many vendors you will evaluate. For example, you may identify 5 vendors and then narrow the choice to the top 2 using a decision matrix (covered in Chapter 3). Or you may have multiple reduction steps, starting with 12 vendors and then reducing the number to 6 and then to 2 finalists.

Define your questions and goals for the visits.

Will you need to perform a pilot project (also covered in Chapter 3) to make your final selection? Define your objectives for the pilot project and create a software specification to define the work to be completed. You can ask for a small pilot project to be completed for free if it is a week or so in length and requires only a few resources to complete. You should be willing to pay for longer pilots when they produce software you can use.

Determine whether you need a complex or simple request for proposal (RFP) for the vendors you will evaluate.

Finally, you should prepare your overall evaluation schedule, with the milestones and tasks to be completed, and identify the internal resources you'll need.

4. **Create the RFP.** Create this document for the vendors you evaluate, so they can respond with the information you need.

    You should include a description of your evaluation process, your required response dates, and your schedule for evaluation. Specify the details of your pilot project if you choose to have one. Vendors want to know how much effort it will take to win your business. Most will respond enthusiastically to receiving your RFP. Of course, how they respond, both initially and with their formal proposal, are key indicators of their professionalism and ability to work with you.

5. **Identify your vendors.** Create a list of the outsourcing vendors and teams you will consider, limiting your selections to the countries and regions you selected in step 3.

    Then, using your contacts, referrals, and directories on the Internet, make a list of vendor candidates. You can reduce the list after reviewing the vendor web sites and comparing the vendors against the list of must-have criteria you specified in step 2.

6. **Distribute the RFPs and collect the responses.** RFPs can be sent by email or made available as a controlled download from your web site.

    After you have distributed the RFPs, you must be prepared to handle questions, issues, and requests for clarification from the vendors. The proposals you receive in response will likely vary widely in their timing and pricing, especially if you provide a specification for a pilot or entire software development project.

You will need to ask questions and get clarification of the responses. This is a good opportunity to test the vendor's ability to handle questions and communication in general.

You should schedule vendor presentations at your offices when possible. It is good to meet as many people from the vendor as you can and to hear about the vendor's approach and mission. For example, a four-year-old startup company downgraded an outsourcing vendor after the vendor CEO's presentation emphasized that their target market was Fortune 500 companies. The startup felt it would not get the attention from the vendor that it needed.

7. **Make your first vendor reduction.** This could also be your reduction to the semifinalists in a small field of vendors.

Review all the vendor proposals and create an evaluation matrix for each one. You may reject some vendors immediately based on a combination of their poor communication and a time or cost proposal that is either too good to be true or much higher than the other vendors and than what you expected.

Host the vendor presentations for the vendors that can travel to your office. You may need to have a series of follow-up phone calls and meetings to clarify vendor responses. Then reduce the field to the top vendor semifinalists.

This is also the time to schedule visits to the semifinalist vendor sites offshore and/or to schedule your pilot project, if you're using either or both of these techniques in your final vendor selection process.

8. **Evaluate your semifinalists.** This is your "short list" of candidates.

Now is the time to make to calls and send emails to check the references of the vendors. Also you will carry out your site visits and complete the pilot project with each vendor if used in your evaluation process.

An initial negotiation of the financial and business terms should be made to be sure that each vendor is willing to work with you to provide the proper level of value.

9. **Select the finalist.** This is the vendor that you judge to be the best outsourcing partner.

Stay on good terms with the runner-up vendors. If your negotiations with the finalist fail, you want to have an alternative vendor to fall back on. If the pricing seems high, you can select two finalists to enhance your final negotiations. However, I recommend that you focus on the relationship and not on squeezing the last nickel, rupee, or ruble out of your vendor.

10. **Sign your outsourcing agreement.** This agreement contains the terms, conditions, and expectations for the relationship.

   You will want to review model agreements from the vendor and other sources to discover the terms and conditions you want in your agreement. Review by an attorney experienced with outsourcing agreements is advisable when the relationship is critical to your company's success.

   Important items include clear language concerning nondisclosure and ownership of your intellectual property, pricing, payment terms, and termination provisions. These are discussed further near the end of this chapter.

11. **Bonus next step: Launch your outsourced software development.** To get your outsourced software development off to a good start, you may have one or more vendor engineers assigned to your project visit your U.S. office. This is desirable when your specifications are limited and direct communication is required.

   At launch you will also implement your project management structure by introducing your employees and managers to the outsourced engineers who will develop your software. Exchange names and digital photos of all team members to facilitate communication and teamwork.

12. **Bonus next step: Manage your outsourcing well.** Doing so will keep your software development on the track to success.

   Closely monitor your software development process and the progress your vendor is making to ensure you have a proper definition of the requirements and specifications for your software. Clearly define project milestones and receive a commitment from the vendor to achieve them. Track the delivery of milestones to measure vendor performance and escalate problems and issues as needed.

Make sure the outsourced team is creating quality code with unit tests and an overall QA process.

You can also use an online system to create an audit trail of communications to retain the knowledge created during the process of developing your software. Such a system can also give you instant access to project status.

These last two bonus steps are discussed in more detail in chapter 6.

Becoming a Micro-Multinational

Creating your own offshore operation has been standard procedure for a long time at large corporations. Now you can do the same, starting out with a just a few employees. Choose your new country based on the strategic advantage it gives you—India to access a huge talent pool, China to enter a huge new market, Eastern Europe to deliver good support to your customers in Western Europe, or Latin America to support your Spanish-speaking customer base.

The major task you will face in setting up a subsidiary, without exception, is recruiting. Much of the work is in finding the best candidates to be your engineering manager or managers. Software engineering candidates must also be gathered for selection as your employees. The establishment of an outsourcing contract, or a legal company and office location if it is a subsidiary, needs to be done carefully but does not nearly approach the work of recruiting the personnel. After hiring, employee training and the planning of initial projects are crucial. Working with a partner is recommended as a way to quickly overcome these challenges.

Once you begin development of your software, you will need to communicate with your offshore engineering team and describe to them what they should do. This remaining challenge exists for all forms of offshore outsourcing. The design of your software is a critical element of outsourcing success and is covered in the next chapter.

Chapter 5

Describing Your Software for Outsourcing

A common mistake that people make when trying to design something completely foolproof is to underestimate the ingenuity of complete fools.

—Douglas Adams, author of
The Hitchhiker's Guide to the Galaxy

What if you could outsource your software development and have a guarantee that the results would be successful? That would be very powerful indeed.

A guarantee is one of the most attractive enticements you can offer your customers to help them decide to buy your product. Actually, marketing folks give such incentives the fancier name of "risk reversal," since they are meant to reverse the feeling of risk within your customers. Whatever you offer as a risk reversal should make them feel that it is less risky to do business with you than it is to continue on their present course. The customer should feel that they have a great deal to gain and very little to lose.

The most common risk reversal is a guarantee. (A free trial is another common risk reversal technique). With a guarantee, not only will your customer get the benefits of your product or service for a reasonable price, but they are also promised guaranteed results.

Do you offer some kind of risk reversal for your business? Perhaps you guarantee the major benefits offered by your software. Or you may offer a free trial for some limited period of time. The more you work to earn the trust of your customers, the easier you will make it for them to do business with you.

Why don't most software outsourcing service firms offer a guarantee? Because developing custom software on time is notoriously difficult to do. An on-time delivery guarantee is virtually never offered for software development, and it would seem hard to believe if it were.

This is mainly because the end goal of a software development project is difficult to define and is not often completely known at the beginning. The competence and ability of the software engineers is rarely the issue, especially if you have carefully selected your vendor using the techniques described in Chapter 3.

The key, you might think, is in defining your software as carefully as possible. If you do this well, it seems, you will reverse your risk in outsourcing your software development. But it is not always so simple.

A Modular Approach

You need to make a fundamental choice concerning your outsourcing. Will you outsource your entire software application? Or just software modules you then assemble into a complete application yourself?

Outsourcing individual modules works well if the modules require specific technical expertise. It can be easier and more cost-effective to find the expertise you need outside your company compared to hiring expert employees. In this case you have to take responsibility for managing your outsourcing team and integrating their work with the software you create internally.

You must also take responsibility for good specifications for your outsourced modules. Typically in this situation, the more traditional "waterfall" techniques of software specification are used.

The Old (and Obsolete?) Waterfall Method

In the past, efforts to make the software development process more productive focused on creating better specifications. As the theory went, you should first try to do a better job of capturing the requirements of *what* your software is supposed to do, including both features and responsiveness.

Second, you should create a good design and description of *how* the requirements are to be achieved. Then you can start coding. With enough detail in your specifications and design documents it seems you should get guaranteed results.

The waterfall[22] approach is still the recommended way to communicate the desired behavior of your software when you are outsourcing individual modules or reimplementation of an existing system. But it is rare to know all the details of what your software should do when you are at the beginning of a new project. It seems crazy to expect guaranteed results in this kind of situation.

And it is.

Observant software engineers have realized that they jump back and forth between the different waterfall boxes during the course of developing new software. Enforcing a sequential process of requirements specification, design, and then development is artificial and counterproductive for new software application development. Techniques for specifying new software applications using agile methods are discussed later in this chapter.

Architecting Your Software for Outsourcing

One reason to choose the modular approach is to identify the software modules and subsystems that can safely be outsourced, while keeping most of your software private. Intellectual property is the lifeblood of a company, and your software ideas should be guarded carefully.

Most offshore software development companies will fiercely defend your intellectual property as part of their normal business procedures. Nevertheless, you may want to carve out the most sensitive parts and develop them internally.

Or you can parcel out the development of your software to multiple independent outsourced teams. That way no one team will have all of the intellectual property.

---

22. This old style of software design is called the waterfall method because when you draw boxes around all of the sequential steps and then pour water into the first one, it will fall through each box—from the Requirements box to the Design box and so on down through the Coding and Testing boxes until you get to the end of the project.

The architecture of your software represents a high-level view of its internal structure. It defines how the various modules and technical components of your product are related. Your software architecture should also take into consideration how the software will be developed. Both the structure of your software and whether all or part of your software development will be outsourced have a tremendous impact on the architecture of your software.

Similarly, the architecture of your software will have a major influence on how you outsource and your decision to use outsourcing at all. If you want to keep your core intellectual property in-house, you must have an architecture that supports isolation of the core intellectual property from any outsourced development you want to do.

Three Architectures for Outsourcing

There are three ways to architect your software to take advantage of outsourcing. The first is to partition your software into pieces that can be developed independently. Some of the independent modules can be developed with outsourcing, and others can be developed with your internal team. An integration step is usually handled by the internal team before product release. Loose "coupling" between these modules is required to make this work well.

For example, one company outsourced the development of a new product based on existing technology created by their internal programming team. Both teams worked independently because the original product architecture had a well-documented set of modules (the internally developed technology) that was used as building blocks for new products (like the one created by the outsourced team).

A second approach is to integrate the work of your internal and outsourced development teams in a truly collaborative effort. This approach works best when both teams are involved with the architectural decisions. The architecture not only identifies the technical modules of your product, as in the first approach, but also reflects the areas of technical strength in the development teams involved.

As an example of this second approach, suppose your product has both an HTML human interface and an XML file interface. If your outsourced team has great expertise with XML file processing, your internal team may then focus on the user interface. If the teams are equally skilled, you can divide the work by use cases and let each team develop all levels of the product for independent sets of functionality. In an online catalog system, for example, one team could do the buyer interface and the other could create the catalog maintenance features used by the seller.

The third approach is to outsource the development of your entire product. In this case, the architecture should be defined with input from the developers and is an important tool for communicating the design of your software to new members of the team.

Marchitecture and Tarchitecture

Many software executives are most comfortable with the approach of outsourcing individual modules. If the programming tasks are well defined, then not much thought or creativity (and therefore potential for delay) is necessary.

However, many outsourcing teams are smarter than this and actually seek out challenging assignments. They understand what is important in the process of creating your software and contributing to the success of your company. If you treat outsourced developers like cattle, as with cattle, you may not be satisfied with what they leave behind.

So far I have been talking about the technical architecture of your software, sometimes called its "tarchitecture." The tarchitecture is defined by a technical architect—an engineer with a strong programming background.

Sometimes your software architecture will be at such a high level that it will not seem very technical at all. There is also another less technical and more marketing-oriented architecture that helps define the customer options for your software product.

The two architecture types are sometimes confused, as they were at a visit to a client. A venture capitalist interested in investing in the company was also present at the meeting. Actually, the VC was really excited by the technology and was effusive in his praise of the technical co-founder of the company.

I also thought the technology was interesting, but I was having trouble visualizing how the software would be used. So I created a diagram showing how all the modules fit together. This was a tarchitecture diagram.

The technical founder did not see much need for documentation, but he showed the VC my diagram anyway. "Oh that's just 'marchitecture'!" the VC said, his tone of voice clearly indicating that it was of little value. He did a good job of intuitively sensing what the techie wanted to hear.

That was not the first time my work has been dismissed by a VC, and I am sure it will not be the last. But there are two problems with this situation (three, if you count how his emotions were being manipulated by the VC).

First, the company really did need a good description of the architecture to better communicate the product requirements, both to customers and newly hired engineers. A well-defined architecture enables engineers to "own" the piece of the software they will develop.

Second, my diagram showed how the internal technical modules were interrelated. As such, it was not a marchitecture diagram. Even if it was, it should not be so easily dismissed.

According to Luke Hohmann in *Beyond Software Architecture,* "Marchitecture is the business perspective of the system's architecture." It shows the structure of the software from your customer's perspective, indicating what options are available and how it can be licensed and installed.

Clearly, your marchitecture is critical to the success of your software and possibly your entire company. When you develop a product to sell, it is best to have some idea of how it will be positioned and offered for sale in the marketplace.

Marchitecture is related to outsourcing when it affects what licensing and installation options need to be developed. Both marchitecture and tarchitecture should be designed collaboratively with your outsourcing team when they are developing your entire software application.

Define the marchitecture and tarchitecture of your new software carefully if you want to take advantage of outsourcing. If you already have an existing software application, your architecture can help you decide which are the best portions to outsource.

In addition, as discussed in Chapter 1, if you have an existing version of your software, you can consider three ways to use outsourcing: (1) create your new version in-house and outsource maintenance of the existing version, (2) outsource development of your new version and continue to maintain the old version with an in-house engineering team, or (3) outsource both and use the internal team to manage your outsourced resources effectively.

The Whole Enchilada

What if you decide to outsource the creation of your entire software application? Can you really specify your software application completely? Will you know all the details of what you and your users will want the software to do? Sometimes you can.

If you are rewriting an existing application—perhaps converting a client/server application to a web application—then you have a well-defined goal. You want to make the web application behave as much like the client/server application as possible. Your existing software functionality, user documentation and old specifications are a great start for defining the new system. You have a pretty good chance of defining the software completely.

However, if you have only broadly defined goals with limited details about what your software will do, the old waterfall techniques are not the best approach. I will discuss this issue in more detail later in this chapter.

What Will Your Software Do?

Software requirements tell *what* your software should do. The design describes *how* the requirements will be implemented. But there is another "how" lurking within your software requirements: How will your users use your software to achieve their goals? Describing the desired behavior of your software is a key part of your software requirements.

There are two approaches to creating software. First is the "build it and they will come" *Field of Dreams*[23] approach. In this case, you do not have to write a description of the software; you just build it yourself. End users and customers are expected to find value in your creation. This actually works sometimes, with eBay and Friendster[24] being notable examples.

---

23. *Field of Dreams* was the very popular 1989 movie starring Kevin Costner, who plays an Iowa farmer who plows under most of his corn crop and builds a baseball field. He did this after hearing a voice that tells him, "Build it and he will come." Many programmers act as though a similar voice delivers the requirements of the software they write.

24. Who knew we needed online auctions before eBay and that the Internet could enable more efficient use of our social network for dating until there was Friendster?

The second, more common approach is to first gain a reasonable understanding of a market or department/business unit need. Sometimes the market need will only be recognized in the future. Either way, you must first describe the need or goals of the future users of your software application so the software you create has a chance of being successful.

Nobody, least of all programmers, wants to spend an excessive amount of time writing *about* the software. But you must write something in order to have an increased chance of success. What is the minimal amount of writing you need to do to describe your software product effectively? Of course, the answer is, "It depends."

Your software may be simple or complex, mission-critical or intended for casual use. In all cases, it is important to describe what users can expect to accomplish by using your software.

Using Use Cases

The use case is the main tool of the business analyst, marketing professional, and software designer to describe how your software is used. Written use cases are an extremely useful tool for describing your software. They explain how users interact with your software and attempt to achieve their goals. Use cases should be a major part of the requirements of your product.

Use cases are part of the Unified Modeling Language,[25] or UML. UML is a set of tools and techniques to define and describe the behavior and architecture of a system and has great popularity in the design of software applications and systems. Use cases include both a high-level diagram as well as a detailed description in text. The level of detail and precision of use cases is discussed in the next section.

The length and number of your use cases depends on two primary factors: your software's complexity and the expertise of your development team with the application area.

For example, I once managed an outsourced development team that had previously developed a software application very similar to what we needed, but with a different style of user interface. All the major use cases were already well understood by the developers,

---

25. Describing all the elements of the UML in detail is not appropriate here, but the bibliography and the book's web site contain references to excellent books that explain all the diagrams, methods, and tools in the UML toolbox.

and we needed only brief descriptions of use cases for a few new features.

A significant amount of time was spent designing the new user interface however. Actually, use case writing and user interface design are separate tasks, which we will discuss in more detail later.

When you are creating a new software application then you need to create your use cases from scratch. The best way to start is to identify the kinds of users, or actors, that will interact with your software.

Acting Like a User

Actors are the various users of your software and the roles that they play. For example, an order management system might have buyer, salesperson, and shipping clerk as actors. The goals of the buyer actor might include looking up past orders placed, placing a new order, changing an order, canceling an order, and so on.

In some cases, actors can be other systems and equipment that your software interacts with. For example, the Enterprise Resource Planning (ERP) system sends a purchase order document to your software, or a heat sensor sends a message about an excessive temperature.

Your software should help your users (actors playing roles) achieve specific goals. These goals must be aligned with the benefits your software delivers. Who are the users of your software, and what are their goals? Are there multiple user types, or is every user the same?

What Do You Mean, Precisely?

One of the best books about use cases is Alistair Cockburn's *Writing Effective Use Cases*. This book covers all the elements of good use case writing, and the emphasis is on writing—how much detail, what you should say, and how you should say it.

The material in this section draws on the content of Cockburn's book. It is summarized and paraphrased here to give you a good overview of this important tool for defining what your software should do.

Use cases tell your developers what they cannot discover for themselves, especially if they are several oceans away. Use cases tell them what your users want, need, and expect your software to do.

If you can explain that, then good engineers can figure out how to build the software.

But how much detail do you need to provide? If you are spending more time describing your software than it would take to write it, something is wrong. You should start out with a low level of precision in your use cases and then increase the amount of detail needed to communicate with your engineers effectively. There is no point in providing more detail than is needed.

In Table 5-1, the amount of precision you need in your use cases is described as low, medium, or high. Low levels of precision are okay for a development team familiar with the application area, or to get started quickly on a prototype when details are not yet known. In the software project needing just a new user interface that I described earlier, I was able to use low precision for use cases and medium precision for the user interface.

In another project to create a web application product, we used medium precision for the use cases and high precision for the user interface. Error scenarios were straightforward and were added later as they were encountered in the development of the product. The user interface was created in HTML before any coding was done. Then the HTML pages were linked together as a demo to show early customers and investors.

Medium or high levels of precision are often required to effectively outsource software development offshore. The lowest level of precision for use cases involves listing the actors and their goals in using your software product. If you provide only low-precision use cases, you will need more frequent iterations and a higher level of collaboration with the offshore software development team.

Table 5-1. Amount of Precision Needed in Use Cases and User Interface Design

	Precision		
	Low	**Medium**	**High**
Use Cases	List of actors and goals	Use cases with success scenarios	Use cases with success and error scenarios
User Interface Design	Screen flow diagram	Screens with data entry and display items and actions defined	Screens defined in HTML or other useful code

Table 5-2. Basic Template for a Use Case

Use Case Element	Description
Scope	The portion of the software under discussion.
Primary actor	The stakeholder or user who initiates an interaction with the software to achieve a goal.
Goal level	The level of the goal (low, medium, or high, as described in Table 5-3).
Stakeholders and interests	People and entities having a vested interest in the behavior of the software
Preconditions	What must be true before the use case runs?
Guarantees	What must be true after the use case runs?
Main success scenario	What happens when nothing goes wrong?
Exception scenarios	What can happen differently during each scenario?

The Gory Details

For medium and high levels of precision, each use case requires more information. The basic template for a use case includes about eight elements, as shown in Table 5-2, with only the first three used in an abbreviated, low-ceremony use case.

In complex products with many actors, goals, and/or scopes, you may feel overwhelmed by the potential number of use cases. One way to organize them is to assign priorities (high, medium, and low) by scope and goal level, as shown in Table 5-3.

Start with the use cases that describe the interaction of individual users with your product. If you have scenarios that involve multiple users or actors using your product, describe them next. Then describe scenarios in which a single user interacts with multiple systems within the environment in which your product runs.

Table 5-3. Setting Priorities by Scope and Goal Level

		Goal Level		
		Multiuser	User	Subfunction
Scope	Environment	medium	medium	low
	System	medium	high	low
	Component	low	low	low

Of lowest priority are interactions between users, subfunctions, and low-level components. Subfunction-level goals are those required to carry out user goals. They are usually shared by other use cases and are separated out to simplify the design. For example, a software system that archives every database transaction in a second database could have low-level components that automatically carry out the data copy. The sequence of steps to do the archiving is important but unlikely to be complex or of high priority for detailed use case specification.

Of course, if your product is complex and its behavior is described by use cases that cover all of the scope/goal level combinations, you will eventually need to write them all. You can use the table to organize and structure your efforts.

Each use case has multiple scenarios. The main scenario is called the success scenario, in which the user does everything correctly and nothing goes wrong. Variations of the main success scenario describe errors and exceptions that can occur and how they are handled. A high level of precision requires you to describe as many of these scenarios as possible.

Use cases are similar to user stories, used for planning in the agile development methodologies discussed later. They may also be decomposed into subfunctions or sub-use cases that are reused in other parts of the software. Subfunctions may also be used as story points for more accurate estimation of programming time required.

Get a Handle on Your User Interface

Writing use cases is different from designing the user interface for your software. If you have a user interface designed, it is best not to let your use cases degrade into descriptions of how to work the user interface (click this, then that, etc.).

This is because a use case is supposed to describe, at a higher level, the goals and intentions of your software's users. Creating use cases is a way to draw out desired software behavior from the users and stakeholders, not a lecture on how the system will work.

However, designing the user interface concurrently while writing the use cases will provide valuable insights into the behavior of your software. New functions will be discovered, and others may be found to be impractical.

Furthermore, as the old saying goes, "A picture is worth a thousand words." Providing screen shots or screen sequences is a very effective technique for communicating the desired behavior of your software to an outsourced development team.

I recommend developing the user interface while capturing the use cases as a way to confirm what you are hearing from users and stakeholders. The user interface design is a common device for both confirming system function and specifying the software to developers.

A Picture Is Worth a Thousand Words

The point of this section is not to show you how to design an auction web site. I am using eBay as an example of a familiar web site to illustrate the visual technique I recommend for specifying your software.

Even if you are not developing a web application, you should use some sort of visual approach when specifying your software. You can use HTML to emulate your actual user interface. Or you can use a drawing program like Visio or even PowerPoint to design your screens and specify their logical sequence.

First let's look at the standard, non-visual, text-based approach to specifying use cases.

Imagine that you are building an auction web site and you need to specify the functionality to your outsourced software development team. You have done some reading and have decided that use cases describing how the buyers and sellers will carry out auction activities are the best way to define what the software should do.

So far, so good. Let's see what a use case will look like for a buyer (the use case actor or role) who wants to place a bid on an item.

Suppose the buyer is a stamp collector. He does a search and finds a stamp to bid on. There can be multiple ways to search for a stamp, and these could be covered in separate use cases.

By definition, use cases consist of text. They contain the sequence of steps the user carries out to accomplish the task. Here is how a buyer bids on a stamp:

1. The user Steve Stamps[26] finds a collectible postage stamp to bid on in the system. (Use cases 8 to 14 describe searches.)

---

26. Cute and memorable names can make your use cases easier to read, and they make it easier for both the target user and the programmer to visualize how the software will be used.

2. Steve displays the page containing a stamp auction item. This page contains an image of the stamp, the starting bid, the time of auction close, and the number of bids on this item.

3. Steve decides to try to buy this stamp. He clicks on the Place Bid button.

4. A page is displayed with the item title, the current bid, and a text field where Steve can enter his maximum bid.

5. Steve enters his bid in the text field and clicks on the Continue button.

6. A new page is displayed showing the item title and Steve's bid. There is a Confirm Bid button and also other text stating that Steve must agree to purchase the item if he is the winning bidder. Steve clicks on the Confirm Bid button.

7. The original item page is displayed as before, except that the number of bids has increased and Steve is now the high bidder if his maximum bid is higher than the previous bidder.

This is a simple use case that shows how a buying user named Steve places a bid on an item in the auction web site. From this text we learn several things. For example, a bid is carried out in a sequence of different pages. The item for sale has several attributes, including title, picture, minimum bid, number of bids, current bid amount, and end time.

It should also raise some questions, especially from a reader who must figure out how to implement these pages. Can an item have more than one picture? Should the picture(s) be shown on the bid page (step 4)? Does Steve need to be signed into the auction site? What happens if he is not signed in? And so on.

Then there are the exceptions, when not everything goes according to plan. The steps presented in the use case assume that Steve is a rational person and generally knows what to do. But suppose he makes a mistake—like not signing in before bidding. Or what if he puts in a bid amount that is less than the current high bid? These and other exceptions will need to be dealt with when the software is written.

Sometimes the way to handle an exception is straightforward and can be left to the software engineer to create. Other times, you will need to specify in detail what the software should do.

Now, are you ready to start coding this feature?

Maybe. Maybe not. You may want to see a couple more use cases to get a better sense of what the software will do.

And if you are writing the use cases, you need to have them reviewed by the actors, the buyers and sellers in this example, to make sure you have the functionality they need.

That leads to the next problem. It can be tough to get your target users to read through a bunch of use cases and have them visualize what the software is supposed to do. It will take some dedication on their part to keep focused and give you good feedback.

After a while their attention will wander. You will probably need to spend time with them in a live meeting to read the use cases with them, hold their interest, and then judge their true reactions. If they are your future customers, or users within your own company busy with other tasks, it is unlikely that you will get them to volunteer the feedback you need to validate the use cases.

What would be better is a demo of the software. But how can you do that if the software is not written yet?

Here's how. You can create mockups of the pages or screens of your user interface in HTML. Then you can link them together in a storyboard kind of demo that shows the use cases in living and moving color.

Here is that use case again, now illustrated with screen shots of a demo made up of HTML pages as a mockup of the user interface.

1. User Steve Stamps finds a collectible postage stamp to bid on in the system. (Use cases #8 to 14 describe searches.)

2. Steve displays the page containing a stamp auction item. This page contains an image of the stamp, the starting bid, the time of auction close, and the number of bids on this item. (See Figure 5-1.)[27]

3. Steve decides to bid on this stamp. He clicks on the Place Bid button. If Steve is not signed in, he is asked to do so. (See Figure 5-2.)

---

27. Okay, I am obviously cheating here. I did not craft these pages in HTML; I just took screen shots of eBay. But you can easily design your web pages from scratch. If you are artistically challenged, as I am, you can use low-cost HTML templates to add nice graphics and menus to your pages. Go to the book's web site, www.SoftwareWithoutBordersBook.com, for links to sites where you can obtain these kinds of templates.

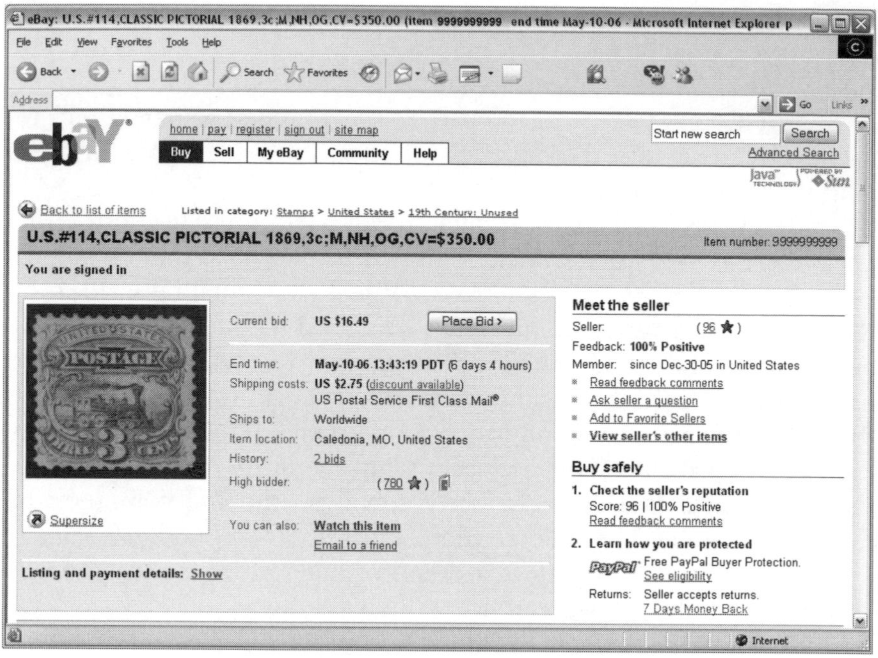

Figure 5-1. Auction Listing

4. A page is displayed with the item title, the current bid, and a text field where Steve can enter his maximum bid. (See Figure 5-3.)

5. Steve enters his bid in the text field and clicks on the Continue button.

6. A new page is displayed showing the item title and Steve's bid. There is a Confirm Bid button and also other text stating that Steve must agree to purchase the item if he is the winning bidder. Steve clicks on the Confirm Bid button. (See Figure 5-4.)

7. The original item page is displayed as before, except that the number of bids has increased and Steve is now the high bidder if his maximum bid is higher than the previous bidder.

Now isn't that a whole lot clearer? Isn't it more interesting to look at? Of course, these screen shots are rich in additional detail. This detail comes from other use cases that use the same pages.

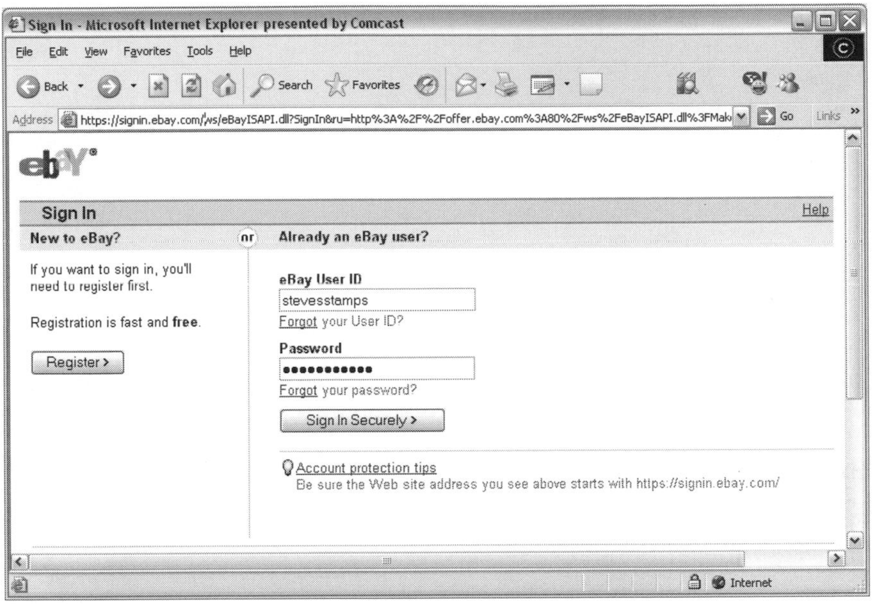

Figure 5-2. Sign-in Screen

For example, the item display page shows a lot of information about the seller. That wasn't mentioned in the use case. And the sign-in page says something about Microsoft Passport. Another use case can describe how that is used.

As you can see, there are many, many use cases that you could specify to completely define your software. But all that text by itself would be very boring!

I recommend that you start with the design of your pages and add details to the pages as new user scenarios are defined. Link the pages together to tell the story of your use cases as a demo. That will bring them to life and simulate how your software will actually run.

Then later, take screen shots of the pages and put the text of the use cases around them, as I have done here. Now you have a relatively complete specification on paper and a demo in color that shows what your software should do.

You can share the demo with your outsourced development team on the web using webinar software like WebEx or GoToMeeting. Or you can record your demo using software like Camtasia that captures the screens as well as your voice to tell the complete story and bring your most important use cases to life. See the book's web

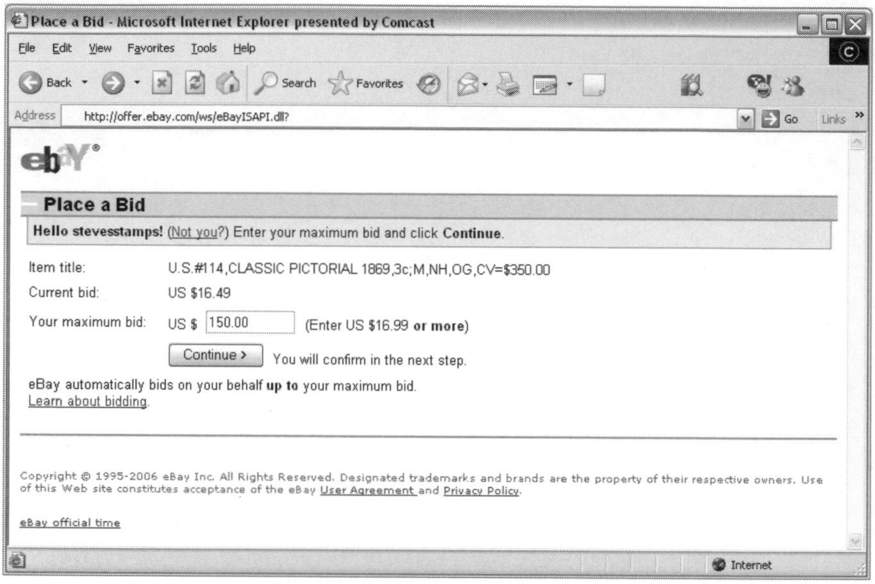

Figure 5-3. Initiating a Bid

site for links to these and other tools you can use to document your software design.[28]

However, designing the user interface does not provide enough information about user intentions and goals. Effort must also be put into creating written descriptions of product behavior. Screen shots or diagrams are not enough.

Business Vision and Technical Skill

Creating a software product requires two kinds of skills. Let's call them business vision and technical expertise. Excellent business vision provides a deep understanding of market needs, and technical expertise is the ability to create quality software.

Either one by itself is insufficient to guarantee success. Successful organizations recognize that these two skills must be married together in a collaborative team effort to create great software in a timely fashion. The key is for the business visionary half of the team to effectively communicate what the software should do and the

---

28. Links to these and other software services and products are listed on the www. SoftwareWithoutBordersBook.com web site.

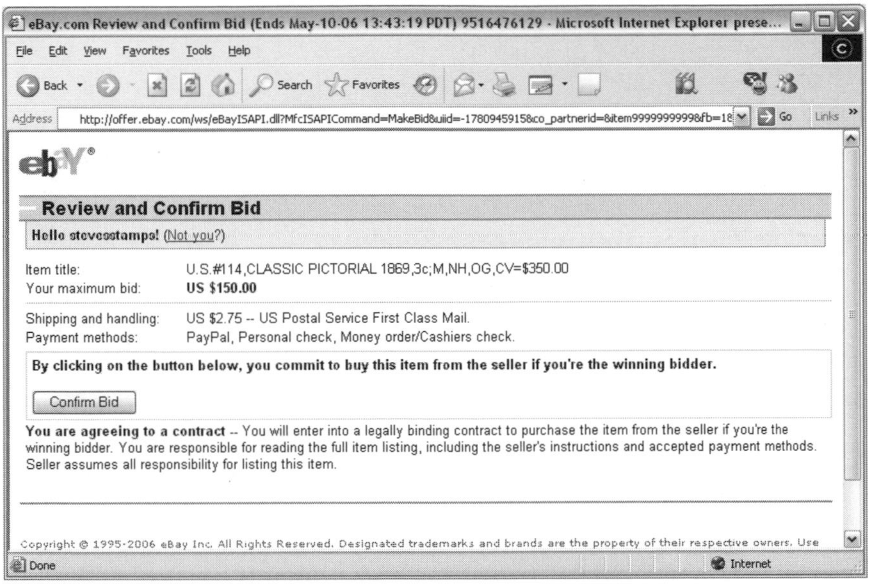

Figure 5-4. Confirming a Bid

technical half to manage engineers to deliver quality software as efficiently as possible. Without this balanced contribution, the vision of the business becomes a hallucination that never becomes a reality for others, and the application created by the technical expert becomes a science project that no one will ever want to use.

There are many good techniques and methods for describing the requirements and the design of software. For example, UML, discussed earlier in this chapter, contains many diagrams and methods for describing software functionality and architecture. These methods are usually used by the technical half of a successful team, which also makes choices requiring technical skill, such as software architecture, computer languages, and databases.

In contrast, someone possessing business vision does not usually care about these technical details. Whether the software uses Oracle or MySQL, Java or C# probably does not matter. Instead, the business visionary knows that Mary over in purchasing is up to her elbows in alligators with the problems of getting her job done. A new software system with three specific features will rein in the alligators, deliver the benefits Mary needs, and save her company money. A person with business vision knows how much money Mary's company will save, how much Mary will pay for the software, and how many Marys are out there in the world with the same problem.

You need both technical and business vision to create great software. And if you want other people to write and/or test your software, you need to describe what the software needs to do.

Creating Your Software Release Roadmap

Your software release roadmap is where you plan out the future releases of your product, along with the major features and benefits they will provide. Your product roadmap usually comes out of the process of gathering product requirements.

For example, at one of my software companies we had product releases planned out for a year and a half. This was mainly because our minds went wild imagining the product features customers would want. Or what we thought they would want.

We knew customers would not wait for a super-duper product release containing all the features we envisioned. We budgeted out the features according to need, difficulty, and customer desire. It is also difficult to design and develop a large software system all at once. Divide and conquer is a better strategy.

We assigned features to the releases in a product roadmap according to our estimates of their usefulness and difficulty of implementation. Features that were less useful and harder to implement were pushed out to a later release. Then we would show customers and prospects the roadmap. If they drooled over a future feature, we would try to move it up to a more near-term release.

Having a product roadmap is important for outsourcing because it helps you accurately judge the size of the engineering team you need and how long you will need them. Defining future features and releases also helps you avoid architecting yourself into a corner. You don't want to have the, "Oops! I didn't know it had to run on a Macintosh!" problem.

Extracting Use Cases from "Experts"

It is common for "subject matter experts" to be unaware of software design techniques. In such cases, outside help is required to create a useful description that communicates product requirements to developers.

A series of meetings is usually required to brainstorm and document the desired behavior of a software product. It is best to start with a low level of precision and then increase the level of detail and precision as details become known.

In the early stages of one project, the company founders worked in the supply chain group at a large company. They were frustrated in their attempts to get materials and parts to the right location at the right time to support the manufacturing process. Based on their experience, knowledge, and difficulties, they wanted a software product to track shipments made between companies. They envisioned at least two user types: the shipping and the receiving clerks.

They were asked how the information about the shipments got into the system. "Shipments usually come from orders," they said. They then realized that buyers and sellers were additional actors needing to interact with the product.

That led to the realization that the orders existed in other computer systems used by their prospective customers. What started out as a simple system to track shipments blossomed into a sophisticated product requiring integration with multiple enterprise systems.

In another situation, the company founders were experts at managing the construction of retail stores. Their computer skills were limited to occasional use of Microsoft Excel, Project, and Outlook for email. They had no experience with editing HTML to create a user interface. However, there were many tabular displays of data in the construction management product they envisioned, and they found Excel useful for drawing mockups of the screens.

Another effective technique is to bring together the subject matter experts and your offshore team for several direct communication sessions. This can occur in either direction by sending the expert(s) to the offshore location or bringing one or more key technical leaders from your offshore team to your facilities. Generally it is better to send one or two people offshore where they can interact with your entire offshore team.

The Requirements of Good Software Requirements

The waterfall approach will divide the overall process of product definition into the creation of two documents—a marketing requirements document (MRD) and a functional design specification (FDS). Some people combine the two into one big document that covers marketing issues as well as a relatively complete description of the software functionality. Or they ignore marketing issues entirely and jump right into the details of software features.

Separating the process into two strands is useful. There are important marketing issues that should be addressed in the MRD. You don't want to distract yourself with the gory details of the software's functionality at this point.

Sometimes the MRD is the only definition of the software and is called a PRD, for product requirements document. In this case, more emphasis is placed on software functionality, and it is easy to overlook the marketing issues that may be critical in defining a new software product.

For example, one company was very focused on software features. The founding team designed a software system and wrote the PRD and FDS without considering potential partners in the marketplace. The system had a sophisticated approach to capture information that tracked shipments sent out by customers using the software.

Later, after most of the software was written, they realized that much of the functionality could have been implemented with an interface to the FedEx and UPS web sites. Such an interface would have had many more features to begin with. Furthermore, an alliance with one of these big companies would have been more important than any set of features the founders could have dreamed up.

In contrast, your MRD may be heavily weighted toward the size and texture of your market. Your opportunity may be the weaknesses of several competitors. The MRD can describe the market situation and indicate how your software will overcome these weaknesses and achieve a significant market share. It may go so far as to prioritize features in terms of their ability to gain market share.

Another recommended component of an MRD is a detailed comparison of competitors by product features in a matrix. You can use the matrix for customer presentations. Of course, your software column should contain the most checkmarks next to the feature descriptions. It is even better if you can have checkmarks in entire categories of features that your competitors have neglected to implement. Internally, this is a tremendous tool to motivate the developers and to describe what the product needs to do. "If we don't have this feature in the next release, we won't be any better than Brand X!"

How you write your MRD depends on what you consider your most important innovation. Is the software by itself so new and cool that customers will beat a path to your door? If so, a feature-centered MRD or PRD may be sufficient.

Or will you need to include specific features that your competitors do not have? Is your innovation the use of a different sales channel that works only if your product is easily self-installed by the customer? If so, requirements like these must be included in your more marketing-centered MRD.

There are multiple formats of MRD to choose from. Two standards that cover requirements are as follows:

- IEEE Std 1220-1998—IEEE Standard for Application and Management of the Systems Engineering Process
- ANSI/IEEE Std-830-1984—IEEE/ANSI Guide to Software Requirements Specifications

    These standards cover the specification and design of large systems and are heavily influenced by the defense industry. Standards like these are usually overkill for most companies and IT departments.

    Here are the major sections I recommend be included in an MRD for most software companies and projects:

- **Introduction or executive summary.** Describes the purpose of the software or the problem it solves, the market opportunity, and a general plan for product releases and revenue. The introduction describes a vision of success achieved after the software is released.
- **Functional requirements.** Lists the major features and capabilities that must be included in the software. It can include a definition of user roles and high-level use cases.
- **Performance**. Describes the required speed of the software in terms of number of users, page views per second, and so on. Also includes the disk space and memory requirements or restrictions of the product.
- **Technology.** Describes requirements such as system architecture, databases, and computer languages. It can be combined with the "environment and integration" section in some MRDs.
- **Hardware.** Lists supported computers, network equipment, and so on.
- **Environment and integration.** Describes the environment or context in which the software will be used. Usually this

means specifying sources of data that the software must tap and other existing software packages that the product must integrate with.

Optional sections you may include in your MRD include the following:

- **Market opportunity.** Market size, segments, and competitor and partner information.
- **Schedule requirements.** Needed if your product must be released for an industry show, customer-specified date, or other date that defines your window of market opportunity.
- **Assumptions and dependencies.** Covers dependence on other companies' products or your own technical breakthroughs.
- **Glossary**. Defines the specific terms unique to your software category that may not be familiar to the development team, investors, and other stakeholders.

It is critical not to get hung up in an overly formal process when it comes to requirements and specifications. Requirements will change. They will evolve. Don't churn in your efforts to create an MRD. Set a time limit on the process. For many projects, the process of creating a useful MRD should take no longer than a week or two.

The MRD describes what the software *must* include and not how it is implemented. The "how" is described in the FDS.

Most of your writing time should be spent in creating an FDS after the MRD step is completed. The FDS contains more detailed uses cases, a sketch of your user interface, definitions of internal objects used to model information in your software, and many other details.

Is That Spec Done Yet, Tolstoy?

You can also gather requirements and write a specification as a way to explore and explain what your software needs to do. People have different emotions about specifications, however. Some consider them dreaded and dead-end programming artifacts that quickly become out of date and are never read anyway. Others are overly formal and treat the specification as if it is more important than the software itself.

A major myth of outsourcing is that you need a huge and detailed specification to do it effectively. The more detailed the specification, the more of an insurance policy it becomes for getting exactly what you want. Therefore, the thinking goes, you can safely outsource only the creation of modules or the rewrite of an existing software application for which there is a complete specification.

It's just not true.

Your specification should be a guide to the development team, describing how to get started designing and developing your software. Involve the outsourced team in the specification process. They can ask probing questions and offer insights into your software design.

For example, one VP of engineering told me he starts his outsourced software development by sending the outsourced team a page or two of product requirements. He then carries out an online discussion during which the product details are fleshed out. The outsourced team asks questions, he answers (or gets the answers), and after a week or two there is enough information to begin coding.

It's like designing software using the Socratic method.

Most people start off with more of a specification than this. I recommend that you at least start by specifying the major use cases with low precision.

Designing a Completely New Software Application

We have covered several techniques for specifying your software and ways to capture your software's requirements. Unfortunately, such techniques are often not enough to ensure success when you are creating a completely new software application. Specifying every detail ahead of time is difficult, bordering on impossible.

It requires tremendous forethought to create a specification that covers the details of use cases, exceptions and error handling, performance requirements, and many other details that are often simply not known at the beginning of software development. And the specifications created are often ponderous documents that few will read before they become out of sync with the software under development.

Most software engineers are not dummies, and you don't need to specify every single detail. Doing so often takes the "fun" out of writing software anyway. Use the innate intelligence of your engineering team, either in-house or offshore, to your advantage. The ability to create new software applications is a critical criterion for hiring employees and it's the same for selecting an offshore outsourcing vendor.

Be More Agile

It is rare to see software accurately specified the first time. It always changes because you get new ideas as you see the software application start to take shape. Or your customers and users change their minds about what the software should do.

And yet many companies treat offshore outsourcing strictly as a business decision. They give a general description of what the software should do and then ask for the lowest possible price. If you are developing a new software application, this can be a recipe for disaster.

Or you can spend months debating what your new software application should do and what should be in the specification. However, you are better off selecting an offshore vendor with experience developing new applications using agile software development methods with whom you can collaborate.

Agile software development methods and user stories embrace change and are recommended for creating new software applications. Agile methods get your offshore vendor developing software as soon as possible. Frequent releases—every three to four weeks—gives you steadily increasing amounts of high-quality working software. A funny way to think of it is—Agile methods lets your programming team do something useful while you figure out what your software is supposed to do.

User Stories and the Planning Game

The techniques described earlier for creating use cases provide structure to the process of describing your software's behavior. This is a major part of capturing the requirements of your software.

Another approach called user stories is described well in the seminal book by Mike Cohn called *User Stories Applied for Agile Software Development*. This section gives you an overview of the ideas presented in greater detail in that book. The main idea is to integrate the software design and development process and delay getting into details until just before implementation.

The main goal of the software development process is to organize and optimize the collaboration between subject matter experts, the people who have the vision for a new software application, and the programmers who will bring the software to life. In extreme programming (XP),[29] this process is called *the planning game*. I think

---

29. See *Extreme Programming Explained: Embrace Change* by Kent Beck.

of it as the development game, since it covers both planning and development activities.

The planning game has four major activities:

- Exploration
- Release planning
- Iteration planning
- Task planning

Exploration is the process of creating stories. You write stories about how your customers will use your product. These stories are very similar to use cases. Then you estimate how long it will take to implement each story.

A concept of story "points" is used to achieve a consistent granularity of stories. For example, you might have a story that describes the login process for a web application. Logging in and looking up past activities or account information for display can be separate points in the story.

If a story is too complex, it should be split into multiple stories. The goal is to explore the functionality of the system by defining stories made up of story points that all take approximately the same amount of time to implement.

The number of story points that can be implemented in a given amount of time is called the *velocity*. Developers may need to spend a few days prototyping a story to estimate velocity. Sometimes work on similar projects may be used. Other elements, such as the number of screens, screen controls, and database tables involved with each story point, can also be used to estimate velocity.

Release planning involves determining the priority of the stories. These are business decisions. Users will be more interested in some stories than in others. You will usually want to implement the most important stories in the first or second release of the software.

During *iteration planning*, you choose an iteration size and decide which stories to implement. An iteration size is the amount of time (usually two to eight weeks in length) that the engineers will work to deliver some number of implemented stories. Both business and technical experts plan the iterations, using velocity to determine which stories to implement in each iteration. To improve accuracy, the actual velocity achieved in the last iteration is used for the next iteration.

Task planning is where developers divide the stories in an iteration into development tasks. The developers then sign up or are assigned tasks, and make a commitment to complete their tasks by the end of the iteration.

If commitments cannot be met, this should be known halfway through the iteration. At that point adjustments are made with the business experts to determine which stories should be completed. It is more important to have completed stories at the end of an iteration than it is to have a maximum number of completed development tasks.

As iterations are completed, more and more user stories are implemented. Users can be shown these iteration results to make sure the product contains functionality they really want. As the product takes shape, new features and functions are discovered, by both business and technical resources. These new features may appear in stories implemented in future iterations.

For example, a new software application enabled the user to define a schedule for a construction project. After an early iteration was complete, a user could log in, select a project, and display the schedule. The schedule milestones and their order were fixed. A later iteration allowed the user to define new milestones and enter estimated and actual completion dates.

In fact, during this later iteration the subject matter experts realized (and then told the developers) that multiple dates per milestone were required. They described a new user story in which the construction manager could update the completion date of a milestone while preserving the original estimated date. No problem! It was easy to add this new functionality during an iteration when the focus was on just a few features for several new user stories. The developers were able to complete the iteration on time.

Another big user story involved updating the milestone dates by importing a schedule from Microsoft Project. This complex feature had a lower priority and was put off to a later release. The developers started with small chunks of functionality supporting complete user stories that they knew they could implement easily. As the developers learned more about the application, they were able to tackle larger tasks with the same level of confidence.

Outsourcing and Collaboration

Collaboration between business resources and technical resources, such as an outsourced software development team, is critical to success. You begin the process with a handful of important user stories.

Each iteration of development implements some of your stories and increases the accuracy of the velocity estimate and the predictability of the subsequent major release dates.

In the beginning of this chapter, I wrote that you are unlikely to find any guarantees in outsourcing your software development. Although you may not have a true guarantee, you can now see that it is possible to reduce the risk involved. You cannot guarantee that your original software idea (which may be inaccurate and incomplete) will be implemented in a fixed period of time. However, you can be assured that you will get a predictable amount of software in a predictable amount of time, and that the software will be likely to deliver a product that your customers will actually want to buy.

The point of a guarantee is not to get something for nothing, but to remove risk from the development process. Whether you develop your software with offshore outsourcing or your own development team, you can use these principles of agile software development to obtain your own reliable results.

Techniques for Estimating Your Schedule

Have you ever been surprised when your software takes longer to develop than you expected? Who hasn't?

If only there was a way to accurately estimate how long it will take to develop your software, and therefore how much it will cost.

Over the years, several techniques have been created to estimate the effort needed to complete software projects. Function Point Analysis, devised at IBM in the 1970s, defines function points in five groups: outputs, inquiries, inputs, files, and interfaces.

Each function point is defined as a business function, such as the user entering an input. This makes it easy to map function points into user-oriented requirements, like use cases. But it can also hide internal functions, which take time and resources to develop.

In 1981 another method, the Constructive Cost Model or COCOMO, was created by Barry Boehm[30]. It was updated in 1997 and renamed COCOMO II. It uses a formula based on the number of lines of code expected to be in a software project to estimate the effort required to complete the development.

---

30. Software Cost Estimation with Cocomo II by Barry W. Boehm, et al, Prentice Hall PTR, 2000

I don't know about you, but I find it difficult to make the leap from a software idea or a page in a user interface to the number of lines of code needed to implement it.

The COCOMO formula also uses 5 values to estimate the scale of the software project, along with 17 cost drivers. But estimating the scale and cost of your software is also an art.

These methods are a bit formal and require research, skill, and a little guesswork. They are suited for large software projects in which you have a good grasp of the requirements and effort required to begin with.

For many software projects, the requirements are not as well defined. In these cases, other, less formal techniques are used to create rough estimates. For example, you can estimate the time needed to implement each of your user screens or pages. Screens may be complex or simple, and you can make three different time estimates for each screen based on its type.

You can also use the number of functions contained in your software or the number of database tables as other factors for making your estimate. Clearly, experience developing similar software will enhance your accuracy.

If you are using agile methods, you can use the planning game described earlier to calculate story points when you employ user stories.

An advantage of the planning game is that it helps you plan tasks, iterations and releases, and gains in accuracy as your software is developed over time.

Vendors use both formal and informal methods to estimate the effort needed to create your software. Estimating the time and effort required to develop your software is not a science, to say the least. If you are faced with a tight budget that will not accommodate delays and extra costs, you need a fixed-price bid, at least to get started.

A fixed-price bid needs to have a good specification of what you need. The downside of fixed price is the lack of flexibility. If you need to collaborate with an outsourced engineering team to design your software, a fixed price will not work.

Your alternative is to select a great outsourcing team with an excellent track record of carrying out software projects for other clients, and to work with them to create an estimate you can both believe in.

Using a fixed-price project is a good way to limit your financial risk when you are getting started with an outsourcing vendor.

However, it requires a good specification and should not be an excuse for judging the validity of their estimates. Work with your outsourcing team to develop and improve the accuracy of your estimates for both fixed-price and time and materials engagements.

Keep Your Eyes on the Prize

The ideas and techniques described in this chapter can get you on your way to using an outsourced software development team effectively. Your software will be well enough defined to start the development process, and your programmers will have a good sense of what you need. As the saying goes,

> Success is getting what you want
> And happiness is liking what you get.[31]

Your outsourcing can proceed well from this good start. Your next challenge is to keep things on track. That is covered in the next chapter, "Controlling Your Outsourced Software Development."

---

31. Attributed to H. Jackson Brown, author of *Life's Little Instruction Book.*

Chapter 6

Controlling Your Outsourced Software Development

What man's mind can create, man's character can control.

—Thomas Edison

A software executive who was originally from India and is now working here in the U.S. complained about his experience with outsourcing. "I'm from India, I know the regional accents, and there is no confusion about what the software I need is supposed to do. And still I do not get the software I asked for!"

Most communication issues with an offshore team are caused by language and cultural differences. Clearly, that is not the problem faced by this gentleman. Instead, he was dealing with an immature team made up of individuals with limited software development experience.

His frustration has been experienced by many others. Most of it can be eliminated by choosing a good vendor. However, even with a good vendor, you want to have some way to control their activity—some way to track their progress and make corrections when things get off track.

This chapter looks at ways to avoid these communication problems. It contains an overview of several tools, techniques, and methodologies.

Entire books have been written about some of these techniques, but this overview will get you started and point you in the right direction.

Software Management Tools

Like a futuristic George Jetson, going to work and pushing a button all day, CTOs, CIOs, and IT project and program managers want a button of their own. The button they seek controls all aspects of their offshore software development, including collaboration, project management, and IT governance. When pushed the right way and the right number of times, the button produces perfect results every time.

Unfortunately, not even a NASA control room full of buttons, switches, and monitors could encompass the variety of issues that can surface in offshoring projects. Still, a vast array of software tools is available that can monitor the status of various aspects of the offshoring process. In fact, so many software tools have become available that it would be difficult even to list them all.

Several categories of tools have emerged to serve key areas of the management of offshore projects: software development, collaboration, project schedule and cost management, and IT governance.

What can these tools do for your organization? And must your organization change its approach to managing projects or outsourcers just to use them? We will take a look at some of the most popular tools, as well as some lesser-known, high-value ones.

Software Development Tools

Software development tools can help you manage the nuts and bolts of requirements capture, software design, source code control, and defect tracking.

Outsourcing software development is a complex human activity with a bidirectional flow of ideas, knowledge, and intellectual property. Some go so far as to compare modern-day software development to a manufacturing process consisting of a "supply chain" of programmers and assemblers who put together the final product.

If software development has truly become a supply chain, then software tools are needed to organize and optimize this effort. Here are three areas where such tools can help you.[32]

Requirements Management and Software Design

The single most important factor in the success of software development is defining and managing the requirements of what the software should do. You don't necessarily need a software tool to do this. However, in large projects with many requirements and many programmers working to satisfy them, a tool is valuable to ensure that details don't fall through the cracks before the project is completed.

The Unified Modeling Language (UML), discussed in the previous chapter, contains many techniques for defining requirements. Most marketing requirements documents (MRDs) and software specifications use UML diagrams and prose to describe how the software should be written and behave. Therefore, most MRDs and design documents are written in Microsoft Word and are then illustrated with diagrams created in Visio and other drawing tools.

More advanced and expensive tools link the requirements to the source code and the test plans for performing quality assurance (QA) after the software is written. Sophisticated tools are now available that will link your use cases and other design elements directly to modules of your source code.

Source Code Control

Any software development project with more than one engineer requires some sort of source code control system to help keep track of the multiple versions of each source file of computer code.

A major decision you must make when offshoring is where the central repository of your source code will reside. Should it be local, on one of your servers, or offshore? Your decision depends on the trust you have in the offshore team and the level of support you have in your own organization to maintain a source code control system.

If you do let your outsourcing vendor host the source code control system, you should obtain copies of the source code upon each release, at a minimum.

---

32. A list of open-source and commercial tools for software development are listed on the web site for this book.

The power of a commercial tool may be required for large bodies of source code and complex products. Offshore vendors will usually adapt to the source code control tool you choose. For most projects, free open-source tools such as CVS and Subversion are sufficient, and any offshore vendor should be familiar with them.

Is an open-source tool like CVS good enough for your software development? Usually it is. Commercial tools requiring a license for each software developer are necessary when you need speed to process large amounts of source code and when complex relationships exist between different versions of your software modules.

Some complex software systems will use different versions of some modules for different customers and at different times. For example, suppose that one customer or set of users is running an existing version of your software that contains modules A, B, and C. Then a new customer comes along and requires new functionality that you put into module D. Finally, you have customers that want to use features in modules A, B, and D but do not want or will not pay for C. You now have three versions of your software: A+B+C, A+B+C+D, and A+B+D.

Things get complicated very fast if you have different versions of these modules installed at different customer sites. If you have a situation like this, in which you need to combine different versions of multiple modules for each customer, you need more sophisticated tools to keep things organized. You need a commercial source code control tool that also does configuration management.

In most cases, however, it is possible, and advisable, to keep things simple, so that low-cost or free tools will have enough power to keep your software development organized. In the example just given, you could send the latest version of each module (A through D) to every customer and then just configure the software during installation to enable or disable the features as needed. Avoid custom versions of your source code, to keep things simple, manageable, and low in cost.

Defect Tracking

Once you start editing source code, introducing defects is inevitable. Defect or bug tracking software is used to enter, organize, and close out bug reports. It is another critical tool for managing the software development process and can also be used to manage enhancement requests from your users.

Most defect tracking programs now have a web interface that enables secure use via the Internet. Most also support attaching documents containing screen shots, lengthy error messages, and other files to each bug report.

Bug tracking software is also used to prioritize bugs, assign them to programmers, and close them out when they are fixed. In this sense it is a mini-project management tool for organizing the bug-fixing process. Therefore, your defect tracking software should allow you to assign a severity level to each bug. A scale of four or five levels is usually sufficient. Here is an example of one way to define several severity levels:

- Severity 1: A critical software bug that causes an unrecoverable software crash or that loses data. The software cannot be released with any level 1 bugs.
- Severity 2: A serious bug that is often an important feature that did not get implemented and where there is a difficult or no workaround for the user. Special approval is required to release the software with a level 2 bug.
- Severity 3: A major bug that has a workaround but makes the software difficult to use. Only five level 3 bugs are allowed in a release.
- Severity 4: A minor bug with an easy workaround. No more than ten level 4 bugs are allowed in each release.
- Severity 5: A nuisance bug such as a misspelling or cosmetic defect. No more than ten level 5 bugs are allowed per release.

It is important to define how many bugs at each severity level your users will tolerate and that you will allow in your releases. This defines from the start an objective criterion for the release of your software and for acceptance of the software from your outsourcing vendor.

Many open-source tools are available to track issues and defects. Commercial tools are required only if they give you more capabilities to tie defects to your requirements and QA process. You may want to see reports showing the number of bugs per module over time, which required features have the most defects, and how quickly bugs are being fixed. Reports like these can give you a more accurate picture of your software development than just the list of open bugs at a given time.

Collaboration Tools

Collaboration software provides messaging for software design and issue resolution, knowledge management, and knowledge transfer. Also known as groupware, this type of software integrates work on a single project by linking several concurrent users at separated locations.

Collaboration is a necessary means of satisfying two important concerns of the offshoring process. In the beginning, it is important to clearly communicate the requirements of the software. Conversations by voice or email are often necessary to tell the user stories and clarify the use cases. Later, collaboration is used to resolve issues after development begins.

Groupware and collaboration tools can be divided into three categories:

- Communications: Email, faxing, voice mail, web publishing, wiki, instant messaging. Techniques in this category are usually not live or in real time.
- Conferencing: Telephone conference calls, instant messaging, electronic white boards, chat rooms, discussion forums, video conferencing.
- Collaborative management tools: Electronic calendars, project management schedules, knowledge and document management.

Regardless of the communication technique used, it is ideal to have an audit trail to capture the knowledge that is exchanged. This transcript can be shared with others who may not have been available during the live session as well as to document changes and commitments.

Project Management Tools

Wrong features, bugs, and project delays are the three big dangers in software development. Project management tools help you avoid the last of these. Delays can come from unexpected interrelationships and dependencies between tasks. Unexpected delays may also occur when people and resources are assigned to too many tasks.

Project management tools enable you to assign people and resources to tasks and combine the results of those tasks to complete milestones. Resource leveling helps you avoid overextending re-sources that are assigned to multiple concurrent tasks. Finally, most project management tools enable you to track progress in terms of percentage completed and the financial value of tasks. The critical path of tasks that must be completed on time in order to meet a mile-stone is also identified and monitored by the software.

Organizations are increasingly managing their activities and business processes as projects, to monitor performance more closely and make better business decisions. Part of the Microsoft Office suite of tools, Microsoft Project is the most widely used project manage-ment software. Although niche products exist to address specific market needs, Microsoft Project is a standard tool that satisfies most project management requirements—especially for scheduling. It is suitable for managing offshore projects, given that such management is often done by tracking high-level milestones and drops down to the detailed task level only if there is a problem.

A weakness of Microsoft Project is that the schedule exists in a file that must be shared. As versions of the project schedule change, it may be a challenge to ensure that every team member has the correct version of the schedule file and even the correct version of Project. It also requires a certain amount of discipline to coordinate multiple people making updates to the schedule either to restructure tasks and assignments or to track progress at multiple sites.

Microsoft has designed solutions that enable you to share proj-ect documents over the Internet. A web-based interface using the Microsoft Sharepoint server provides controlled access to schedule documents for updates.

Detailed tracking of day-to-day progress by resource and task is usually left to your outsourcing vendor. You will more likely be focused on software features and achieving major milestones. It is important that your outsourcing vendor use some kind of project management tool to track progress. In most cases you will need to see reports only on a weekly basis.

IT Governance and Portfolio Management

There are good strategic and tactical reasons to use tools to track IT and outsourcing projects. They give your company a way to measure whether these projects are in line with your company's business objec-tives. Many IT and line-of-business executives need to juggle multiple projects and make decisions about which ones are of the highest priority and value. When a new project is proposed, executives need to determine whether to move resources from other projects already underway. This is all part of good corporate governance.

How can you compare one project to another in your portfolio? And how can you compare resources, such as different offshore vendors, to make good choices regarding who should be working on your projects? (For instance, it may be possible to track which vendor has the most qualified resources available.) Software tools that help managers rate projects and track resources promote good IT departmental governance.

Metrics and Risk Assessment

Using the right software tools, your organization's managers should create a scorecard to evaluate and compare outsourcing providers based upon their actual performance. You can then eliminate those vendors that do not perform well and assign critical projects to those vendors with a good track record.

Another aspect of IT governance software is risk assessment—evaluating and categorizing risks and devising strategies to mitigate those risks. And a large part of risk reduction is removing uncertainty. The risk of an event can be generally defined as the probability of the event's occurrence multiplied by some measurement of the possible impact of the event. Once you identify the risks associated with your projects, you can devise strategies for minimizing them.

Software Development Methodologies

Your software development methodology defines the processes and procedures used to develop your software. It also includes the details of source code control and defect tracking as well as acceptance tests and release criteria.

The history of software development is only about 50 years old. We have come a long way from the early days of machine language programming and assembly language. Compiled languages have improved individual programmer productivity.

In the early days of software, ideas for programs often came from the programmers themselves. In fact, most programmers dreamed of ways to make their programming work easier. For me, this desire is captured by the aphorism I first saw as a graffiti in the computer center at Worcester Polytechnic Institute in 1978: "I would rather write programs to help me write programs than write programs."

Today, sophisticated interactive development environments (IDEs) like Visual Studio and Eclipse give a tremendous boost to programmer productivity. In addition to individual programmer productivity, the productivity of programming teams has also improved in the last few years. There are now multiple processes and methodologies for you to choose from.

Will you use pair programming and test-driven development? Do you prefer agile development methods over the rational unified process? Are you using Microsoft technology and following a model-driven architecture approach?

There is no one right answer that suits every product or software development project, outsourced or not. Consider various approaches and choose a methodology that you have had success with before or that feels right to you. You don't need to religiously follow all the elements of any particular methodology or even adopt a label for the one you choose.

Personally, I recommend agile development methods because of the commitment to frequent software builds and releases. It is a great way to track the progress of your software development and make corrections if results veer from the plan or if the plan changes, as it inevitably will.

Whatever software development methodology you choose, you must make sure that the outsourced team understands your process. In fact, the ability to work with the methodology to be used should be an important criterion for choosing your outsourced team to begin with.

Define Your Engineering Management Structure

Professional software development teams have a structure for effectively managing and achieving success with software development. When you are outsourcing, that structure applies to your in-house team as well as the offshore team.

Should your CEO be in charge of the day-to-day activities of your outsourced software development? Probably not. But it is important to make someone in your company responsible for the successful delivery of your software. To get the job done, he or she needs to have the authority to deal with the in-house employees responsible for various aspects of your software, as well as the authority to deal with the outsourced team.

You should have a core technical team within your organization that does product or project management rather than coding. It is a mistake to hire very technical, hands-on programmers to manage software development when using outsourcing.

Your core technical team will be comprised of experienced product and engineering managers to handle the coordination of your outsourced teams. Do not rely exclusively on the project management resources within the outsourced team to guide your product to successful release. Only your employees have the proper perspective that comes from proximity to your customers to play this role.

A good rule to follow is: outsource your software development, but not the entire responsibility for success.

CMMI Maturity Levels for the Software Development Process

Some offshore outsourcing companies tout their CMMI rating of level 4 or 5. Others offer an ISO 9001 certification. What are these ratings, and are they important to developing your software?

Back in the 1980s, the Software Engineering Institute (SEI)[33] at Carnegie Mellon University began studying the software development process. The SEI and others investigated how to improve budget and schedule estimates and improve quality. This work evolved into the Capability Maturity Model for Software, or CMM, and is described in the paper of the same name by Mark Paulk and colleagues. Since the year 2000, the specification has been upgraded to CMMI, standing for Capability Maturity Model Integration. The CMMI defines five levels of software process "maturity."

Determining your level of maturity may bring back bad memories from junior high school. However, here is how the paper uses this concept:

> A software process can be defined as a set of activities, methods, practices, and transformations that people use to develop and maintain software and the associated products (e.g., project plans, design documents, code, test cases, and user manual). As an organization matures, the software process becomes better

---

33. References to CMMI web resources are on the book's web site.

defined and more consistently implemented throughout the organization.

The CMMI also defines key process areas for each of the maturity levels. Level 1 really has no process and is included as a base reference. Table 6-1 describes the five levels in the CMMI.

Can every software development organization make use of these guidelines? Are new software development groups immature by definition? The CMMI paper defines "immaturity" this way:

> . . . software processes are generally improvised by practitioners and their management during the course of a project. Even if a software process has been specified, it is not rigorously followed or enforced.

That sounds like the situation at many software organizations and outsourcing vendors to me! I have been there—up at midnight,

Table 6-1 Capability Maturity Model for Software Development

Level	Name	Description	Key Process Areas
5	Optimizing	Continuously improving process	• Process change management • Technology change management • Defect prevention
4	Managed	Predictable process	• Software quality management • Quantitative process management
3	Defined	Standard, consistent process	• Peer reviews • Intergroup coordination • Software product engineering • Integrated software management • Training program • Organization process definition • Organization process focus
2	Repeatable	Disciplined process	• Software configuration management • Software quality assurance • Software subcontract management • Software project tracking and oversight • Software project planning • Requirements management
1	Initial	No standard process	• Ad hoc and heroic efforts of individuals

converting Diet Coke and doughnuts into working software. We called it bipolar candle combustion, a twist on the old saying about burning the candle at both ends. CMMI calls it level 1.

For example, a founder at one software startup wanted to create a long specification and then do focus groups before creating a product. This is a big-company approach that most software startups cannot afford. He was hooted down by his co-founders. An overly formal process is usually not welcomed by wild-eyed entrepreneurs in the early days of a startup. But some process is required to keep things organized. In my experience, good software development organizations operate somewhere near level 2½.

There is a tension between creating an innovative software product and following a more formal process to get predictable results. It's like the old joke about the railroad whose trains always ran late. Finally, a passenger went up to the ticket window and complained, "Why do you even bother publishing a schedule when the trains are always late!?" The station master replied, "Sir, if we didn't, we wouldn't know how late the trains are."

Sometimes your customers or users will want to see whether you have a well-defined software development process. They don't want to get stuck with an ill-defined and poorly created piece of software that is difficult to use and support. You don't need to be CMMI or ISO certified, but you should at least have implemented most of the processes found in level 2.

If you are seeking funding, your potential investors will want to know how you develop your software. Venture capitalists will often hire consultants to investigate your software development process.

Of course, it is always better if you, or someone you have hired, has experience developing software and a plan based on that experience for successfully delivering your next software project. However, there is an old saying: "Anything worth doing is worth doing badly." The point is, you should get started with bringing your software to life and implement more formal development processes as you and your organization "mature," rather than waiting to develop the perfect specification and plan. A good offshore outsourcing vendor will help you do this.

Should you select an offshore firm with a high CMMI rating? If your present organization is at level 1 and you hire an offshore company at level 4, you will have some catching up to do. It will not be a good fit.

I recommend choosing an offshore company that is near your current level or at the level you would like to achieve with your own organization.

Often the benefits of a high CMMI rating go to the offshore vendor rather than to you. You may never see the benefits of continuous improvement gained by the vendor unless they continue to build future versions of your software. If the vendor is your long-term partner, you will usually gain benefits and efficiencies when they develop future versions of your software anyway, because of their familiarity with your application, whether they are CMMI rated or not.

Qualifying for a CMMI rating is not a trivial process. Offshore firms deserve to charge a premium for their ability to execute a more formal design process. If you do not need the benefits of a high CMMI level, you will be paying too much and adding delay in releasing your software.

The Agile Alternative

If the features of your software are likely to change as development proceeds (and whose don't?), you will derive great benefit from a process that accommodates these changes smoothly. Agile development approaches embrace change and are a better fit for developing new software in situations where the requirements are not completely known.

Agile approaches do this by having the development team work on a small set of features that you determine are of the highest priority. They work on as many features as can be completed within a predefined window of time or "time box." The features should be completely implemented and tested when the end of the time box is reached.

Each time box is usually only 2 to 4 weeks in length, so your software development does not get too far off track before you know it and can't do something about it. And "off track" means that your software is late because either you misjudged the productivity of your development team or you prioritized the features wrong and other features turn out to be more important. In the latter case, you can easily implement the newly important features in the next time box or iteration.

Agile and CMMI are sometimes presented as opposing or at least different approaches to software development. The approach that is best for you will depend on the experience and structure of your software development organization, the completeness of your specifications, and ultimately on how you like to develop your software.

Keeping in Touch with Your Outsourced Team

Keeping in touch with your offshore team is critical to the success of your outsourcing. That idea seems pretty simple, but when you factor in accents and time zones, your ability to communicate well can be seriously hurt.

Poor communication can be a concern bigger than security or the safety of your intellectual property. When it is daytime here, you want to move documents back and forth, but the servers can be shutdown at night in India. The engineers in each country can have trouble understanding one another. The accents and the fatigue of late-night or early-morning conference calls reduce your ability to share ideas and brainstorm. These are common frustrations you can encounter with offshore outsourcing.

Much is lost without the intimacy of direct communication. And without good communication, barriers are created between your local people here and "them": the guys one or two oceans away who are supposed to be writing your software.

The overhead required to make outsourcing work depends on the skills of people both offshore and in your organization. You need to put processes in place and use tools to minimize that overhead.

Many companies that outsource use weekly conference calls and then exchange emails and instant messages as needed, usually every day. In addition there are bug tracking and source code control systems, and each software release is delivered as a zip file of source files.

Here is a summary of the tools that you should be using:

- Project management: Keep your outsourcing on course by tracking delivery dates, scope, and budget. You can manage milestones, project and subproject plans, tasks, and resources. It should be compatible with Microsoft Project and support import/export of Project files.
- Resource management: Identify and track the engineering talent on your project and rate their performance.
- Time recording: Track the progress of your software projects by viewing the actual time spent on tasks and comparing it to planned estimates.

- Document management: Unify your teams by enabling them to share and manage key documented information affecting your software project's outcome.
- Requirements management and traceability: Capture and analyze your requirements and trace their progress throughout the project to ensure that they're being delivered as agreed upon. Notify relevant team members and stakeholders when a requirement has been changed, completed, or approved, to help you head off issues before they affect your bottom line.
- Issue tracking and defect tracking: Successfully manage the life cycle of each issue and defect to its resolution.
- Change management: Keep expectations in line and prevent going over budget by managing each stage of a change request, including tracking its cost and schedule implications.
- Test management: Achieve the level of quality your software requires by managing your testing cycles. You can track and confirm the status of test plans, trace test cases to requirements, review the results of all test scripts, and analyze and audit current test results against historical results.

You can put together a collection of tools like this on your own by cobbling together tools and systems from open-source offerings. Easy, low-cost alternatives also exist that are online hosted solutions allowing you to keep in touch with your outsourcing team. Some have a roles-based dashboard, used by everyone from testers and programmers to the high-level executives responsible for the software development. The dashboard enables you to keep on top of and manage the critical factors affecting your outsourcing from start to finish.

Whether you use a commercial offering or put a collection of tools together yourself, the list just given contains the functions you need to implement.

Examples of Well-Managed Outsourcing

Let's look at four basic techniques used by software development organizations that are outsourcing successfully. See whether any or all of these approaches will fit your situation.

Milestone Tracking

To keep things simple, one software development company is setting clear milestones with its outsourcing vendor. Rather than micromanage the software development done offshore to the task level, it sets clearly defined milestones describing the features that are to be completed in each. Then it receives a commitment from the offshore vendor as to when the milestone will be completed.

Managing by milestone is much more efficient than watching for the completion of each module or other programming task. For this approach to be practical, your outsourcing vendor must have a management infrastructure. You don't get this if you view your outsourcing simply as a way to get more programmers.

Some vendors view their role in the relationship as simply providing the programmers. These vendors are sometimes called "body shops" and can play a useful role if you need just a few programmers and have the management resources to direct their activity every workday.

Sometimes the distinction between hiring an outsourcing team and hiring individual programmers is not understood between a software development organization and the outsourcing vendor. The client sees a chance to hire programmers cheap, for well under $20 per hour. Meanwhile, the vendor sees an opportunity to hire out individual programmers and make a tidy profit without having to provide any oversight to the software development process.

But if you have limited resources in your organization to manage your software development to begin with, hiring cheap programmers just won't work. It is the opposite problem expressed by the old saying, "Too many chiefs and not enough Indians." Having too many Indians and not enough chiefs doesn't work either.

One U.S. software company learned this the hard way. After promising a complete software development team, the outsourcing vendor provided only a group of junior programmers. The project managers at the U.S. company had to stay up late to check the source code as it was delivered from the offshore team.

They also had to stay up late to communicate what the software needed to do. The ability of the offshore team to understand the specifications was extremely limited. The U.S.-based managers found that they had to send pseudocode, essentially designing and writing the software themselves, to enable the offshore team to deliver any kind of useful code.

This is not outsourcing—it is a nightmare of micromanagement made ridiculously difficult by the distances involved.

For projects where you need more than a couple of programmers, you should find a vendor that has a management infrastructure that enables you to delegate your software development. Manage your offshore team by milestones, and don't take on the day-to-day management of programming tasks. Professional offshore software development teams will make commitments to deliver milestones by specific dates and then live up to those commitments.

Use of Audio and Video for Collaboration

The traditional method of audio communication is the telephone through the public-switched telephone network. Today this is still the most reliable but also the most expensive way to talk long-distance. The quality of low-cost Voice Over Internet Protocol, or VOIP, services is lower, but they enable you to talk to anyone in the world for pennies per minute.

VOIP calls from offshore can also be made to the U.S. through free conference call services that enable the entire team to be available on one call. The quality is sometimes poor, and multiple attempts may be required to get a good connection. The quality of the speaker phone on either end of the call also has a big impact on the ability to understand what is being said.

Most people today are using free services like Skype, Yahoo Messenger with Voice, or Google Talk for free computer-to-computer voice communication. This is a very useful and workable way to talk, since both sides are likely to be using computers when outsourcing software development. However, a high-speed Internet connection is also required for best results. DSL, a T1 line, or an even higher-speed line is not an issue for most offshore outsourcing vendors, but it could be too expensive for some individual freelance programmers.

Of course, the reason to use voice communications is to clarify issues and to answer questions more quickly than by written email or instant message.

For example, a company exchanged multiple emails attempting to explain the difference between a purchase order and a backorder and how they were to be handled within the software application being developed. A purchase order is the order a buyer places with a seller. The backorder is not an order at all, but a notification by the seller to the buyer that an item already ordered by the buyer is not presently available. A backorder may include information as to when the item will eventually be shipped.

A real-time discussion of the differences was required to resolve this issue efficiently. This was probably because the meanings of backorder and purchase order were so well understood by the client that the words to describe them were difficult to come by. Meanwhile, the Russian developers had limited experience placing orders and receiving shipments.

Luckily, the Russian developers were able to understand and speak English well enough for the phone call to be successful. This will not always be the case. If you think you will need to rely on voice communication to clarify your outsourcing requirements, you will have to make the ability to communicate with spoken English an important vendor selection criterion.

Remember that spoken communication with all engineers working on your software may not be necessary; the ability to speak with your project leader may be sufficient.

At another extreme, you may have a close working relationship between the members of your local engineering team and individuals on your offshore team. A company with programmers working together in this way uses an open Skype connection to enable long-distance pair programming. Pair programming, as defined by the extreme programming method, usually has the two programmers working on a single computer in the same room. In this example, the two programmers are across an ocean and are sharing the screen with GoToMyPC.

As broadband Internet access becomes more widespread, real-time video connections will become practical. An immediate full-screen video connection to your offshore software development team will make the distance shrink even further.

Face-to-Face Visits

After several months of communicating by email and instant messaging, the engineering director and CEO flew to India to meet the software development team.

Was there a problem? No, things were going great. And now things are going even better because of the improved communication they have gained from meeting face to face.

During the visit, not only were names matched with faces, but personalities and individual interests also became known. Friendship and mutual respect has developed between working members on both sides of the world.

Have they eliminated all problems and miscommunications? Of course not, but issues and problems are much easier to resolve now that the individuals involved know each other better.

Do you have to travel to make your offshore outsourcing work well? Not necessarily. Many software development organizations are spanning the globe, and yet the individuals in different countries have never met.

Sometimes the travel occurs in the other direction. Another company had the leader of its offshore team in Russia fly to the U.S. before software development began. The specifications were discussed and several questions were answered. When the offshore team leader returned to St. Petersburg, additional questions and issues arose, but a firm foundation of understanding and a personal relationship with all the U.S. team members enabled questions to be answered with a minimal amount of time and typing.

You usually get the most benefit from bidirectional travel, having people from each side visiting the other. If time and budget are limited, you will probably get more benefit for the dollar by visiting your offshore development team at their site and communicating directly with them explaining what your software should do.

Travel is not a strict requirement for success in offshore outsourcing. But it does help things go more smoothly.

Test-Driven Development and Continuous Builds

Have you ever faced the nightmare of integrating software created by multiple developers? The software is supposed to be released on Friday, so a few days beforehand you try to combine all the modules so testing can begin. Of course, nothing works.

Your testing is supposed to actually run the application, enter data, and verify the results. But you cannot even create a running application because the modules created by your programmers don't link or work together.

Unfortunately, some software development organizations fail to account for the issues that arise from integration. A programmer creates a module to behave one way, and the rest of the programmers expect it to behave in another. The bugs can be subtle and difficult to find.

That's why most experienced software development teams have frequent builds of their software, where integration problems are caught early rather than letting them pile up to be dealt with later.

The next step in making software integration go smoothly is to automate testing to avoid the tedious and error-prone process of manually testing each software release. This *regression testing* should confirm that existing functionality is not broken by the new release. Over time, the regression test suite grows by including tests of new functionality.

These are basic steps of modern software development, and most offshore software development vendors will already know how to do integration and regression testing. However, automated regression testing takes time to implement, and not every software development project starts with such a framework or even uses it before the software is released.

But complex and long-term software development projects with a plan for multiple releases benefit greatly from the time invested in automated integration and regression testing. They do not eliminate the need for overall testing of your software's functionality, but they at least ensure that basic functions are working and that bugs are discovered quickly and fixed.

Another big benefit that automated testing enables is test-driven development, or TDD. TDD promotes the process of testing to the point of beginning each implementation of a software feature with testing. Of course, the test will fail when run, because the software does not yet contain the feature that is being tested.

The benefit of this approach is it has the programmers thinking about testing right from the start. The tests contain the definition of success, of what it means for each feature under development to be completed.

TDD is an extension of *unit testing,* the testing of each module or unit independently to detect and eliminate basic bugs that occur at a low level before they become more difficult to detect in the fully integrated software application.

Ideally, all programmers do some unit testing during development. TDD makes unit testing mandatory and an integral part of the software development process.

Unit tests that are defined by the programmer are checked into the source code control system, along with the code of the module itself. The unit tests are then made part of the automated regression tests. They are executed each time programmers check in code (and the accompanying tests) and integration occurs.

A test-driven development process usually enables integration to occur without error. Therefore, integrations can occur frequently— every time a programmer checks in code, in fact. This continuous building of the software gives you access to working software at almost every point of the software development process.

If your software is a web application being developed offshore, then with proper authorizations, you can point your web browser into the development environment and see the current state of development at any time.

Of course, the biggest benefit of TDD is eliminating the integration nightmare that has been the cause of many delayed releases over the history of software development on all continents.

Strictly Agile

TDD is part of the agile approach. You can also take a strictly agile approach and abandon the artifacts of requirements, specifications, architecture designs, and so on described in previous sections. Instead, your focus will be more purely on the collaborative process of sharing user stories about how the software will be used, and you will interact with your outsourced software development team to clarify details and prioritize their activities.

Agile was originally conceived as a way to improve communication with software engineers, and it requires close collaboration with the business/marketing/product managers and customers themselves in daily meetings. There are also several case studies and reports of *distributed agile* software development[34] that describe excellent results using agile software development with teams in multiple locations around the world.

The low-cost hourly rates of offshore programmers are not a key theme in these studies. Instead, the studies show the tremendous increase of productivity these teams achieve because of the agile

---

34. One report is "Distributed Agile Development and the Death of Distance" by Matthew Simons.

methods. They consistently show faster results and produce higher-quality software compared to conventional methods requiring more formal specifications and management approaches.

One study[35] describes use of the scrum version of agile development, in which a daily meeting—the daily scrum—is carried out at the same time with both the onshore and offshore teams. The scrum is at the beginning of the workday in the U.S. and the end of the workday in Russia. The scrum meetings focused on explaining details of the user stories for the library information system under development. The system is for use in American libraries, which have different procedures than the libraries in Russia. Therefore, the Russian programmers do not have an innate understanding of how an American library management system would be used, just as American programmers are not likely to be aware of how libraries are run in Russia.

This is the fundamental challenge in all software development—to convey the purpose and goals of what the software should do so the engineers can create it. The agile methods have proven to be the best way to handle this critical information flow between humans.

A major inspiration for agile software development methods comes from the lessons learned about manufacturing from Japanese auto makers in the 1980s. The concepts of lean manufacturing used by Toyota in particular are nicely mapped to software development by Mary and Tom Poppendieck in their book *Lean Software Development: An Agile Toolkit*.[36] They identify seven lean principles from the manufacturing world that should be applied to software development. Decision-making power is distributed to the software development engineers in the same way that power is distributed to workers on the modern manufacturing assembly line. Gone are the formal processes and procedures that centralize decision-making power and encourage wasted time spent creating specifications and documents that few will ever read.

Are distributed agile methods of offshore software development right for you? It is a dramatic change from the traditional software

---

35. *Distributed Scrum: Agile Project Management with Outsourced Development* by Jeff Sutherland, Anton Victorov, and Jack Blount.

36. This and several other books and studies that describe various principles, practices, and methods of agile software development are on the Software without Borders web site: www.SoftwareWithoutBordersBook.com.

development methods. But the results are impressive and the methods themselves are built on sound experience and principles. They are growing in popularity and acceptance, and you should give them serious consideration.

How Will You Manage?

Is TDD right for your offshore outsourcing? Do you have to fly to India or China or Russia to properly kick off your software development? Or can you handle any problem or issue with a flurry of free Skype calls from your computer?

These are the questions you must answer for your situation, based on the complexity and timing of your software development projects. Discuss them with your outsourcing vendor as part of your vendor evaluation process.

Most of these techniques are required for large software development engagements that go on for years, and for situations in which multiple software projects are completed over time. They give you tools to monitor progress and keep your outsourced software development on track.

Over these longer time spans, it is also a good idea to measure the productivity and progress of your outsourcing in some objective way. The next chapter covers how to define and make these measurements or metrics.

Chapter 7

Software Outsourcing Metrics

You can observe a lot just by watching.

—Yogi Berra

How do you measure the success of your outsourcing? There are several ways to look at it. First, if you are a technical professional—a VP of engineering or a programmer or project manager responsible for outsourcing—one way you can measure your success is your ability to communicate with the offshore team. Your "gut feel" for how things are going is based on the quality of the software you are receiving, the kinds of bugs being found in it, and how many crises must be fixed via conference calls.

If you are more comfortable running your business with quantifiable objectives, a gut feel is not enough. That is where metrics come in. They give you a way of quantifying the results of your outsourcing so you can judge objectively whether your software development is succeeding or not. Better yet, they let you focus on ways to improve the productivity of your outsourcing for greater cost savings.

Peter Drucker is often quoted as saying, "If you can't measure it, you can't manage it." And he is correct. However, in small organizations, metrics may seem like overkill. If your offshore team meets its commitment to deliver the software on time, and the code contains a reasonably small number of bugs that get fixed quickly, then what is the problem? Do you really need to spend time inventing formulas, adding up lines of code, and dividing by man-hours? After all, you may not bother with fancy metrics when your programmers are right there in the same room with you.

Stroke, Stroke!

When I worked as a programmer in the 1980s, my boss used to joke that he was going to hire a guy with a kettle drum and put him in the corner of the room. Every time the kettle drum was hit, we had to have written a line of code!

Today there is a different drumbeat. Now that outsourcing is more popular and promises huge cost savings, the drumbeat drives executives to measure the real savings. They want to be sure that outsourcing of software development is as cost-effective as it can possibly be.

This desire is driven partially by the huge growth in business process outsourcing (BPO). Business processes such as accounts receivable, inbound support calls, and outbound sales calls are easy to outsource. They can be well defined, and you can accurately measure performance in terms of dollars, transactions, and time.

Outsourced business processes are carefully measured and analyzed to detect problems and inefficiencies. New software tools not only help detect problems but can also predict and show how to fix problems before they arise.

The process of developing software is also pretty well understood. Is it possible to measure software development to make it more predictable and reliable, like BPO? That is what business executives are asking. And in organizations where software development has a significant budget, it seems like a fair question.

What metrics should you use, and what should you do if your outsourced software development process does not measure up?

What to Measure: Efficiency or Acceleration?

For a simple example, consider the Toyota Prius hybrid car I purchased last year. The EPA sticker on the window promised 61 miles per gallon (mpg) of gasoline, but I am getting only 45 mpg. Oddly, my wife gets 50 mpg when she drives it! Anyway, it seems to me that my Prius is not meeting the service-level agreement (SLA) originally implied by the numbers on the window sticker.

Of course, the EPA rating of my Prius is not a legal agreement that I can use to seek better performance from Toyota. It just feels disappointing because my mileage is not meeting the expectation set by the EPA rating. But 45 mpg is a lot better than the 13 mpg I was getting in my old SUV!

Similarly, outsourcing's detractors claim that the savings actually realized by outsourcing will not be as great as those advertised on the "window sticker" of a vendor's rate sheet. Extra costs for management and delays due to poor communication, they say, will eat away at the huge savings promised by outsourcing vendors.

On the other hand, many managers who are now outsourcing offshore often feel content knowing that the $25 hourly rate they are paying is much cheaper than the $100 per hour they used to pay contractors in the U.S.

Before we look at metrics more closely, let's review. The SLA describes the level of performance the client expects from the outsourcing vendor. It is useful only if it is backed up by meaningful and objective metrics, like the mpg for my Prius or the number of features in and the release date of your software application. Without objective metrics, an SLA does not make much sense.

SLAs can be complicated and require the collection of many details to compute the metrics that will track progress accurately. Many managers don't bother spending the time to define metrics or just don't know where to get started. But if you don't measure progress at all, you are setting yourself up for trouble. One CEO spent most of his budget of $300,000 before realizing the outsourcing of his software development was going nowhere. You cannot just go on faith alone.

The kind of work you are performing offshore will influence the kind of metrics you should use. At the risk of stretching a metaphor too far, let's compare my hybrid Prius to a sports car. I was driving my Prius behind a candy-apple red Ferrari (do they come in any other color?) the other day. The Ferrari accelerated up the freeway on-ramp and left me in the dust. I realized that mileage was probably not an important metric for Ferrari owners.

Likewise, there is no one metric for all software development. It is difficult to know how to measure creativity and innovation when you are outsourcing the development of new software—especially if new features are always being introduced and changes are occurring constantly.

Metrics of New Development

It turns out that you can measure the process of new software development, and it is done differently than the way you measure the maintenance of existing software. Table 7-1 compares the metrics involved in tracking both processes.

To measure new software development, you track the number of new features added over time. Some metrics do this by splitting the programming required into work units and then tracking the number of units completed over time. It is best to measure results daily or at least weekly.

Engineers are notoriously optimistic about their ability to create working software. So another metric measures how accurate their estimates are regarding the time required to finish the software development. Initially, their ability to estimate will likely be poor. You can set a goal for the engineers to improve this skill as your development continues, so that you can improve the predictability of your process.

For maintenance programming you need to track the work units or bugs fixed over time. In addition, you should measure the amount of rework required for bugs that fail the QA step after fix attempts.

Remember: The purpose of the SLA is to guide your software development to success and to detect and correct problems as they arise. It is not to support micromanagement or a blame game or to create an adversarial relationship with your outsourced team.

Your offshore software development team should commit to a schedule for completing the programming work. As part of this

Table 7-1 Typical Metrics for Software Development

Metric	New Development	Maintenance
New features per week (or daily)	X	
Work units (use cases, functions, story points, bug fixes) completed by the team per day	X	X
Delays in meeting scheduled releases	X	X
Mentoring time for junior engineers	X	X
Amount of rework or repeat bug fixing		X
Average time for bug fixes		X

schedule, they must also agree to the definition of work units and the productivity level they believe they can achieve. Their commitment allows them more independence and frees everyone involved from the need for specific, detailed instructions for each work activity.

You will typically measure the throughput of your outsourced team as a whole. A team generally consists of both junior and senior members. Junior engineers will need guidance and mentoring from the senior engineers. This is normal and should be expected and encouraged. But it should also be measured over time. A senior engineer can be expected to spend from 5 to 25 percent of his or her time with junior engineers, depending on the complexity of the project and the prior experience of the junior engineer.

Today most people use common software tools, such as spreadsheets and the basic features of Microsoft Project, to track the metrics of their outsourcing. More sophisticated tools are also available but are expensive and best applied when you have a large portfolio of software development projects.

New tools are now becoming available that offer automatic tracking of metrics as you develop your software. For example, you will be able to track the amount of time source files are checked out of your source code control system to help measure the productivity of your engineers.

Will software development become as predictable as BPO, and will you be able to fix problems before they occur? I doubt that we will ever have that much control over the creative software development process. But who knows? The guy with the kettle drum may not be far off!

How the Big Boys Do It: Balanced Scorecards

The balanced scorecard[37] was developed in the early 1990s by Drs. Robert Kaplan (of Harvard Business School) and David Norton. It is a method for measuring the effectiveness of strategies used by a company as they attempt to achieve their goals.

---

37. A very brief overview of the balanced scorecard method is presented here. Additional references are available in the bibliography and on the Software without Borders web site.

Financial goals and measurements typically dominate corporate management. Kaplan and Norton pointed out, however, that financial measurements describe past events, and that to achieve corporate goals, managers need a system of measurement that will enable them to direct corporate activities and employee behavior going forward on a day-to-day basis.

Furthermore, financial measurements do not tell the whole story of the complex interaction of internal business processes and external results. Thus, measurement of financial performance should be balanced with three other perspectives. The balanced scorecard is a tool for measuring how all four perspectives contribute to achieving overall corporate vision and strategy.

Whew! Pretty highfalutin' stuff! Especially when your vision and strategy are to work all weekend to get out the next release of your software. So let's see how a balanced scorecard relates to software development and outsourcing.

The balanced scorecard method views the organization from four perspectives, and develops metrics for each one:

- Financial perspective
- Business process perspective
- Customer perspective
- Learning and growth perspective

Financial considerations are definitely at play when software development is outsourced, especially from within an IT department of a larger company. This is the environment in which balanced scorecards have found support. After all, saving money is a major reason that companies outsource, especially offshore. So it seems reasonable to measure these savings, along with quality and customer satisfaction.

Cash Is King

Besides the promised cost savings of offshore outsourcing, which you can measure objectively, there are other financial elements to consider. In larger IT projects, the value of the software to the organization can be measured. This is particularly useful when you must prioritize multiple software development projects by determining which will have the biggest impact.

In a software company, the business value of your software is more obvious. The sale of the software being developed is the revenue and lifeblood of the company. For small companies, the ability to release quality software on time will mean the difference between success and disaster. In larger software companies, the financial impact is more complex. You have to decide whether to allocate resources to a new product or use them to fix up an old one, for example.

Clearly communicating the business value and financial impact of your software development work is important. It creates a strong motivation and sense of shared mission in developing the software on time, compared to the less meaningful and isolated achievement of meeting a project deadline. Why not share the financial impact of your software development with your offshore team members? Making them aware of your important financial goals makes their own work more important.

Metrics from the three other perspectives will also contribute to good software development. Of course, the business process perspective is really the process of creating software.

The Customer Is Also King

The customer perspective is often overlooked by software developers. I still hear of software development done in stealth mode and then released by the company with the expectation that grateful customers will beat a path to their door. But it rarely works out that way. It is better to involve your customers or users in the software development process to ensure that you create something they will actually use.

You can devise metrics to monitor the amount and type of customer activity you want in your software development process. It can be as simple as customer surveys or as complex as having them participate in design reviews with your developers.

Agile software development methods involve customers in the requirements gathering and validation process as the software is developed. Each iteration contains features that have been prioritized with input from the user community. The results delivered in each iteration should similarly be reviewed by the users to ensure that their expectations are being met. Your customer metrics can simply document the customer participation you want.

A Lifetime of Learning

With respect to the learning and growth perspective, forward-looking organizations recognize the importance of developing the skills and knowledge of their employees. If your own programmers are developing your software, you want them to be using the latest tools and techniques to improve their productivity. This takes an investment of time for them to keep current by attending seminars and trade shows.

The professional development of your programmers can seem less important when they are offshore and an ocean away. But is it? If you embark on a long-term partnership with an offshore vendor, you will want to make sure that it treats its engineers well. After all, in such a long-term relationship, the vendor's programmers are really your programmers. You will want to make sure they stay on your team and increase their productivity over time beyond the initial savings of a lower offshore rate.

Measuring the Achievement of Your Strategy

The use of the balanced scorecard adds metrics to your software development process that go beyond the monitoring of your schedule and counting of bugs. It has the most impact when you measure your software development in the context of your company's overall strategic goals.

The balanced scorecard captures the measurements you will make to determine if the strategies you employ for achieving your goals are working or not. It is a way of linking your strategies to objective metrics.

Of course, to do this, you must have a set of goals and then defined the strategies for achieving them. Work on goals and strategy is a prerequisite for using the balanced scorecard technique.

Scorecard for Your Company or Department

If you are developing software in a larger organization, you may not have the authority to influence or measure broader business goals like customer satisfaction across a complex product line and achievement of revenue goals. However, you can still apply the balanced scorecard method to your software development organization.

**Table 7-2 Balanced Scorecard Model
Applied to Application Development**

Balanced Scorecard Perspective	Focus Within Application Development Organization
Financial	Business value of the application development projects
Business process	Operational effectiveness and excellence in creating software
Customer	User satisfaction, service level, up-time, etc.
Learning and growth	Future orientation of learning and improvement, positioning to take advantage of future opportunities

In the Forrester report "Metrics for Application Development," author Liz Barnett maps the balanced scorecard perspectives to their use within an application software development organization. This mapping is shown in Table 7-2.

The report goes into more detail on the kinds of goals and metrics that can be used in each of these areas of application development.

Applying Balanced Scorecard to just your own department or organization is not as powerful as applying it to track your overall corporate strategy but still valuable. You will be speaking the same language as other business leaders and will be well positioned to help your company achieve success by applying this popular metrics model beyond your own software development organization.

Practical Software Measurement

The experience of several groups in government, military, and university software development has been gathered together in a Practical Software Measurement (PSM) project sponsored by the U.S. Army and the Department of Defense. The results have been presented in a number of papers, books, and software.[38] PSM includes an iterative process in which you plan what you want to measure, perform those measurements, and then evaluate the results. That's pretty basic, but it does point out that any useful metrics program will evolve over time and should be planned for from the start.

---

38. Several of the books and papers describing PSM are listed in the bibliography and on the Software without Borders web site, along with a link to the PSMI software.

PSM also points out that if you are going to collect metrics you need to make effective use of them. For example, if you discover that half of your programmers are producing bugs at a rate of five per hour and the other half are fixing them at a rate of only three per hour, you are eventually going to have a serious problem on your hands. The purpose of metrics is not to document failure but to make decisive changes and improve your software development process. The aim is to evaluate not the performance of individual team members but the overall software development process.

PSM Insight (PSMI) is a free PC-based software tool that automates the Practical Software Measurement (PSM) process. It is worth a look as a way to get started with your metrics implementation.

Measure for Measure

Some software development organizations still resist using metrics. This is especially true of young companies in which time is short and success is often determined by a single software release. They wonder whether the time it takes to measure and analyze metrics is worthwhile. Some are concerned that they will use so much time and energy pursuing "excellence" that the real business of getting things done will be neglected.

Finally, some fear that the use of metrics will put a damper on creativity. It is as though there was a Heisenberg uncertainty principle of software metrics—if you try to measure the performance of your software development activity too closely, you will reduce the amount of innovation and creativity that can be delivered.

It depends on which metrics you choose. If you measure how quickly the engineers fix bugs, then their focus will be bug fixing. If you measure function points per week, then their focus will be on adding working features to your software quickly. Your software should not be as elusive as electrons. Tracking a moderate number of the right metrics should enhance the creative spirit.

This review of several methods of software metrics is only an introduction. At a minimum, you should be monitoring your software development with the common metrics that track feature creation and bug fixes over time. The use of metrics in other areas, as recommended by the Balanced Scorecard approach, gives you a more holistic view of your software development and company progress.

Chapter 8

Protecting Your Intellectual Property

Chico: Hey wait, wait! What does this say here? This thing here?

Groucho: Oh that. Oh that's the usual clause . . . that's in every contract. That just says . . . eh . . . it says . . . eh . . . "If any of the parties participating in this contract are shown not to be in their right mind, the entire agreement is automatically nullified."

Chico: Well, I don't know . . .

Groucho: "That's in every contract; that's what you call a sanity clause."

Chico: "You can't a fool a me; there ain't no 'Sana-tee Claus.'"

—The Marx Brothers in the movie
A Night at the Opera, 1935

The Usual Disclaimers . . .

This chapter discusses the issues surrounding the protection of your source code and other intellectual property (IP) when you use off-shore outsourcing. I am not an attorney, and the content of this

179

chapter is not a replacement for good legal advice for your specific outsourcing situation. My goal is to give you some grasp of the issues so you can discuss them intelligently and make good decisions. Do you need a sanity clause in your outsourcing contract? That's up to you and your attorney!

Software companies are concerned about putting their intellectual IP at risk when using offshore outsourcing. But you can also be so protective of your IP that you can overlook the opportunity to use low-cost offshore resources. How do you give your IP the right amount of protection? Are you being promiscuous with your IP, or overprotective?

Many years ago I worked for a software company that licensed a copy of its software to the U.S. Navy. I flew to San Diego to do the installation. Even in those days, security was a notch higher than at most companies I visited. After checking in at the guard shack and meeting my escort, I was ready to get to work.

But first my escort had to find a third person authorized to bring my tape into the data center so we could read in the software. Then more authorizations were needed to allow installation of the software on their Univac computer. The installation process dragged on.

During one of our many breaks, I was escorted to the men's room. Along the way I passed someone's cubicle with a big sign on the wall. It said "My job is so secret, I don't even know what I am doing!" That pretty much summed up my experience that day. The point is that sometimes the need, or perceived need, for confidentiality and security adds a great deal of inefficiency and cost.

Software company executives consider their software IP to be their highest-value asset. But is it? How about your sales contacts and deep knowledge of the market you sell into? The actual software and the work that goes into creating it are often just a commodity.

But IP risk is an important criterion you can use to decide whether outsourcing your software development is right for your company.

What Is Your Tolerance for IP Risk?

One way to determine the extent of your risk is to give it a score on an increasing scale from 1 to 5. Here is the meaning of each score value:

1. **Very low IP risk.** You are using standard or old technology that is widely available and understood.
2. **Low IP risk.** Some IP is exposed, but your significant market knowledge and innovation limits its practical use by others.
3. **Neutral IP risk.** Some of your IP will be exposed, but you can partition your software to limit exposure during outsourcing.
4. **Moderate IP risk.** You must be careful about partitioning your software and should possibly use multiple outsourced teams to limit access to all of your IP.
5. **Serious IP risk.** You cannot separate out your critical IP. It will be exposed to any outsourced team used. This risk may overwhelm the benefits of outsourcing in some cases.

You can enter your score for IP risk in the decision matrix presented in Appendix A, along with 16 other criteria to evaluate five different outsourcing strategies. A sixth strategy of using in-house development with employees is also included.

Here are the six software development strategies:

- **In-house**—using your own employees or contractors.
- **Onshore**—outsourcing to a company in your country.
- **Offshore**—contract outsourcing outside your country.
- **In-house plus offshore blend**—having your internal team and an offshore team program the same software together.
- **BOT**—build, operate, and optional transfer to create your own offshore subsidiary after two or three years.
- **Subsidiary**—create an offshore subsidiary immediately.

IP risk is a very sensitive and important issue. Let's look at how this specific criterion is used in the decision matrix and what its overall impact is on the score computed for each software development strategy.

When IP risk is serious, creating your software with an in-house team of employees is ranked highest and offshore strategies are all ranked very low. In-house development is ranked lowest when your IP risk score is low. A low IP risk score lets you take advantage of offshore outsourcing.

Onshore outsourcing is ranked low in the matrix for all scores of IP risk. Here's why. If your IP risk is *low,* you will save money by

Table 8-1 Ranking of Software Development Strategies Based on Your Level of IP Risk[*]

	Low IP Risk	High IP Risk
Software Development Strategy	You are using standard or old technology that is widely available and understood.	You cannot separate out your critical IP. It will be exposed to any outsourced team used. This risk may overwhelm the benefits of outsourcing in some cases.
In House	Low ranking because your very low IP risk does not justify in-house development	High ranking since your IP will be within the confines of your own company
In House Plus Outsource Blend	Very low ranking, very low IP risk gives no justification for any in-house development	High ranking—use in-house development on sensitive IP and outsource what you can
Onshore	Very low ranking, very low IP risk gives limited justification for keeping outsourcing onshore	Lowest ranking for putting your sensitive IP at risk
Offshore	High ranking since exposing IP with offshore outsourcing poses very low risk	Lowest ranking for putting your sensitive IP at risk
Offshore BOT	Very high ranking since exposing IP to possible offshore subsidiary poses very low risk	Very low ranking for putting your sensitive IP at risk
Offshore Subsidiary	Highest ranking since exposing IP to offshore subsidiary poses very low risk	Less than neutral ranking for putting your sensitive IP at risk

[*]A complete table with all five levels of IP risk is included in the outsourcing decision matrix described in Appendix A and available on the book's web site, www.Software WithoutBordersBook.com.

going offshore. If your IP risk is *high,* any outsourcing is ranked low. Onshore outsourcing can gain in ranking from other criteria in the matrix, such as your need for technical expertise and fast ramp-up of software development.

When you have a neutral IP risk, the strategy of using a blend of in-house and offshore teams ranks highest. You should be able to partition your product or architect your software to enable the development of sensitive software in-house and outsource the rest.

Creating a subsidiary is also ranked high when you have a neutral IP risk, since you will have more control over your IP in your own subsidiary.

If your IP risk score is low or very low, the offshore outsourcing strategies are ranked high as good choices for your software development. Creating a subsidiary is ranked highest, with BOT and offshore outsourcing only slightly lower.

Of course, having a low tolerance for IP risk does not mean you have to create a subsidiary. The overall ranking given to creating a subsidiary and the other five software development strategies depends on your scoring of all 17 criteria in the decision matrix.

Belt, Suspenders, and Safety Pins

When offshore outsourcing is the highest-ranked software development strategy for your company, there are three ways to protect your IP: legal, physical, and technical.

- **Technical protection.** Basic firewall, VPN, and encryption technology is widely available to protect electronic assets like source code and electronic documents. Make sure both you and the outsourced vendor use them.
- **Legal protection**. Use the right kind of agreements (as explained in this chapter) with local jurisdiction, always seeking to specify the laws of one of the United States as the governing law to protect your interests. It is helpful for any offshore firm you select to have a U.S.-based legal entity, such as a corporation, that you can seek to hold responsible for any disputes.

  Copyrights should be properly assigned to your company in the agreement, which is crucial in order to get what you pay for. You may also want to seek patent protection on your software in the U.S. and other countries where possible.
- **Physical protection.** You probably have some sort of physical security for your computers, servers, and source code. Make sure your outsourced vendor has the same. Keeping the computers in a locked room, with card key access, will be sufficient. Security guards may also be necessary in larger facilities and in some parts of the world.

The bottom line is, don't be promiscuous with your IP. But don't overlook the power of offshore outsourcing either. Most offshore firms will fiercely protect your IP as a normal part of doing business.

Who Owns What?

When you hire an outsourcing vendor, you want to make sure you will own the software they develop for you. There are two factors that influence this important requirement—your agreement and the provenance of your software. The word "provenance" is a fancy way of saying where your software came from. The point is that even if your agreement says you own all the software created for you by your outsourcing vendor, you could still have a problem if preexisting source code owned by the vendor or a third party gets included with yours.

Inclusion of other software can happen when open-source components or modules previously developed for other projects are used in your software. It is most likely to happen on fixed-price projects in which the outsourcing vendor is motivated to cut costs by reusing existing modules. Other times, a well-meaning individual engineer might accidentally include such a component.

I'll give more details about the use of open-source modules in your software later in this chapter. Let's look first at the agreements and what needs to be in them to protect your software IP.

Work Made for Hire

The creator of a work, such as software, is the default owner of the copyright in that work (which arises as soon as the work is created) unless the work is created by an employee within the scope of his or her employment (which is a "work made for hire" owned by the employer). But if the employee can convince a court that he or she created the work outside of the scope of employment, the employee is free to copy, distribute, sell, or modify the work, subject to any relevant patents, without the permission of the employer and without sharing any profits obtained. That is why employees are normally asked to assign, in writing, the copyrights, patents, and all other rights of invention in the copyrightable software they author, to the employer as a condition of continued employment, even though in most situations of employee/employer relationships, the ownership of the software created by the employee goes to the employer as a work made for hire.

The concept of *moral rights* is the ability of an author to control his or her creative work and is applied to literary and artistic works, including software. In the U.S., the Visual Artists Rights Act of 1990 recognizes only moral rights applied to works of visual art. It is more broadly applied outside the U.S. to include software. Even if the author, artist, or programmer assigns their other rights to a work to their employer or a third party, they still maintain the moral rights to the work.

When you hire a contractor or an outsourcing vendor to create your software, copyright ownership, moral rights, and other property rights must be expressly assigned to you or your company in writing. Be certain that the assignment agreement clearly covers all of the software you are paying for. When the vendor is a foreign-based entity, you also need to be aware of which country's laws will govern your agreement (as discussed later in this chapter).

Fortunately, the copyright and "work made for hire" provisions of the law are generally similar in most countries when your software is being developed by employees of the offshore vendors you hire. You should try to confirm this with your attorney for the country in which your vendor is performing the work. However, a careful attorney will advise you to require that the outsourcing vendor include in your outsourcing agreement, copies of the signed employee IP assignment agreements, as well as contractor agreements your outsourcing vendor has with the engineers developing your software.

Is this overkill? Perhaps, because most companies hiring an outsourcing vendor rarely request this level of detail regarding the engineers working on their software. But if you do not see the agreements, how will you know whether the software you have paid to create is owned by your company or by an individual programmer offshore? You will have to judge whether the cost involved in reviewing these employment agreements is worth avoiding the risk of having a problem later.

Subcontractors

When your offshore outsourcing vendor uses subcontractors, the situation gets a little more complicated. Work by contractors is usually not covered by "work made for hire" rules, and all ownership rights, including copyright, must be explicitly assigned in writing to the offshore vendor by the contractor. Then the rights should be assigned to you by the offshore vendor as part of your written agreement with the vendor. You should either prohibit the use of subcontractors to protect your IP or require that your offshore vendor notify you if contractors are used to develop your software and that they demonstrate that all assignments of ownership rights have been made properly.

For example, if your offshore vendor hires a contractor to help develop your software and the contractor has *not* assigned the copyright to the vendor, the individual contractor would own the copyright for the work he or she was paid to create for you. You may own a copy of the work, but you could not prevent the contractor from also licensing the work to third parties.

Registration and Recordation of Copyrights

As I just described, the assignment of copyright requires a written agreement signed by the owner of the copyright. For additional protection, a copyright can also be recorded with the government copyright office. Recording the copyright of your software in the U.S. requires sending in a hard copy of some or all of your source code along with an application form and $30 fee.[39] Your source code must also contain the notice of copyright for the recordation to be accepted.

Recording creates a public record of your copyright and provides an advantage if a dispute arises over infringement. Also, without recordation, a subsequent assignee may obtain priority over the earlier assignee.

Recordation should be done by each party and in each country associated with the copyright. Here are several examples[40] that use India as the offshore location, but the ideas apply to any country.

---

39. See the U.S. Copyright Office web site at www.copyright.gov for more details. Links to specific pages and documents describing the copyright process are on the Software without Borders web site, at www.SoftwareWithoutBordersBook.com.

40. These diagrams of copyright assignment and recordation scenarios are based on the work of Joel Riff at GCA Law Partners, LLC in Mountain View, California (www.gcalaw.com).

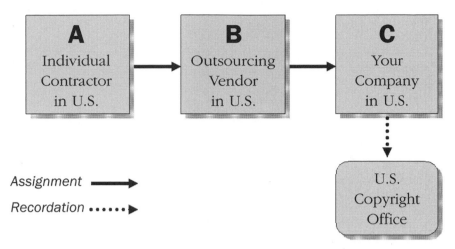

Figure 8-1. Copyrights for Onshore Outsourcing

Onshore Outsourcing Example

Your U.S. company (C) outsources to a U.S.-based outsourcing vendor (B) that does all programming in the U.S. The outsourcing vendor hires an individual contractor (A) to perform programming work.

Two written assignments of copyright are required, one from A to B and one from B to C. In addition, C is advised to record the copyright with the copyright office at the Library of Congress. Figure 8-1 illustrates this scenario.

Offshore Outsourcing Example: India

Your company (C) hires an outsourcing vendor (B) in India. The Indian outsourcing vendor hires a contractor (A) to develop some of your software.

Two written assignments of copyright are required, one from A to B and one from B to C. In addition, C is advised to record the copyright with the copyright offices in the U.S. and India. Figure 8-2 illustrates this scenario.

Offshore Outsourcing Through Multiple Entities

Your company (D) hires an offshore outsourcing vendor through its U.S. subsidiary office (C). All programming work is performed in India by the parent company (B). The parent company in India hires a contractor (A) to develop some of your software.

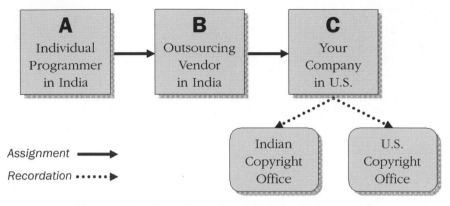

Figure 8-2. Copyrights for Offshore Outsourcing

Three written assignments of copyright are required, one from A to B, one between parent and subsidiary B and C, and one from C to D. In addition, C is advised to record the copyright with the copyright offices in the U.S. and India. Figure 8-3 illustrates this scenario.

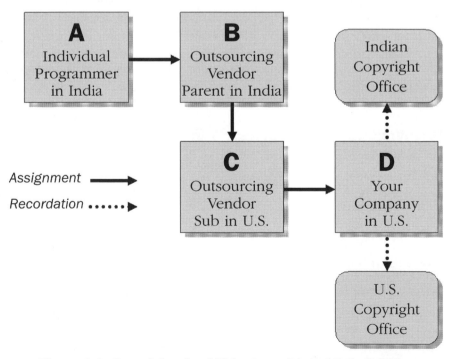

Figure 8-3. Copyrights for Offshoring with Multiple Entities

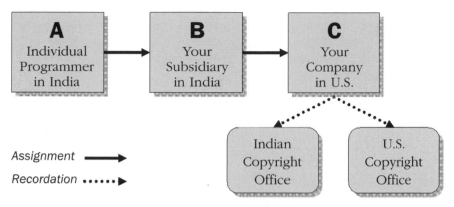

Figure 8-4. Copyrights with Your Own Subsidiary

Offshore Contracting at Your Own Subsidiary

Your company (C) has an offshore subsidiary (B) in India. Program-ming work is performed by employees and contractors (A) at your Indian subsidiary. This is the same flow as in the second example, where you hire an offshore outsourcing vendor directly.

Two written assignments of copyright are required, one from A to B and one from B to C. In addition, C is advised to record the copyright with the copyright offices in the U.S. and India. Figure 8-4 illustrates this scenario.

Offshore Outsourcing Through Your Own Subsidiary

Your company (D) has an offshore subsidiary (C) in India that hires an outsourcing vendor (B), also in India. The outsourcing vendor hires contractors (A) in India.

Three written assignments of copyright are required, one from A to B, one between B and C in India, and one from your own subsid-iary C in India to the parent company D in the U.S. In addition, D is advised to record the copyright with the copyright offices in the U.S. and India. Figure 8-5 illustrates this scenario.

Be sure you have a complete and total chain of assignment in all of your contracts with the business entities and individuals involved with your outsourcing. It is usually worth the small amount of time and expense to register your copyrights in each country so that you will have a good public record of your copyrights and minimize the chance of a future lawsuit.

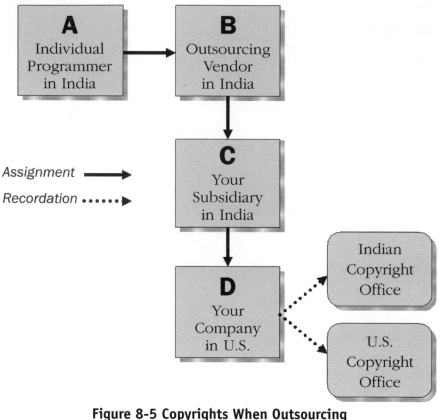

**Figure 8-5 Copyrights When Outsourcing
from Your Offshore Subsidiary**

Choice of Law

I somewhat glossed over the issue of "choice of law" earlier in this chapter. It is a very complex and ever-changing legal area that you may have to confront if you need to use the judicial system to enforce or defend a copyright, or other property rights, in a foreign country. Generally, local law is used to resolve copyright disputes However, a judge may need to decide which country's laws—for example, Indian law or California/U.S. law—will govern the specific aspects of the dispute.

In addition, you may need to consider jurisdiction—that is, the court or courts in which you should bring your dispute for judgment. And if you receive a judgment in one country, can you rely on the judgment to be enforced by the courts in another?

Judges rely on prior judicial decisions, articles, and scholarly treatises to resolve choice of law issues. The goal is to make decisions that are fair and lead to predictability in future cases and to eliminate any possibility of "forum shopping," where different jurisdictions would apply different laws to the same dispute, giving the party that initiates the court proceeding an advantage when choosing one venue over another.

What choice of law rules will apply in a property dispute, such as a copyright infringement case? Judges may consider some or all of the following:

- The laws of the jurisdiction that has the most significant relationship to the property.
- The laws of the jurisdiction where the property was located at the time of the disputed assignment (except that intangible property, like a copyright, has no specific location).
- The laws of the jurisdiction where a violation of property rights harmed the plaintiff.
- The laws of the jurisdiction where the new property, such as IP, was originally created if its initial ownership is in dispute.

All this is very interesting in an abstract, theoretical kind of way, but let's hope it stays theoretical for any software you might contract to develop offshore. After all, you are developing the software to use or sell, and not to make interesting future case law.

Therefore, you should involve legal counsel in the early stages of structuring a significant offshore engagement. Hire an attorney familiar with international property rights issues or at least one familiar with the laws of your offshore destination. Larger law firms have offices in some foreign countries, and others will often partner with an existing firm there.

It's Not Free, It's Open Source

Open source as a way to create software has been around for over two decades. Its success proves that developing software with a distributed, international team of engineers, like those you can hire for offshore outsourcing, works well. And in some cases, an open-source strategy can be an effective marketing tool for your own software product.

"Open source" is defined as the process of delivering a software application or product by making the source code freely available. This used to be known as "free software," a name with a somewhat negative image. So in 1997, the name was changed and the open-source movement was born.

There are two ways to create open-source software. One is to create the software as the collection of efforts by developers around the world. This is the way Linux was developed. The second way is the usual way software is created. You hire your own team of programmers, and your company retains ownership of the software but makes it available as an open-source product. The mySQL and SleepyCat products are developed in this way. In both cases, the software is "given away" but is subject to a license that may restrict further use of the software.

Larger companies support open source as a way to create innovative ideas. Employees of the larger company are paid to contribute to one or more open-source projects. Customers using the open-source software often buy other hardware and software from the same vendor to implement the open-source innovation.

They Lose a Little on Each One, but Make It Up in Volume

Successful open-source companies use one of two business models—the service and support model or the dual license model.

Red Hat and Cygnus Solutions (Cygnus provided a supported version of Gnu software and is now part of Red Hat) are companies that provide service and support for software that is otherwise completely free. Customers are able to spend time and save money by using the free version, or they can spend money to save time by licensing the supported version.

The "dual license" model enables a company to provide software as both free open source and under a paid license. Your use of the open-source version is usually restricted by a license that requires derivative works to also be made available as open source. This may not fit your business model if you intend to charge your customers to license your modified version of the software. Hence the second type of paid-for license, offered by dual-license open-source companies, places little or no restrictions on your distribution of derivative works.

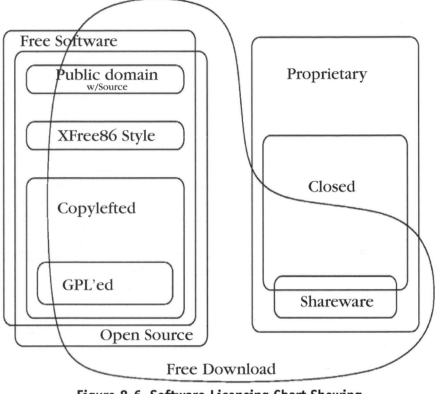

**Figure 8-6. Software Licensing Chart Showing
the Not Quite Overlapping Categories[41]**

Copyleft

The Gnu[42] General Public License (GPL) gives everyone permission to use, copy, and distribute an open-source software offering, but requires subsequent distribution of the software, and derivative works, to also be distributed under the GPL. This is the GPL's famous "copyleft" requirement. It forces you to use the GPL for your own software when you incorporate other GPL software into your

---

41. This chart is available on the Gnu web site, www.gnu.org/philosophy/categories. html.

42. Gnu is a recursive acronym for "GNU's Not UNIX"; it is pronounced "guh-noo," like canoe.

product. Of course, this is the opposite of a copyright that protects your software from being copied.

There are many other, less restrictive, open-source licenses. The Lesser GPL, the MIT license, and many others, have no restrictions on the distribution of derivative works.

Furthermore, most (perhaps all) free software licenses are open-source licenses, and most (but not all) open-source software licenses are free software licenses.

"Open source" usually refers to the 10-point guidelines published by the Open Source Initiative, a nonprofit organization whose stated purpose is to "own and defend the Open Source trademark." They approve (via the certification mark "OSI Certified") various software licenses, ranging from the BSD license to the GPL that meet the guidelines they advocate.

"Free Software" usually refers to licenses meeting the guidelines published by the Free Software Foundation.[43]

Additional work has since been done to create and promote various types of new open software and intellectual property licenses. New licenses grant various amounts of freedom for distributing and modifying works.

For example, the work done by the Creative Commons[44] is very interesting. This organization was born to explore and create new licenses for digital content such as writings, images, and music.

The Creative Commons web site has an interactive license chooser to compose a license that protects and grants freedoms to your property as you see fit. For example, Sleepycat Software, Inc., uses an open-source license for their software and a Creative Commons license for some of their documentation.

The Catch

All this free and open-source software is a great way to bootstrap your own software development. It can reduce the cost of your software development and speed your software to market. But you have to be careful of what open-source software you are using and know what the associated licensing requirements are. If you (or one of your

---

43. FSF guidelines are online at www.gnu.org/philosophy/free-sw.html.

44. See www.creativecommons.org.

offshore engineers) incorporate open-source code into your product, you must comply with the license required by that open-source software. This problem of source code provenance is something venture capitalists look for during due diligence for their investments.

Several software tools are available from companies like Palamida and Black Duck Software to watch over your source code to make sure you are not surprised later by the discovery of an open-source module you did not know you were using. Even if identifying license text and comments are removed from the open-source code, you must comply with their associated license. These tools will recognize the "fingerprints" of the open-source code even if the license information is removed. These tools help you avoid nasty surprises and also help you comply with the open-source licenses for the modules you do want to include in your software.

I Rest My Case

Find a vendor you can trust that offers the right kind of agreements and the service you need. For larger projects, you will want an attorney to review your agreements. Make sure your outsourcing vendor is aware of open-source license issues and will not include random modules of software that have been developed elsewhere without letting you know where they came from and what licenses apply to them.

Chapter 9

Outsourcing Your Quality Assurance

Quality . . . You know what it is, yet you don't know what it is. But that's self-contradictory. But some things are better than others, that is, they have more quality. But when you try to say what quality is, apart from the things that have it, it all goes poof!
— Robert M. Pirsig, in *Zen and the Art of Motorcycle Maintenance*, 1974

I t is common for quality assurance, or QA, to be given short shrift in a software development organization, especially when budgets are tight. Or as one cynical software manager told me once, "QA? Isn't that what beta customers are for!?" (More about alpha and beta releases later.)

Sometimes QA seems like a luxury. When debating the software development budget at one of my startups, the CEO finally asked, "Well, do you want to hire a programmer to add features to the software, or do you want to hire a QA guy?" At the time, I had to hire the programmer because we had a huge list of features to implement. It was a tough choice. But we could not afford to implement a QA process without hiring a significant staff of QA engineers and someone to manage them.

In another example, a company had developed software and was getting ready for a beta release with their first customers. But the company had neglected QA. Although the work of their individual programmers was good, the entire system needed testing after the work of their individual engineers was integrated together.

The VP of engineering realized that going to market without a comprehensive test of the system would be a major disaster. An obvious indicator of the impending doom was the missing data on different screens of the application whenever he tried to use the software. Their target market consisted of average consumers who would be confused and frustrated by any missing data, odd behavior, or unexpected error messages.

How could such good engineers create such lousy software!?

It is often because QA is the ugly stepsister of software development. Your software development team does not want to be bothered with testing the entire application. It is not considered a creative or "fun" part of the process. Consequently, QA is often neglected, causing mediocre software and unhappy users.

Another reason is the complexity of testing a large software application. If there are many different ways to use the software, you can find yourself without the people and time required to do a thorough job.

Perfect for Outsourcing

Outsourcing is an excellent solution to the problem of nonexistent or incomplete QA. Sometimes people are surprised to learn that QA can be outsourced. But it absolutely can, and outsourcing your QA is a terrific first step to taking advantage of low-cost offshore outsourcing.

One reason QA is such a good place to start your outsourcing is that you do not necessarily need to divulge your source code. You can deliver a binary version of your software for installation and testing by your outsourced QA team.

Five Types of Testing

You can look for a team with experience performing the type of QA you need. QA can be broken down into five different types of testing:

- Requirements testing—making sure your software does what you designed it to do

- Usability testing—specialized testing that may require focus groups of target users
- Load or stress testing—testing to ensure that your software has the required performance
- Environment testing—testing your software on different operating systems, browsers, etc.
- Regression testing—an automated process of repeating tests quickly on each new release of your software to make sure it does not "regress" to a state where previously working features are now broken

Regression testing is often used with unit testing. Unit testing is performed during programming and requires access to the source code. Other separate regression tests can exercise the user and programmatic interfaces defined for your software without the need to view the source code.

Avoid outsourcing too much testing at once. Pick the type of testing that will give you the biggest benefit. For example, regression testing may be valuable because you can reuse the tests yourself after they are developed by the outsourced QA team. On the other hand, environment testing requires executing a large number of test cases manually, and low-cost outsourcing is the only practical way to complete them.

Keeping QA in the Family

Another way to outsource QA is to do it with the same team you use for the software development. For example, one company outsourced the development of a web application they offer to customers for use in their sales departments. Each customer will have thousands of salespeople using this software to support their sales activities. Now the focus of the offshore vendor is shifting from adding new features to making sure that the software can support an increasing number of simultaneous users.

The vendor working on this project is expert at QA as well as software development and can support their new testing requirements easily. Whether you outsource your software development or do it internally, you can certainly use outsourcing to add low-cost QA when you need it.

It is important to recognize the value of QA in the software development process. You may start out with a small development team and be satisfied with the quality of their code. As the complexity of the software grows, you can add QA resources, either by outsourcing or by hiring your own internal team.

When you undertake a large and complex software project, it is critical to plan for professional QA as part of the effort. If you don't, you run the risk of making a bad first impression and losing critical early sales, funding for future projects, or worse. Even though outsourcing is criticized for eliminating jobs, outsourced QA may be just the tool you need to help you keep yours.

Avoid the Impossible

Take a pragmatic approach to software QA. It is often impossible to test everything because of limits on time and budget.

For example, I was responsible for the testing of a database product at one of my startups. We received a few bug reports of slow searches, and so I decided we should test every combination of inputs to find out which ones were slow to execute. I found that there were literally billions of input combinations. Even if I could run a search combination each second, it would take almost a year to do all the searches! Outsourcing to all the engineers in China would not be enough manpower to finish testing the software in a reasonable amount of time. I finally created a list of the top hundred likely search combinations to test and found that to be sufficient.

It's Black and White

Some automated tests use random input for black box tests, or use programs to exercise code in performing white box tests. The terms "black box testing" and "white box testing" are often used in software QA.

Black box testing focuses on the external behavior of the software product. It does not consider how the software was written or structured. It is appropriate for use case scenarios and individual feature and function testing.

For example, to use a product function like "place an order," the user must complete a specific series of steps, such as find an item, put it in the shopping cart, enter shipping and payment information, etc. You don't care what the program is doing to complete each step; you care only that each step is completed successfully, with no error messages, until the end result is achieved.

When you design *white box* tests, you use knowledge of the inner workings and structure of the code to design a more comprehensive test. For example, you may know that entering data in a particular field of the screen causes the product to access a specific database table. You can use facts like this to design your tests to cover the access of all database tables.

White box testing also includes writing programs to call functions and modules in all possible ways to ensure that every line of code is executed during testing. This kind of testing is more often done during unit testing as the code is written. It is more efficient for the developer to perform these kinds of comprehensive tests rather than have another engineer try to figure out what the code is doing and test it after it is written.

The percentage of test coverage indicates how much of your product's source code is executed when tests are run. If a series of tests causes every line of code in your product to be executed, you have 100 percent test coverage. This is hard to measure in complex products without the use of software tools.

If you are willing to send source code offshore, or if it comes from there to begin with, you can use offshore QA for white box testing. The extra programming needed for regression and other automated testing is also an excellent choice for outsourcing so you can keep the details of implementing automated QA from distracting your internal software development team.

Tracking Your Bugs

Whether you use offshore outsourcing for development, QA, or both, you should use a bug tracking system that is accessible over the Internet. Both testers and developers should be able to submit bugs and run reports. The ability to attach files to the bug reports is very useful for providing valuable information like tracebacks, output files, and screen shots.

As we discussed in Chapter 6, effective bug tracking involves defining several severity levels. For example, here is a severity classification scheme I have used in the past:

- Critical—crashes or loses/corrupts data, with no workaround
- Serious—missing a feature, difficult workaround
- Major—missing a feature, easy workaround

- Minor—incomplete feature or user interface inconvenience
- Trivial—misspelling, wrong color, or a style issue

Decide ahead of time how many bugs of each severity level will be allowed in a product release. For example, you may decide that your customers can tolerate the following quantities of known bugs in your product release:

- Critical: none
- Serious: none
- Major: 3
- Minor: 10
- Trivial: no limit

Don't have the bug tracking system send bug reports directly to development engineers. You should have a "bug triage" process first, to assign and send bugs. Otherwise, developers will get distracted by bug reports that may be less important than the feature they need to complete for the next release.

Before each release can be made, the software product should pass an acceptance test. Usually, one or two major use case scenarios will show that the basic functionality of the product is intact. Engineering should run these tests, and then someone in marketing or customer support should do the same to confirm that the release is acceptable. The last step is important when you are using offshore outsourcing.

Alpha and Beta Releases

Alpha and beta releases of your product can precede version 1.0. There are multiple definitions for these releases, depending on your goals and customer situation. I consider an alpha release to be a major internal release to ensure that the product development is on track. Basic functions and use cases should be implemented, but the software is not necessarily ready for use by customers. An alpha release can be preceded by multiple other internal releases to monitor development progress.

A beta release can be used as the first release provided to eager and waiting customers. It should provide basic value to the customer and not just be a collection of loosely related features. At beta, customers can tolerate a limited amount of testing and should be told that they will probably find bugs.

QA of your software can be critical to your success. Ensure that your software works and provides a great user experience. Your customers and users will get all the benefits you promise and say, "Wow, it doesn't get any better than this!"

Outsourced QA Strategies

Let's summarize by discussing several approaches to outsourcing QA of your software.

Well-Integrated QA and Development Teams

Whether one or both teams are offshore, it is critical that they work together and avoid any "us vs. them" mentality. A danger in outsourcing QA separately from development is it can create an adversarial relationship between the two teams. There should not be two teams—only one. Both must take responsibility for the quality of their software.

Unit testing and even test-driven development should be used. Manually intensive QA like environment testing with different operating systems or browsers is a good use of outsourcing. Similarly, automated load testing requires a great deal of setup and execution time that is significantly different from development and is also a good fit for outsourcing.

An outsourced QA team should have expertise at testing software. The idea of outsourcing QA is to gain this expertise and not just low-cost resources to pound on the keyboard. Their expertise should be in the sophisticated processes and procedures for testing software thoroughly.

Any outsourced QA resources should be considered part of the overall software development team. Good communication between your offshore QA and onshore software development teams is critical for smooth operation and success.

Software Development with High Ceremony

Software systems that require high reliability and accuracy, because they will bring about terrible consequences if a failure occurs, must be developed with very formal processes. They are often real-time systems that may be difficult or dangerous to test (launching a rocket, for example).

Finding errors in such systems at the end of development cannot be tolerated, and therefore great emphasis is placed on the front-end requirements gathering, specification writing, and detailed design. These design documents are reviewed thoroughly before coding begins. Coding then uses peer reviews, code walk-throughs, string module inspections, module integration, and rigorous testing by the designers.

Such a formal software development process proceeds with great ceremony.[45] It will often use independent verification and validation (IVV) by a third party. Ideally, the IVV should not find major design errors or poor quality. IVV should demonstrate that function and performance will meet high standards of completeness, quality, and contractual obligations.

When the development process is so critical and uses such high ceremony, IVV is one of the few steps that can be outsourced. Clear specifications and documentation enable this type of outsourced review and QA.

QA as a Pilot Project

It is common to begin a software development project by coding a prototype. After that, you can then outsource development of new versions with an offshore vendor. As a first step, select a vendor that is capable of both QA and software development and have the offshore vendor perform QA on your initial version. Then, as your confidence in the offshore vendor grows, you can outsource development tasks as well as QA.

Separate Outsourcing of Development and QA

Another strategy is to use separate offshore vendors for software development and QA. This can be effective in complex systems requiring a lot of manual testing, but it involves too much management overhead for small engagements.

---

45. "Principle 4. Greater ceremony is appropriate for projects with greater criticality," page 151 of *Agile Software Development* by Alistair Cockburn. Cockburn defines four levels of criticality: loss of comfort, loss of discretionary monies, loss of essential monies, and loss of life.

Keep QA In-house and Outsource Your Development

This is the opposite of the other strategies presented in this chapter. You keep your QA in-house and outsource the software development. Your internal team is responsible for specifying the software and verifying that the outsourced software meets the specification. This approach is used when testing is straightforward and requires a few resources. It also makes sense for software that is for internal use only. In this case, your internal team will be the best judge of software quality.

Is Outsourcing Right for Your QA?

Outsourcing QA can make sense. It can be the only thing you outsource or a stepping-stone to use outsourcing for both software development and QA.

In the next chapter we will look at several more situations in which outsourcing software development makes sense.

Chapter 10

Five Situations
Right for Outsourcing

*The obvious is that which is never seen until someone
expresses it simply.*

—Kahlil Gibran

Several types of software development projects are well suited
for offshore outsourcing. Low-cost and knowledgeable offshore
teams are a great way to implement software in these examples,
either as a one-time project or with your own team of programmers
managed by a vendor in your offshore development center. Here are
the five presented in this chapter:

- Transforming your software into a service
- Outsourcing data entry operations
- Implementing the latest technical craze
- Creating embedded software systems
- Developing version 1.0 of your software product

Transforming Your Software into a Service

Today, no one really wants to pay for software. Customers want
the benefits that the software delivers at the lowest cost possible or
even for free with open-source applications. For many commercial

applications, the best way to achieve low cost is to use the software as a service (SaaS) model.

Software as a service is a model in which the software vendor provides an Internet-hosted version of their application (in-house or at a managed third-party site) that customers access via the web site and pay for on a per-use, per-project, or subscription basis. Salesforce.com is a leading example of the SaaS model. The SaaS model offers significant benefits to software vendors and their customers.

Some software companies design and deliver their software as a service. But many others still offer a traditional software license. They are being caught by the SaaS wave and face dwindling sales as customers refuse to pay high license fees.

For example, one software company in San Francisco offers their product for a hefty $300,000 license fee. On top of that, you have to pay another $300,000 for customization. Do they have customers? A few. But the new ones are all asking for a SaaS pricing model.

As SaaS becomes more popular, time is of the essence. The rewards often go to early market entrants. Salesforce.com has broken down the barriers to the SaaS model, and many others are following. Accelerating your time to market is critical to your business success.

Putting your software on the web is not as easy as it sounds. Your software company faces several challenges in offering its software as a service:

- **Delivering a new level of quality** that ensures availability, scalability, and security of both your software and your customers' data.
- **Determining your business model** and how much each customer or user will pay for using the software so the customer gets a good value and your company makes a healthy profit.
- **Modifying your existing software product** without disrupting the flow of new features and enhancements that your present customers expect.

This complete turnaround of your software company can cost hundreds of thousands of dollars and many lost months of time in the market if you make the transformation incorrectly.

Today you can hire an offshore team that is expert at web technologies, and they will transform your software into a service. You can continue using the outsourced team after the transformation is complete, or you can take over development with your existing internal team of engineers.

For example, a U.S. company completed the transformation of its Excel spreadsheet-based product into a full-fledged web application using an offshore software development team. The company never would have created this SaaS product with its already overworked internal engineering staff, and it could not afford to hire a whole new team of engineering employees.

An expert outsourced team can perform these critical steps in transforming your software:

- Convert your client/server application into a web application with a browser-based user interface.
- Use new Web 2.0 and AJAX technology to give your web application the look and feel and functionality of a desktop application.
- Add self-provisioning of user accounts so that new customers can sign up and use your service quickly and without human intervention.
- Ensure that customer data are kept separate and safe in the database.
- Perform stress tests and tune your SaaS so it can handle the required number of users.
- Implement a configurable user interface so your users can customize your software to meet their needs

Let's look at some of these steps in more detail.

Traditional client/server applications are single instance. Each customer must license and install his or her own copy or instance of the software. In addition, the client software must be installed on each user's computer to carry out computations and provide functionality. These clients often implement highly interactive features and enable the user to manipulate large amounts of data. This kind of complex functionality can be very difficult to implement in an HTML, request/reply web application interface that requires frequent page refreshes. The ease of migrating from your client/server model to an Internet-based SaaS model is highly dependent on the complexity of your specific application.

However, new Web 2.0 technologies like AJAX or Flash-based software from Adobe, Laszlo Systems, and others give web applications the look and feel and functionality of a desktop application or client. Web 2.0 requires little or no software to be installed on the user's client computer. The most that might be needed is the Flash plug-in, which is already widely installed. This fundamental change to the user interface converts your client/server application to a single-tenant web application.

Web applications can be single instance or multi-instance. A single-instance configuration, requiring a new server for each instance, cannot be scaled to a large number of customers and should be avoided. The alternative, known as multi-instance, is to install multiple copies of your software on a single set of servers.

An accurate answer to the question "How many copies of your software can you install on a server?" is derived by testing the software as you add additional instances. This is best done with automated software testing tools that can simulate the desired number of users on the system.

The ultimate goal is to modify your single-tenant web application to support multiple customers or "tenants" on the same instance. Multitenant web applications minimize the amount of hardware needed to support multiple customers. Also, customers can self-provision their use of your software by signing up for an account and entering payment information. This minimizes, and often eliminates, support needed to set up a new customer.

Of course, if you start out to create your software as a service, you will design it as a multitenant web application. Software companies have been implementing SaaS for 10 years now. But the changes required to transform your software from a single-tenant web application to a multitenant service are nontrivial. The tasks often exceed the engineering capacity of software companies that must also support existing customers.

That is why outsourcing these one-time changes makes so much sense. You increase your chance for success and lower your costs when you use an offshore outsourcing team to accomplish your goal of transforming your software into a service.

Outsourcing Data Entry Operations

Many software companies outsource software development. Some also offer data products, and those companies that digitize and process their customers' data are outsourcing the data entry operations too. Outsourcing your ongoing data entry is an excellent way to save money and improve quality by using an operation that focuses on just your data entry activities.

Outsourced data entry operations are a subset of the often-discussed business process outsourcing, or BPO. These operations handle the paper shuffling central to many businesses. BPO operations process expense reports, insurance claims, and tax returns and deliver sophisticated evaluation and diagnosis from electronic versions of medical images. As a friend of mine says, the bits are weightless and they travel at the speed of light. There is no reason data entry work cannot be done offshore.

Some software companies feel more comfortable setting up an outsourced data entry operation than they do outsourcing their software development. Actually, data entry operations often require their own software development capability. The software is created for internal use and facilitates accurate entry of the data being captured.

My first exposure to offshore outsourcing was about a dozen years ago at one of my startups. The company had two products: a modern client/server enterprise software product that enabled electrical engineers to search and select electronic parts for systems they design. The second product was the database containing records for more than a million electronic parts—everything from diodes and DRAMs to microprocessors.

The CEO was originally from India, and he had a key business goal of creating a low-cost operation there to build and maintain the database. The Internet was just emerging and had not yet made its way, reliably, even to Bangalore. Therefore, we shipped many paper documents, books, and catalogs to India via DHL, the most reliable international shipping service at the time.

These days, scanning and processing of paper is more easily done in the U.S. The cost of sending electronic images is near zero compared to what we used to pay DHL.

The books and catalogs themselves were cataloged into a carefully designed data entry process. Individual pages were scanned in and then processed electronically. Optical character recognition (OCR) techniques could not be used because of the inconsistent use of fonts, special symbols, and Greek letters commonly used in electronic part specifications.

The data entry process was organized by part category. Each category had its own set of parameters, and rules were defined in the software to help accurately guide the data entry process. For example, valid ranges were entered for each parameter, to avoid having incorrect data sneak into the database. There is no such thing as a 2-farad capacitor. The value must be 2 microfarads or 2 picofarads, depending on what makes sense for the part category.

In some cases, the software could derive data values from other values already entered. For example, a brief part description field was often a concatenation of various parameters describing the device. The description field for a resistor might be "1 mega Ohm, 10%, 100W" and was automatically created from the parameter values entered in other fields.

Because of this complexity, we had to create our own software to facilitate the data entry, and this was also done by offshore engineers. Actually, we brought engineering project managers to the U.S., where they helped design and write the software. They then went back to India to lead the data entry process.

The software to handle this kind of data entry is typically based on a database forms application. The database can also track the person doing the data entry, the number of errors, the amount of time taken for data entry, and other factors for improving operations over time.

Another way to improve data quality is by using a double-entry process. Two people enter data from the same source. The software compares the data entered and flags any differences. The two people then resolve the difference themselves or bring in the project manager if necessary to judge a difficult situation.

Double entry is a common technique for typed text entry. This kind of data entry requires only data entry people who can read and type fast. Consequently, typed data entry is offered at a relatively low cost.

The higher the skill required for data entry, the higher the cost. At the high end, you may want to set up your own offshore subsidiary to train and keep workers who have the skills you need. For example, the interpretation of medical images has become a popular outsourced service requiring a high level of skill.

Other data entry jobs that require educated judgment include research and the gathering of information using the Internet and other resources. Examples include lead generation for sales and screening of job candidates by reviewing electronic resumés and performing phone interviews via low-cost VOIP.

The security of data you have entered offshore can be a major issue. Your sensitivity will depend on the type of data you are entering. Publicly available electronic parts data is of less concern than highly sensitive financial data, like that seen in tax returns.

Using encryption, restricting access to the data, and using computers without removable media (floppy drives or CD-ROM writers) are usually sufficient security safeguards.

As simple as data entry sounds, it must be carefully controlled to get good results. You should control the data entry and use a formal release process similar to what you would use for a software product release.

You can derive multiple data products from one set of carefully entered data. For example, your data may be delivered in multiple database formats, such as Oracle and Microsoft SQL Server. Or you may need to provide a version for Windows and one for Macintosh. Your release procedures should be automated to maintain the integrity of the captured data and provide a final QA procedure.

Final QA should include automated testing that verifies that the data are readable in the release format and are unchanged from what was originally entered. Your automated testing and QA is another programming task that can be carried out by engineers in your outsourced data entry operation.

The frequency of release and the amount of data you need to enter will determine your best approach to outsourcing. Do you have a small amount of data entry that can be handled on a project basis? Contract outsourcing with a reliable offshore vendor is all you need.

Do you need to enter large amounts of data requiring multiple shifts? Do you need to enter and then publish data on an ongoing and long-term basis? In these cases, creating an offshore subsidiary is best. One company is doing this with a build, operate, and transfer (BOT) approach. They used 65 criteria to evaluate and select a partner in India that built them a data entry operation capable of a rapid ramp-up to several hundred people. They want the option of converting this operation to a subsidiary in future.

Creating a quality data product is very similar to creating software. The tasks of design, coordination of resources, QA, and product release must be done carefully. As with software product development, you can take advantage of low-cost outsourcing as an effective approach to creating your data products.

AJAX and Web 2.0: Implementing the Latest Technical Craze

Imagine your software as a dynamic web application that dazzles your users with an attractive display of data and a powerful but familiar user interface. That is the promise of AJAX, a user interface approach that combines several standards and requires nothing on the user's computer except a browser.

AJAX rapidly gained popularity beginning in 2005 as a way to enhance the usability of web applications.[46] It is an example of programming capability that everyone suddenly feels they need. You can use outsourcing to quickly take advantage of new and useful technologies like AJAX.

AJAX's rapid rise occurred because it delivers a compelling user experience but is based on a combination of existing web standards: HTML, JavaScript, CSS, XML, and SOAP.

AJAX stands for Asynchronous JavaScript and XML, an acronym coined by Jesse James Garret of Adaptive Path in his seminal article "Ajax: A New Approach to Web Applications."[47] It is enabling a new kind of web application called a "mash-up" that integrates web content from unrelated web sites using web services. See www. housingmaps.com for an example.

It sounds great, but it does take a bit of programming skill. Several software toolkits, both commercial and open source, are available to make using AJAX easier. Another way to add AJAX to your software is to take advantage of low-cost offshore outsourcing with a team that is expert in new web application technologies.

All outsourcing vendors do is create software for clients, often using the newest technology. You can gain the technical expertise you need quickly by outsourcing.

For example, a U.S. company used a vendor in India to create a web application using AJAX. It rapidly updates one side of the web page with descriptions of computer printer models as the user enters and modifies printer criteria on the other side. Another company had a vendor use AJAX to create a sophisticated and interactive data entry application to accurately collect information about audio CDs and video DVDs.

---

46. Some view the AJAX phenomenon as part of a more general improvement in web application technologies. Tim O'Reilly wrote an excellent overview article of these technologies, which are now given the name Web 2.0. A link to the article "What Is Web 2.0: Design Patterns and Business Models for the Next Generation of Software" is on the Software without Borders web site.

47. Published on the www.adaptivepath.com web site.

The bottom line is that you can use an experienced and low-cost outsourced team of programmers that stays current on all of the latest programming developments, such as AJAX.

Creating Embedded Software Systems

There are many different kinds of embedded systems for which software can be developed, and there is no one definition of what an embedded system is.

Devices that include embedded software are used in many different markets:

- Automotive
- Consumer electronics
- Industrial controls
- Medical
- Networking
- Office equipment
- Communications
- Gaming
- Vending
- Point-of-sale
- Kiosk
- Data security

The devices themselves are very diverse, ranging from PDAs and cell phones to refrigerators and automobiles. Here are some characteristics they generally all share:

- They have limited functionality compared to a PC or web application.
- The software is more hardware dependent or runs closer to the hardware.
- They often use a dedicated or proprietary operating system.
- They perform a dedicated function.

Given the wide variety of markets and applications, it is hard to imagine how software development for these devices could be outsourced.

But it can. There are vendors that focus on embedded system software development, and each has a specialty in the kinds of devices they program, the operating systems they use, and the kinds of applications they develop.

When designed properly, embedded systems will typically have three distinct layers:

- Application software layer
- System software layer
- Hardware layer

Most of us think only of the application software layer in these devices, because that is the layer that controls the user interface. But if you are designing an embedded system, the choice of hardware and system software may be foremost in your mind.

If you are an embedded system designer, chances are your hardware and instruction set architecture (ISA) are determined by market requirements. That leaves the other two software layers of an embedded system—the system and application layers.

The System Software Layer

In a simple embedded system device, the system software consists mainly of device drivers for interrupt handling, memory, bus, and I/O devices. Outsourcing your driver development can be difficult because it depends so deeply on the experience with the hardware choices you have made. Instead, you can consider outsourcing the entire hardware and system software layer design to a vendor that is experienced with the standard architecture you have selected. If you have custom hardware and software, you will have to train your vendor on the details, which is only practical or worthwhile in a long-term relationship.

Most embedded systems use one of more than a hundred commercially available microkernel operating systems. One class of these microkernels provides the ability to deal with events and inputs in "real time" and process them as they occur, with no perception of delay by a human user. There are many real-time operating systems (RTOS), and some are designed to follow standards for their application programming interface (API). Make sure your outsourcing vendor is experienced with the operating system you plan to use.

The Application Software Layer

Embedded system software at the application layer is often written in the C and C++ programming languages. However, use of Java has grown in popularity. There are three standard Java virtual machines (JVMs) that are like an operating system on the device and are used to interpret and run your Java application:

- Personal Java (pJava)
- Embedded Java
- J2ME—Java 2.0 Mobile Edition

There are also three approaches to processing Java byte codes; you select one based on your need for speed and programming and debugging convenience:

- Interpretation—Interprets the code as your application executes.
- Just in time (JIT) interpretation—A compiled version is created as your application executes, and it is used in subsequent execution of the same code.
- WAT/AOT—Way ahead of time or ahead of time compiling. Applications run faster than either of the interpreted approaches.

The .NET Compact Framework from Microsoft is another application programming environment for embedded system applications.

Your choice of software for the system layer of your embedded system or device is a key decision. Using an RTOS with C++, Java, or .NET will dictate the kind of experience your outsourcing vendor will need to have to create your application. You will want to make sure they have the right experience and tools to develop your application efficiently and effectively.

Those tools can include the use of native code simulation on the same processor used by your embedded system or simulation of the ISA with software running on another computer.

You will also have requirements for testing your embedded system. The JTAG, or Joint Test Action Group, standard is a very common approach. It uses a dedicated connection for testing the embedded system.

Narrow Down Your Choices

Developing applications for an embedded system is similar to creating other software for desktop or web applications. The biggest difference is the number of combinations of hardware, operating system, and application area for embedded systems compared to the vast majority of other software created for the Java, LAMP, or .NET technology stacks running on Windows or Linux. On the other hand, regardless of the combination of embedded system technologies you choose, you can probably find an outsourced vendor that is experienced with them. With the right vendor, you can outsource the implementation of the hardware and system layers, just the application layer, or all three.

Developing Version 1.0 of Your Software Product

I have encountered much skepticism from executives and investors who believe that software products cannot be developed using outsourcing. They express even more skepticism at the idea of creating version 1.0 of a product. Yet companies are using outsourcing to create their products right now. What is the secret to using outsourcing to successfully develop a software product?

Many people believe that outsourcing is useless when you are in the Fuzzy Front End—that fuzzy zone between when an opportunity is recognized and when serious software development begins. They think you need to slog through the Fuzzy Front End by coding a prototype of your product. If so, you need the development team here, not several oceans away.

Another assumption made by many is that you need to write a comprehensive specification for your software during the Fuzzy Front End period. Many companies use a very formal product definition process, optimized to remove as much fuzz as possible. How long should you spend designing a software product before development can begin?

Here is a story from the book *Developing Products in Half the Time* by Preston G. Smith and Donald G. Reinertsen that describes how conquering the Fuzzy Front End can be time-consuming and deadly:

> A well managed Fortune 500 company saw a compelling
> opportunity at a trade show. The company did everything by

the book, preparing a business plan, screening through their strategic planning process, and allocating R&D dollars for it in the budget. When qualified engineers became available to do the project, they began work. Unfortunately, it took 18 months before the first engineering hour was invested in the project.

Meanwhile, a small startup company had been to the same trade show and seen the same opportunity. The Chief Engineer of this company, who also happened to be the President, recognized the compelling nature of the opportunity and began designing a product on the plane flight returning from the trade show. The startup company had its entire product designed before the "well managed" company had even begun development. The Fuzzy Front End at the startup was 500 times faster than at the Fortune 500 company, where well-intentioned planning and budgeting processes guaranteed defeat.

This is the classic comparison between the big and bureaucratic company and the agile and clever startup, a story as old as David and Goliath. Of course, the startup could fail for a whole list of other reasons—a buggy product that dies in the market, poor sales channels, no marketing budget, etc. The startup may just fail more quickly than its bigger, slower competitor!

Notice also that the chief engineer designed the product on the airplane. The usual story is that the chief engineer codes a prototype on the plane ride home on his or her laptop.

What constitutes a useful design for a software product? Is it coding a prototype? Is it typing up a marketing requirements document (MRD)? I think it is a combination of both, but more about that later . . .

Documenting requirements should be part of your design process. You never get them right the first time, of course. Prospective customers have a way of ruining the best plans for products.

But what do you show customers? They are not going to read your 50-page MRD. You can't talk to customers until you have a demo, right?

So we are back to that prototype programmed on the airplane. At least you can show a customer the prototype and prove you have a solution to their problem. But then again, we are assuming you know what problem the customer needs to solve.

According to Steve Blank, founder of several software startups and now a lecturer at the Haas School of Business at UC Berkeley, you don't just need a product development process. You also need a customer development process that runs in parallel with your product development.[48] You use your customer development process to discover what ornery problem your potential customers have that will cause them to part with their hard-earned money to buy your software and solve the problem.

The first step of Blank's customer development process is *customer discovery*. Here are his steps for customer discovery:

1. **Create a product** (or product demo).
2. **Meet with customers** and answer these four questions:
   - Have you identified a problem customers want to solve?
   - Does your product solve these customer needs?
   - If so, do you have a viable and profitable business model?
   - Have you learned enough to go out and sell?
3. **Change your product** to reflect what you have learned.
4. **Iterate** until all questions can be answered positively.

The challenge you have is to begin with a product. Also, changing your product may take a great deal of time. Is there a way to shorten these iteration cycles? If you are programming, good tools like an interactive development environment and adherence to software design patterns can help.

What if you don't code up your product or prototype at the start? Instead, use an HTML editor to create screen mockups. Then link them together to tell the "user stories" of your software product (this technique is discussed in Chapter 5). These stories show the major use cases of your product. Demonstrating the use cases in this way is like putting your product requirements in motion. It simulates how the real product will be used.

HTML is easy to edit and requires no programming. You can make quick iterations before committing your product ideas to code.

Here is a five-step formula you can follow to successfully design your product:

1. Describe your product idea and its benefits.

---

48. *The Four Steps to the Epiphany: Successful Strategies for Products That Win* by Steven Gary Blank.

2. Create a demo of the major use cases, showing the biggest benefits of your software.

3. Perform the customer discovery steps described earlier, iterating until you and your customers are satisfied.

4. Write an MRD, using screen shots from your demo as illustrations.

5. Develop your software, test, and release.

In modern business, you should focus on your core competency and outsource the rest. In this five-step process, the first four steps—defining your product idea, completing the customer discovery process, and documenting the requirements—must be part of your core competency. The last step is not.

Anybody can develop software. But only you can figure out what your customers will buy. And that makes low-cost outsourcing an effective way to get your product developed quickly.

Chapter 11

The Future of Global Software Development

Change is the law of life. And those who look only to the
past or present are certain to miss the future.

—John F. Kennedy

We have almost finished our journey to the interesting other shores of outsourcing your software development. Along the way you have seen many advantages and disadvantages of offshore outsourcing.

Is offshore outsourcing of software development for everyone? Will U.S. firms continue to send more programming work offshore?

We reviewed how to decide whether it is right for you back in Chapter 1. The key reason for outsourcing has been the cost savings, and those savings are large—about a million dollars a year for a team of 12 outsourced engineers over hiring employees in the U.S. Now companies are rediscovering the original reasons for outsourcing non-core activities—improved performance and reliability. Yes, the cost savings are there, and still compelling. But the rapid ramp-up and reliability of outsourcing to a professional team, wherever they are in the world, will become the dominant benefit. After all, what is the point of cheap outsourcing if the results are not good?

Will India continue to dominate? Or will rates there rise so high that they are priced out of the market, forcing Indians to outsource to other destinations to keep costs low? Will outsourcing head south, to South America and Africa, where programming services can be delivered in time zones similar to those of the North American and European markets that need them?

We covered many other outsourcing destinations in Chapter 2. It could be easier for you to do your software development in Brazil rather than Bangalore. India will remain the clear leader for some time. Other countries of the world should look to India as a "rich uncle" that can offer valuable advice, wisdom, and even investment as outsourcing services are offered from more diverse locations.

Globalization: Good or Bad?

In his book *The World Is Flat,* Tom Friedman defines three versions of globalization that have developed over time. According to Friedman, we are now in Globalization 3.0, which he believes started around the year 2000. And I think this current version of globalization is a good one.

When I was in high school, my brother gave me the book *Flatland* by Edwin A. Abbott. It portrays Flatland, a world of only two dimensions, in which a square Flatlander discovers the third dimension and tries to explain it to his fellow two-dimensional compatriots, without much success.

Flatland first caused me to feel a sense of superiority over the lowly shapes inhabiting Flatland who could perceive only two dimensions. Then I realized that my arrogance at being able to perceive a full three dimensions would seem pathetic to any creature that inhabited a universe of four dimensions or higher. Humility, or at least caution, was definitely in order.

It is ironic that Tom Friedman has chosen *The World Is Flat* as the title for his book. Like the lonely but perceptive square in *Flatland*, Friedman has become aware of the new global dimensions of our world and how we must adapt to them in order to prosper.

Friedman is certainly not a "square" in the 1960s sense of the word. He is a well-respected journalist who has a knack for making incisive observations that uncover the key human factors of our world, and then turning out memorable prose to drive his points home.

Will his message get through? It seems as though it is. As I write this, *The World Is Flat* is number 4 on Amazon and number 2 on the New York Times bestseller list, and it has been on the list for 49 weeks.

For a while, wherever you turned you would see or hear Friedman's catchy phrases and anecdotes about the "flattening" of our world. Here is a sample:

> It started on 11/9, not 9/11—that is, November 9, 1989, the day
> the Berlin Wall came down. And five months later Windows went
> up—when Microsoft released Windows 3.0.

You can hear an interview with Friedman and get a good synopsis of his book on the *Fresh Air* show with Terry Gross that aired on National Public Radio on April 14, 2005.[49]

A key idea set forth by Friedman is his definition of Globalization 3.0—the ability for individuals and small companies to conduct business easily and efficiently, primarily using the Internet.

According to Friedman, Globalization 1.0 was the discovery of America by Columbus, giving further weight to the theory that the world was round. Global interactions during this era of globalization were dominated by nations dealing with other nations. Globalization 2.0 involved the use of global strategies by nation-states and large corporations, leading to the colonization and exploitation of less advanced countries in the world.

Now, with Globalization 3.0 as defined by Friedman, the Internet has democratized the world economy and given us all access to the resources and opportunities around the globe.

Do you need to raise capital and set up your own software factory in a foreign country to take advantage of a lower-cost work force? No. Any entrepreneur with an idea can find freelance programmers online who will create the software that makes that idea a reality.

And any software company that needs to expand its software development capabilities can do so with a combination of individual freelancers and offshore vendors that can deliver a team of engineers to develop and test their software.

Globalization 3.0 is a good thing. It enables convenient access to excellent resources around the world, which is good for the provider of the services as well as for the provider's local economy. It is also

---

49. A link to a recording of the interview on NPR is available on the Software without Borders web site.

good for the users of those services because it reduces the cost of creating innovative products and services for their local market. It's like the old saying, Think globally and act locally.

The Looming Shortage of Global Engineers

According to a McKinsey report, there may not be enough engineers to satisfy global demand by the year 2011. This could have a serious impact on your offshoring decisions.

Last year, the McKinsey Global Institute published *The Emerging Global Labor Market Report*[50] in three sections covering the demand for employees both locally and globally, the supply, and how supply is meeting the demand.

There are also special chapters on the demand for employees in eight industry segments. The packaged software and IT services are two industry segments that are dominated by software development. Packaged software includes the development and sale of operating systems, accounting software, and other applications that are installed and used by businesses and consumers. IT services include the devel-opment of custom software for internal use by business clients.

Surprisingly, the report predicts a shortfall of suitable young, low-wage professional engineers in India by 2011. In fact, the report says, the U.S. and the U.K. could absorb the entire supply of these young engineers with less than 7 years experience, from India, China, and Philippines by then.

What? We keep hearing about an unabated flow of jobs heading offshore. What's going on?

Good question. The report quotes one observer of the debate as saying, "the plural of anecdote is not data." True, and this report makes up for it.

The report has hundreds of pages that go into the gory details of analyzing, slicing, and dicing global employment data in eight different market segments. Exciting stuff—if you are an accountant! But as we have seen, the analysis and some of the numbers are remarkable.

For example, the flow of "jobs" offshore has been overstated by politicians and the media reporting on anecdotes of actual job loss.

---

50. A link to the McKinsey report is available on the Software without Borders web site

There is no question that some engineers have lost their jobs, but how many?

Of course, it is more accurate to say that "work" is being off-shored, not jobs. The McKinsey report shows that employment is actually increasing in the U.S. in the packaged software segment. Let's look at some of the numbers from this segment.

- 7 percent of the demand for employees in high-wage coun-tries was offshored to low-wage countries in 2003, for a total of 37,000 FTEs (full time equivalents).
- Offshoring is estimated to rise to 18 percent of employees in high-wage countries, or 116,000 FTEs, by 2008.
- The maximum number of FTEs that theoretically could be offshored in 2008 is 390,000.

The report states that a theoretical maximum of 75 percent of all FTEs can be offshored for R&D functions of new product devel-opment, maintenance, porting, support, and integration. This means that at least 25 percent of these positions are expected to stay in the U.S. and other high-wage countries.

Why? The report has a list of the drivers and inhibitors that influ-ence the decision to go offshore.

Strong drivers include cost pressure and the difference in costs between the high- and low-wage countries. Another driver is your existing presence in other countries and experience with global soft-ware development.

Two strong inhibitors are concerns about poor quality and in-tellectual property (IP) exposure. Chapters 5 and 6 in this book give you some tools to address the quality issues, and Chapter 8 covers IP protection. Of course, with a high-quality offshore software develop-ment team and a reasonable tolerance for IP risk, you will frequently see 100 percent offshoring of R&D at companies where budget con-straints are more dominant than these risks.

Are there enough engineers available? Maybe not. The report considers whether the engineers in each low-wage country are "suit-able" for multinational engagements. Suitability is determined by lan-guage skills, cultural differences, and ability to have flexible work hours.

Table 11-1 gives the percentages and total number of suitable engineers estimated to be available in several low-wage countries in 2003 and estimated for 2008.

Table 11-1. The Growing Numbers of
Suitable Engineers in Low-Wage Countries

Country	Percentage of Engineers That Are Suitable	2003 Engineers (thousands)	2008 Engineers (thousands)
Russia	10	49	69
Czech Republic	50	8	11
Poland	50	39	41
Hungary	50	13	34
China	10	159	213
Philippines	20	58	85
India	25	132	177
Malaysia	35	17	25
Brazil	13	21	34
Mexico	42	25	38
Totals		539	731

The table uses the percentage growth in the number of engineers presented in the report to estimate the number of suitable engineers available in 2008. Mexico and Brazil have the highest growth rate, at a compound annual growth rate (CAGR) of 9 percent and 10 percent, respectively.

Here are several conclusions you could draw from these numbers:

- There are plenty of engineers. The numbers show a surplus through 2008. The report extrapolates supply and demand to show a possible shortfall in 2011, but many things could change by then.
- Outsource without shame. Everyone is doing it, and job growth is predicted in the software industry for both high- and low-wage countries.
- Have a balance of in-house technical expertise and offshore technical resources.
- Broaden your search for offshore resources to other countries with suitable engineers.

The supply of global engineers is sufficient through 2008. If we start running short of suitable engineers later, countries may be able to improve the suitability of their engineers for multinational work, through language and cross-cultural training. Of course, you can also use software vendors from other countries emerging as competitors.

Software Development as an IT Service

The packaged software segment discussed in the previous section described the needs of companies that are developing and selling software products and services. Outsourcing of information technology (IT) includes software development as well as the services and support needed by any company to keep their business up and running.

IT services is a larger market segment than the packaged software segment, according to the McKinsey report, with an estimated maximum demand of 3 million FTEs that can be sourced from low-wage countries.

Okay, that's the theoretical maximum. How many of these FTEs will actually be employed offshore in 2008? The report estimates that only 770,000 of these FTEs will actually be employed offshore in low-wage countries in 2008 for the IT services segment. About 40 percent of these are estimated to be software and IT professionals which is 308,000 that are estimated to be employed offshore in 2008.

It is the demand for these engineers, combined with those in the packaged software segment, that may lead to a dwindling supply over time.

A Different World

IT services is a different industry segment than the development of packaged software. Sometimes it seems like a different world. It includes other services besides software development, such as business process outsourcing, IT consulting, system integration, and IT hardware and software support. Vendors that focus on the IT services market are therefore offering a variety of services, and software development may not be their strength.

Because of the size and growth of this segment, more vendors focus on it with a broad array of IT services. If you are looking for a software development vendor, chances are you will run into companies offering other services you do not need.

Then again, maybe you do need them. If your company is developing software for internal use, or to be offered as a service to your customers, you can also outsource the customer support and help desk support with the same vendor that is developing your software.

Another difference is that IT service vendors tend to have an industry focus, while most software development vendors have a technical focus, with a portfolio of projects for clients in multiple industries. If you need industry experience, an IT service company is a choice to consider.

Many customers now prefer to pay for software as a service, instead of purchasing licenses for packaged software. They need to install and maintain licensed software themselves, or hire an offshore IT services company to do it for them. In a sense, your licensed software product is driving demand for offshore IT services. Why not use offshore resources to develop your software and deliver it as a service to your customers directly?

If you are developing software to be used by your clients as a service, then you are a kind of IT services company yourself. You have to consider that a software service can be delivered from anywhere in the world. If you don't make use of low-cost offshoring, competition will eventually appear that will.

A New IT Services Company: Vijay's Story Continued . . .

Vijay's software company was a great success. After two years, he sold the company to an American firm that was offering additional software products and services to the same market. The application developed by Vijay and the development team run by his brother Sandeep back in Bangalore was a niche product that was just what the buying company needed to fill out their product line.

"What's next?" Sandeep asked Vijay with a laugh after the company was sold.

"Can't I at least take a weekend off!?" Vijay complained with a broad smile.

"Sure," said Sandeep. "As long as you are working on that new business plan in your spare time."

Actually, they had already discussed their plans for the new company many times before. Vijay had seen the opportunity developing a few months before. They decided their next company would offer IT services to the pharmaceutical industry to help organize the huge quantity of data associated with the clinical trials needed for the new electronic drug application process with the FDA in the U.S. and EMEA in Europe.

This time the software development team in India would be developing an online system for use by the company's clients around the world. It's just a little different than developing a software application that is licensed to customers, like the product created by their last company. Now they would be able to update all customers instantly.

A bigger change is that the new company will need a large staff of data entry personnel to enter and process the clinical trial data for their clients. This requires new software for internal use and tracking of metrics to monitor the operation.

"I'm telling you," Vijay said to Sandeep, "this is going to be big! And I need the new software team to put the entire security infrastructure together so we will be HIPAA compliant."

"No problem," said Sandeep.

"Oh, I've heard that from an Indian software developer before," laughed Vijay.

Sandeep laughed too and then said, "Wait! Don't forget that we're not another Indian company this time. We're a true global company right from the start."

"You're right." Vijay agreed, and he looked at his brother with a wistful smile. Our parents would be proud, he thought.

Outsourcing's Changing Value Proposition

Rates are rising in India. Some software executives claim that unless they can get a 50 percent cost savings, outsourcing is not worth the hassle.

But the idea that software development work will come streaming back to the U.S. is a false hope. Now that we have had a taste of the cost savings that are possible, the pressure will remain high to continue outsourcing. I predict that this will be done with new low-cost destinations, a more efficient software development process, and better communication with programming teams in far-flung locations around the globe.

The process of selecting an outsourcing vendor will change as well. It will not be sufficient to have cheap programmers in India. You will want a software development team that is experienced with your industry and the application you need developed. You will want 10 Java programmers who are experienced not only with JBoss, Hibernate, and Struts, for example, but with delivering software as a service (SaaS) for your industry or target market. You will want a vendor experienced with financial services or healthcare *and* the technology, like Java or .NET, that you require.

And you will be willing to pay more for your outsourcing—at least when measured on an hourly or man-monthly basis. This is because offshore teams with specialized skills will provide more than just cheap programmers who need to be brought up to speed on the details and nuances of your particular industry. You will get a better value from quick execution and reduced errors and misunderstandings.

New Locations

Let's face it: India owns the brand for outsourcing. Will their domination of the outsourcing mindshare continue? It is possible. But as I mentioned earlier, new low-cost locations for outsourcing will arise, and Indian companies will also take advantage of them. Some of you will bypass the Indian connection and go directly to these new locations in South America, Africa, and Asia.

We may see a segmentation of the outsourcing services market similar to the following:

Tier 0: U.S. and Western Europe, where little software development is done.

Tier 1: India and Israel, where teams manage the development of your software but outsource the programming to less expensive countries.

Tier 2: Other countries where outsourcing is done today, including the countries of Eastern Europe, Mexico, China, and Russia.

Tier 3: New countries not widely known for outsourcing of software today but that could grow in skill and experience over time. These include Peru, Ghana, Uganda, Botswana, and the countries that were former Soviet Republics in Asia.

If you are in Tier 0, you should consider using vendors in Tier 2 and maybe jump to Tier 3 as capabilities grow and offer to greater cost savings.

New Tools for Communication

Since the 1960s we have been waiting for a practical video tele-phone. Today, the camera in my laptop sends my picture along with my voice when I make an online VOIP call using Skype. The picture is jumpy and at a low resolution, but it is an indication of things to come.

Full video conferencing is still expensive. But larger companies are making the investment to improve communications with their global workforce. The cost of these systems is well justified compared to the savings realized in reduced time and cost of travel.

Low-cost screen-sharing services like WebEx, GoToMeeting, and Macromedia Breeze give you a taste of what is possible. As band-width increases and cost decreases, more sophisticated tools will be used and will make the world appear even smaller.

Today it is often recommended that you travel to your offshore team or have one or two of them travel to you when you kick off a project. This will still be needed, because nothing beats face-to-face communication. However, online real-time video will minimize the need for subsequent travel and may eliminate it entirely.

New Software Development Tools

A few years ago, the ideas espoused in extreme programming and test-driven development seemed pretty radical. Yet they came from well-respected principles of lean manufacturing pioneered by the Japanese automobile industry and adopted by most manufacturing companies in the 1980s. Now the principles of reduced inventory, lean manufacturing, and testing throughout the manufacturing pro-cess are being applied to software development.

Some tools, like Cruise Control and Fitnesse, are available as open-source offerings. New commercial tools, like Agitar, RalleyDev, and VersionOne, are also available to ease the transition to a more agile software development methodology. These tools have been adapted to the reality of outsourcing, or distributed development, as it is often called.

Online services used to manage your outsourcing are also here today, such as Artifact Software, CollabNet, MetrixLine, and ReleasePlan.

Shopping the World: Jack and Mary's Story Continued . . .

Jack started the meeting. "Okay, where do we stand?"

"Well," Mary said, "I created a list of about a dozen vendors in India."

"Terrific!" Jack exclaimed. He was worried that finding an off-shore vendor was going to be difficult. They were given the assignment by the CEO at the last operations review meeting, at which the disappointing delays of the data warehousing project in IT were discussed. Going offshore has become critical because of budget constraints and also because there were not enough resources in IT to handle some new projects coming up later in the year. "How did you find them?"

"Google. I spent a couple of hours last night searching the web." Mary explained. "I got lots of hits."

"So maybe finding a vendor won't be so tough after all," Jack said optimistically.

"Not so fast," replied Mary. "I mean I had *lots* of hits—hundreds of web sites. I also found some online directories with literally thousands of vendors. It will be a challenge to sort through them all to try and find the right vendor for us."

"Oh," said Jack. "Let me see the list. Maybe we already know some of them."

Jack looked at Mary's list. It had some of the larger Indian outsourcing vendors with familiar names, and the rest were companies he had never heard of before. "I'm afraid these larger ones won't respond. After all, we only need a few programmers."

"You're probably right, but I thought we should have them on the list anyway. You know the CEO is going to ask about them," Mary explained.

"Hey, I have an idea," Jack said with sudden enthusiasm. "How about that programmer that used to work for us—what was his name?" A second later, he said, "I remember. It was Ravi. I heard he went back to India and is now doing something with outsourcing. I think he is working with family members back in India or something."

"Maybe," said Mary slowly, trying not to be too discouraging. "I remember Ravi, but I am not sure that is the right fit for us. Do you even have his contact information?" Mary continued without waiting for Jack's answer. "Anyway, we have to show the CEO that we made our selection carefully from a list of multiple vendors. Hiring a former employee back in India is not good enough."

"What about ELance?" asked Jack.

"No, Jack. We need *eight* programmers. I don't want to manage a bunch of freelancers spread all over the world," said Mary.

"But that does remind me," Mary continued. "I found vendors in other countries besides India. I am not sure how to compare them all."

"First of all, they have to have experience with the data warehousing software we are using," Jack reminded Mary. "And .NET for sure."

"And some knowledge of our business would be ideal," added Mary. "It seems like a tall order."

"This might take longer than we thought," said Jack. "Somehow we have to get to a short list by the end of the month."

"I know," Mary said reluctantly. "I'll keep looking."

Wanted: A Rational Market

Globalization 3.0 enables individuals and companies large and small to freely transact business internationally. Therefore it is a bit incongruous that Friedman's focus in *The World Is Flat* is on the larger Indian vendors with well-known names—Infosys, Mphasis, Wipro, and so on. These are huge multinational companies, and that puts them in the old Globalization 2.0 category.

You need to be a pretty big client yourself to engage one of these giants. Their target market is large American corporations that are often multinationals themselves.

Of course, I understand why Friedman has this focus. The executives at these vendors have prominence and great stature in the world. They are easy to find, and they are happy to talk about their businesses to someone like Tom Friedman, with his skill and reputation. And it's not as though Friedman can chase down every freelancer in India, China, Russia, and the rest of the world to get their opinion.

In most large, complex, and fragmented markets like the current one for outsourced software development, it is inevitable that the leaders will arise as name brands. But as these brand name companies grow in size, they are unable to address many small and medium-sized potential clients effectively. Decision makers at these smaller companies cannot rely on brand name alone.

What is needed is a way to rationalize the market and make it easy to select the right vendor to develop your software. You need an easier way to compare vendors, so you can make your selection quickly.

Of course, giving you these new tools and techniques is one of my goals in writing this book. I hope you will benefit from the ideas, recommendations, and warnings about some of the risks and gotchas, so your offshore outsourcing will be a tremendous success.

Surviving with Offshore Outsourcing: Kelly's Story Continued . . .

Kelly's startup company never got off the ground. Three months later she took a job at another startup as VP of marketing. A step down perhaps, but she did not feel that way.

"I need to get a little more experience under my belt before I head back up to Sand Hill Road with a 'tin cup' looking for venture capital again," she told her friend Deborah.

They were having breakfast at Buck's Restaurant in Woodside. In fact, it was at the last breakfast at Buck's that Deborah told Kelly about the job at the new startup, after Kelly described how her old startup couldn't get funding.

"Don't worry about it!" Deborah said. "Believe me, there are lots of entrepreneurs in the valley that have failed and then gone on to great success. It's a mark of distinction. Investors actually look for failures to see if you are resilient."

Deborah should know. With her connections to Stanford Business School and the venture community, she had seen many entrepreneurs fly high and then crash and burn, only to get up and do it all over again.

"It was hard," Kelly remembered. "I had to tell everyone their jobs were gone."

"Yes, but they landed on their feet, didn't they?" Deborah pointed out. "Like that VP of engineering you had."

"Oh, Harry? Yes, he joined another startup right away—one that was already outsourcing to China. Now he is even talking about moving there! Can you imagine?" Kelly laughed.

"That's amazing!" Deborah chuckled. "He really turned around his attitude about outsourcing."

"Well, he certainly would have an uphill battle if he continued fighting it," Kelly said. "Heck, even I'm outsourcing now."

"What do you mean?" Deborah asked.

"Oh, we are doing all of our market research and lead generation from India now. And we have all our white papers written in the Philippines. I am amazed at the quality," Kelly marveled.

"Wow!" Deborah said. "It really is a 'flat world,' isn't it?"

Kelly glanced at the pancakes left on a plate at the next table and laughed. "Yes, I guess it is," she said.

The ability to take risks with the knowledge that ultimate success brings great rewards is an American ideal. Outsourcing your software development to another country may seem risky too, but the rewards of cost savings and an improved software development process are also high.

Americans are risk takers. And that unique ability drives innovation and will keep us competitive in the new global marketplace.

Appendix A

The Outsourcing Strategy Decision Matrix

The concept of using a decision matrix to help you decide which software development strategy to select is presented in Chapter 1. Table A-1 summarizes your six software development strategy choices.

The decision matrix is available as an Excel file you can download from the Software without Borders web site:

www.SoftwareWithoutBordersBook.com.

Table A-1. Software Development Strategies

Software Development Strategy	Description
In-house	Software development within your company by employees and/or contractors
In-house plus outsource blend	Software development divided between in-house and external teams working on the same code base
Onshore	Outsourcing to a vendor within your country
Offshore	Outsourcing to a vendor outside your country either far away offshore or relatively close nearshore
Offshore BOT	Offshore outsourcing with an option to transfer your software development team into your own subsidiary later
Offshore subsidiary	Creating a subsidiary in a foreign country and hiring employees there to development your software

You can enter your score from 1 to 5 for the following 17 criteria. Based on your weights and scores, the matrix automatically computes a ranking for each of the software development strategies. Here are the definitions of the 17 criteria, along with the meaning of your possible scores:

1. **Concerns about employee morale.** If outsourcing is used, will it have a significant impact on existing employees or cause major upheaval? If so, will it be more pronounced if offshore outsourcing is selected? Will employees accept outsourcing as an important strategic move for the company that enhances their job stability and improves the overall success of the company?

   1 – Low impact on morale. Employees recognize the potential of outsourcing as a strategic advantage for your company.

   2 – Moderately low impact on morale. Employees may have some concerns over potential job loss but recognize the potential value of outsourcing to the overall success of your company.

   3 – Neutral impact on morale.

   4 – Employees have moderate concerns about outsourcing.

   5 – High impact on morale. Employees have serious concerns about outsourcing. Staff reduction is likely, and care must be taken to maintain morale to retain key employees.

2. **Customer concerns about your outsourcing.** Will your customers care if you use outsourced software development to create and test your products? Outsourcing may be a concern because of perceived risks and issues of quality and responsiveness. Outsourcing is defensible if these issues are neutralized in the sales process. Some customers may perceive outsourcing as a benefit. Does your product involve highly secure transactions or information about your customers? Are you selling to military or government customers? If so, outsourcing, especially offshore outsourcing, will not be welcome or acceptable to your customers.

   1 – Very low concern to customers. Outsourcing is not an issue and could possibly be considered a benefit.

2 – Low concern to customers. Outsourcing is not an issue, but customers might want to know how and where you are using outsourcing.

3 – Neutral concern to customers. Outsourcing is not a major issue, but customers might take it into consideration when selecting your product.

4 – Moderate concern to customers. Outsourcing will be used as a factor in selecting your product. You may need to defend it in the sales process.

5 – Serious concern to customers. Outsourcing may be a deal killer for some customers.

3. **Cultural affinity.** How comfortable are you working with engineers from another culture? Have you had a bad experience in the past with offshore outsourcing? Are you skeptical that offshore outsourcing to a country and culture different than America can be effective? Or are you originally from a foreign country and completely comfortable working with people from other cultures? Are you ready to commit to creating a subsidiary in a foreign country?

1 – You have strong feelings against offshore outsourcing, either because of concerns about jobs going offshore or because you have had a bad experience with outsourcing to a specific country or region and have doubts that outsourcing can be made to work at all.

2 – You are an American, speak only English, and may never have left the country. Your limited exposure to foreign travel makes offshore outsourcing seem risky. You may have had a bad experience with outsourcing to a specific country or region but are willing to consider outsourcing again.

3 – You have a global view and are willing to consider offshore outsourcing if it makes business and engineering sense.

4 – Because of your heritage, familiarity, or direct experience, you are considering outsourcing to a specific country or region of the world.

5 – You were born in a foreign country where high-quality outsourcing talent has become available. You are completely comfortable with your original culture and country of birth. You travel there multiple times per year.

4. **Export restrictions.** How important are export restrictions on your product, if any?

    1 – No export restrictions exist.

    2 – Export restrictions are limited to an independent portion of your product.

    3 – Approximately half of the product is restricted for export, with other parts independent.

    4 – Most of the product is restricted for export.

    5 – All of the product is restricted for export.

5. **Other reasons for going offshore.** Your company may need to open an office in another country for sales and support or to maintain a special relationship with a large customer or a partner in that country.

    1 – You have no plans to go offshore.

    2 – You have long-term plans to open an office offshore.

    3 – You plan to open an offshore office in an offshoring country more than one year from now.

    4 – You plan to open an office within a year in an offshoring country.

    5 – You already have an office in an offshoring country.

6. **Budget.** Of course, cost is always an issue, but is it a major driver in your outsourcing decision? Do you have a large enough budget to develop all of your software in the U.S. with your own employees? Do you want to outsource just to bring in needed technical expertise, and budget is not a concern?

    On the other hand, are you looking to take advantage of a high-quality outsourced team and to cut costs at the same time, if you can?

    Are you are in an emergency situation in which costs must be cut immediately? Do you have a limited budget and need to launch a new product?

    1 – Budget is not an issue. Enough money is available to develop your software product by hiring employees in the U.S.

    2 – Budget is an issue but not as important as control and quality.

    3 – Budget is important, and you have a goal of cutting some development costs.

4 – Budget issues are very important, and software development costs should be minimized.

5 – Budget issues are critical, and software development costs must be minimized, both now and over the long term.

7. **Concerns about risk to intellectual property.** Outsourcing will expose the intellectual property (IP) of your product to people outside of your company, potentially in other countries. This is a risk that must be evaluated in selecting outsourcing as a strategy and in selecting which portions of your product development to outsource.

Does your product use standard technologies that are easy to obtain and use elsewhere? In that case, your product innovation is the application of the technology to a target market you understand well. This is difficult for anyone to duplicate, even if they have access to your IP.

At the other extreme, your IP may be unique programming algorithms, possibly encoding research results only your company has access to. Does outsourcing necessarily divulge your IP and pose a large risk to the survival and success of your company? For most companies the risk is somewhere in between. Can you limit what is outsourced to reduce this risk?

1 – Very low IP risk. You are using standard or old technology that is widely available and understood.

2 – Low IP risk. Some IP is exposed, but your significant market knowledge and innovation limits its practical use by others.

3 – Neutral IP risk. Some of your IP will be exposed, but you can partition your product to limit exposure during outsourcing.

4 – Moderate IP risk. You must be careful about partitioning your product and should possibly use multiple outsourced teams to limit access to all of your IP.

5 – Serious IP risk. You cannot separate out your critical IP. It will be exposed to any outsourced team used. This risk may overwhelm the benefits of outsourcing in some cases.

8. **Speed of ramp-up.** Do you need to start developing your software right away? It takes time to hire employees. Outsourcing

is a way to get an excellent team working quickly. However, creating a subsidiary can take months to complete.

1 – No urgency; you have a longer-term need greater than six months.

2 – Your need is in four to six months.

3 – You need a team in place within three months.

4 – You want to move quickly and have a team in place within a few weeks.

5 – You want to start development yesterday.

9. **Leeway in schedule.** Can your product release schedule tolerate slippages? Sometimes critical customer delivery dates must be met and bug fixes need to be made quickly. You may also need to bring on additional engineers to meet schedule requirements.

1 – Schedule concerns are minimal.

2 – The schedule cannot be delayed more than one month.

3 – The schedule can suffer a delay of no more than a week.

4 – The schedule can be late in time measured only in days.

5 – The schedule is extremely tight and critical.

10. **Length of project.** Are you planning to continue development with outsourcing over the long term or just filling in to make a deadline?

1 – You have a short-term need of three months or less.

2 – You hav a short-term need of less than six months, with chance for continuation.

3 – Software development will take at least six months.

4 – Software development will continue for more than one year.

5 – Software development will continue indefinitely.

11. **Impact on value of company.** What is the long-term plan for your software company? Do you plan to go public in a few years or be acquired? Are you looking to use outsourcing to enhance the valuation of your company? Or are you looking to cut costs on one or more short-term projects that do not add strategic value to your company?

1 – Your software development capability adds little or no value to your company.

2 – Your software development capability adds some value to your company.

3 – Your software development capability is measured equally as both process knowledge and your ability to minimize costs.

4 – Control of your software development capability is more important than cost savings.

5 – Your software development capability is considered a critical corporate asset and a significant part of your company value.

12. **Need for domain expertise.** If your product is built from standard software technology and has a user interface that is easily specified, no domain-specific expertise is needed. On the other hand, you may want to outsource to a team that has domain knowledge to improve communication of requirements and take advantage of insights the outsourced team may have in your application area. Are you looking to address a new market in areas where your present development team lacks domain expertise? Outsourcing can be used to gain that expertise quickly, and potentially at a low cost.

1 – No domain expertise is needed.

2 – Domain expertise would be helpful but is not strictly required.

3 – Domain expertise would be useful for some development work and may be used as a criterion for team or employee selection.

4 – Domain expertise is required for some development work.

5 – Domain expertise and knowledge are required.

13. **Need for technical expertise.** Do you have a product written in Java and you want to create a special .NET version? Do you need specific technical expertise quickly or for a short-term project?

1 – No special technical expertise is needed.

2 – Special technical expertise can easily be acquired if not present.

3 – Special expertise is not required but will be used as a criterion for team or employee selection.

4 – Special technical expertise is an important requirement.

5 – Special technical expertise is critical, and level of expertise will be used as a criterion for team or employee selection.

14. **Status of requirements and specifications.** How well have you captured the requirements of what your product will do? Have you described the required product functionality as well as the performance and environments required?

    Have you specified how your product will work? Are you using elements of UML like use cases and state and LOVEM diagrams to design your product? Have you defined the user interface? Have you created a demo with HTML or coded a prototype?

    1 – Little or no written specifications. You may have white papers and business plans but nothing that translates directly into software.

    2 – Some requirements are written. Limited or no software design documents exist, although a prototype may be coded and running.

    3 – Most requirements are written, and major use cases and actors are named. The reader will have a good idea of what your product will do but will not know how all features will be implemented.

    4 – Requirements are complete, and major use cases are defined. The user interface design is well defined. Some object classes may be designed and coded, but design is incomplete.

    5 – Complete written requirements and specifications have been captured, with all use cases, object classes, and dynamic behavior defined. You may have a running prototype or demo.

15. **Need for process compliance and ceremony.** You may have a specific process in mind for developing your software product. How well defined is your methodology? Do you have specific steps and milestones defined? Do you expect to have a formal process (high ceremony) for document, code, and product reviews?

1 – No compliance with a specific methodology is required. Little or no ceremony is required during development. Comparable to CMMI level 1.

2 – Some software development methodology is required, and you may rely on the development team to define it.

3 – A specific software methodology is required, but the development team has influence over the process. Minimal ceremony is required for development steps. Comparable to CMMI level 2 or 3.

4 – You require a well-defined methodology for developing your software, with some ceremony in the QA and release process at least.

5 – You have a well-defined methodology for developing your software, with strict compliance required. Can include day-to-day compliance with code walk-throughs and coding standards as well as QA and release procedures. Comparable to CMMI level 4 or 5.

16. **Team size.** How many engineers do you need to hire to develop your software?

1 – Small team of 1 to 5 engineers.

2 – Small team of 1 to 5 growing to medium team of 10 to 20 engineers.

3 – Medium team of 10 to 30 engineers.

4 – Large team of 20 to 50 engineers.

5 – Large and growing team of 30 to 100+ engineers.

17. **Project type.** The type of software development project you have can influence your outsourcing strategy. Here are five project types; the order is not meaningful.

1 – New software development.

2 – Maintenance of existing software

3 – Enhancements to existing software

4 – Testing and QA of existing software

5 – Hardware/software development

The matrix will use your weights and scores to compute a total ranking for each software development strategy. A summary of the results are presented on a separate sheet so you can see how the scores for each strategy compare. There are also separate sheets for each strategy where you can see a detailed analysis of how your criteria scores affect the rankings of each strategy.

The matrix is a guide to help you consider and evaluate all the criteria important to making your decision. It is a tool, and in the end your decision on how to develop your software is still yours.

Appendix B

The Outsourcing Readiness Test

The questions and multiple choice answers of the Outsourcing Readiness Test are below. You can make your selections and add up your score manually. Here is how to interpret your score:

1 to 20   You desperately need help. Your outsourcing will fail unless you make several improvements and get help

21 to 40   Your outsourcing is likely to fail with out help

41 to 60   You have a chance of success on your own but could use help in a few critical areas

61 to 80   You are doing well and could use help in just a couple of places

81 to 100   Congratulations! You are an outsourcing expert.

The Outsourcing Readiness Test is also available on the Software without Borders web site where your score is automatically computed. Here is the URL:

www.SoftwareWithoutBordersBook.com/readinessTest.php3

It takes only a few minutes to complete and your score may surprise you. When you provide your name and email address you will receive a complete analysis of your test results showing the outsourcing risks you face. The analysis will also help you discover the areas of outsourcing knowledge you should improve before you outsource your software development.

Good luck!

Your Outsourcing Experience

#	Question	1	2	3	4	5
1	Have you outsourced software development before?	No	Know Someone Else That Has	Once	Several Times	Expert
2	Was your past outsourcing successful (zero if never outsourced)?	Disaster	Poor	OK	Pretty Good	Fantastic
3	How do you plan to select an outsourcing team?	Not Sure	A Friend	Trusted Referral	Careful Evaluation	Previous Vendor
4	How experienced is your outsourcing manager?	Limited	Junior U.S. Software Manager	Senior U.S. Software Manager	Some Outsourcing Experience	Extensive Outsourcing Experience
5	How comfortable are you working with engineers from another culture?	Concerned About It	Not Sure	OK with It	Worked with Foreign Engineers in U.S.	Already Out-Sourcing

Your Technology

#	Question	1	2	3	4	5
6	Do you have use cases for your software?	Not Needed	What's a Use Case?	Some	Most	All
7	What is your software development methodology?	Not Needed	Not Sure	Waterfall	Rational	Agile
8	How will you manage your source code?	Don't Know	Copying Files	Source Code Control System	Source Code Hosted in U.S.	Well Defined Process & Control
9	Do you know what technology your software needs (Java, .NET, etc.)?	Not Sure	Outsource Team Will Specify	Outsource Team WIll Confirm	Pretty Sure	Completely Specified
10	Are you outsourcing to gain technical expertise not available on your current engineering team?	Not Sure	Yes	Some	Yes, But Well Known	No

Your Business Situation	1	2	3	4	5
11 What contract terms do you require?	Don't Know	Will Rely on Vendor	Will Use An Attorney	Have An Old Contract	Have Model Agreements
12 How much are you concerned about the protection of your intellectual property (IP)?	Concerned & Not Sure What To Do	Some Concern	Can Keep IP Safe	Can Separate Critical IP	Not An Issue for Your Software
13 What is your understanding of the costs of your outsourcing?	Don't Know	Need a Quote	Have Cost Estimate	Have an Estimated Budget	Have a Realistic Budget
14 Does your organization fully support outsourcing?	Don't know	Some Resistance	Have Executive Buy-In	Most Support It	Support at All Levels
15 Do you have a plan for multiple releases of your software?	Not Yet	1 Release After 4+ Months	Outsource Team Will Plan	Releases Expected, Not Yet Planned	Release Plan Complete

Your Management Approach

	1	2	3	4	5
16 Will your existing engineering team and the outsourced engineers work on the same code?	Not Sure	Yes	Small Changes	Small Changes & Bug Fixes	No
17 Does your outsourced project need a larger team of engineers than you have used before?	Much larger	Larger	Same Size	Smaller	Much Smaller
18 How will you measure the quality of your outsourced software?	Don't Know	Manually Tested	Test Plans & QA Team Defined	Out-sourcing QA	Automated Test Process
19 Do you need to re-purpose your existing engineering team?	Entirely	Half	A Few	No	Hiring More
20 What metrics will you use for your outsourcing?	Not Sure	Don't Need Metrics	Schedule Milestones	Schedule & Quality Goals	Productivity, Throughput, Return Rate

Avoiding the Seven Deadly Dangers of Outsourcing

Thousands of people have downloaded the content of this Appendix as a free report on the Accelerance web site www.Accelerance.com. It is included in the book as an excellent summary of the do's and don'ts of outsourcing your software development.

⚠ Danger # 1—You Ignore Outsourcing

Ignoring outsourcing is not a realistic strategy. You and I both know that outsourcing is not going away anytime soon. The use of outsourcing is growing rapidly. But here are some reasons why people choose to ignore outsourcing.

- **You don't know how to select an outsourced team**. It's tough to select a team—there are many, many teams out there, and choosing the right one is a challenge.
- **You think only a big project is worth the time and trouble.** You may think that you can just hire a few engineers for your project. But as you will see shortly, this can really add up and bust your budget.
- **You believe that all of your software must be developed "in-house" to get the best results.** Sometimes this is true. But why do you believe that you *have* to develop your code in-house? Is it fear of the unknown due to a lack of experience with outsourcing?

- **You overlook the slow ramp-up to build your employee team.** How long does it take you to hire a team of engineers? Two or three months? That's a long time to wait until you start to write your software.
- **You overlook the high burn rate to support your employee team.** Salaries are one thing. Then there is the cost of benefits, offices, computers, and so on. Recruitment costs, benefits, and overhead can easily add 30 to 50 percent or more to employee salaries.

Here are some numbers. Suppose you have a team of 20 engineers developing your software over a period of a year, working as paid employees in your offices. As shown in Figure C-1, the difference in a year's cost between in-house development (at a rate of $64 per hour that includes benefits and overhead) and offshore outsourcing (at a relatively high $32 per hour) is about $1 million. You are spending at least a million dollars more than if the engineers were offshore! As you can see, deciding to outsource, *or not*, is truly a million dollar decision.

The savings of offshore outsourcing are too large to ignore. The cost of outsourcing is 25 to 50 percent of what it costs to develop software in-house. So the question is not whether you should outsource but rather how you can make outsourcing work for you and your company.

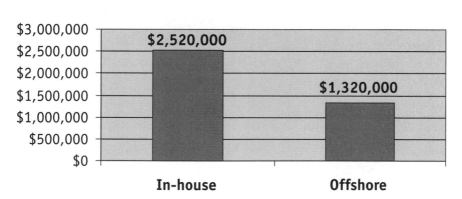

Figure C-1. Cost of 20 Programmers for One Year

⭐ Risk-Free Strategy #1: Make Your Optimum Outsourcing Decision

- **Consider all your options.** Choose the best of the six software development strategies for you.
  — **In-house.** Don't outsource. In some cases, in-house development is the best approach because of IP protection and other reasons, despite the higher cost.
  — **In-house/outsourced blend** of both in-house and outsourced development teams working on the same code base.
  — **Onshore outsourcing** to a software development company here in the U.S.
  — **Offshore outsourcing.** By far the most popular choice of American companies is to choose contract outsourcing to an offshore team in another country.
  — **Offshore subsidiary.** Jump in with both feet and commit to creating an offshore subsidiary right from the start.
  — **Offshore build-operate-transfer (BOT)** gives you the option of creating a subsidiary and transferring the team into the subsidiary after a year or two of contract outsourcing.
- **Use an analytical, objective tool** to help evaluate the business and technical issues of your situation.

"OK," you say, "I am convinced. I will start outsourcing right away!" But hold on. What about all those nightmare stories we hear about slipped schedules, wrong features, bugs, and stolen intellectual property? Why would anybody outsource if it is so risky!? What about the remaining six deadly dangers? Let's look at how to overcome each one.

⚠ Danger # 2: You Hire the Wrong Outsourcing Vendor

Considering only your friend's roommate's brother in Bangalore or his cousin in Kiev is unlikely to produce the "A" team that best matches your software development needs. It is a common, and very human, mistake to look only among your immediate circle for resources. Similarly, being pressured into hiring the colleagues or friends of your investors puts the ease of creating a relationship ahead of the hard work of finding the best match for your project.

But it can take months to find and evaluate outsourced teams. That's why many companies avoid outsourcing to begin with. Here are some of the dangers encountered in selecting an outsourced team when you do it yourself.

- **You don't diligently check multiple references before hiring.** When a recommendation is made by someone you know and respect, additional reference checks seem superfluous or even insulting.
- **You scrutinize only the firm, not the individual developers assigned to your project.** Your outsourced development work will be done by a team of developers. The makeup of the team and the strength of each individual will affect the quality and time-to-market of your software.
- **You hire a team that is not dedicated to your project.** You're supplementing your workforce with an outsourced team to speed up the development process, not slow it down or confuse it. An outsourced team that is overextended with other contracts, or that is developing its own products, will not be able to deliver. In addition, a team working on its own product may, knowingly or unknowingly, threaten the security of your intellectual property. Will your IP end up in their product? Will their IP end up in yours?
- **You don't use a pilot project.** Experienced business people know that, when embarking on any new business process, it is prudent to start with a small independent pilot to decrease the overall risk and the impact on your ultimate project.

⭐ Risk-Free Strategy #2: Hire the Right Vendor

- **Carefully check references** with other North American clients or English-speaking clients elsewhere. You should have at least two positive references and no negative ones.
- **Hire only a team** that has a stable core of expert engineers. It is okay for them to hire a few new programmers to expand your team, but the new hires should not exceed 40 percent of the team, as a guideline. Critical questions you should ask include, Are there junior members of the team who will get

on-the-job training on your project? Is there frequent turnover, requiring someone (you?) to bring new members up to
speed? Do the team members have the specific skills and experience to quickly deliver your software? Have the members
worked together as a team before with outstanding results for
other clients?

- **Hire a team with several senior members** to guide and
  shepherd the development of your software.
- **Look for a team with experience** developing software
  similar to what you need.
- **Ensure that there is a core group on the team** that is
  focused exclusively on your software.
- **Consider running a pilot project** for 3 to 6 weeks to confirm that you are selecting a team that works well and meets
  your needs. A pilot allows a safe trial and a chance to move
  up the learning curve over a reasonable time period while
  minimizing risk. You can make and learn from small mistakes
  rather than large ones.
- **Use a prime contractor,** to save time, money, and the hassle
  of selecting your outsourced team on your own, and to manage the process of developing the outsourced software. A
  prime contractor with connections to multiple outsourced
  teams can cut the time and cost of your selection process by
  as much as 90 percent.

⚠ Danger # 3: You Are Promiscuous with Your Intellectual Property

The dangers of not emphasizing and protecting your unique intellectual property are multiplied when you are working with outsourced vendors. Here are some specific mistakes that put your IP
in danger.

- **You put off developing and communicating IP protection policies and procedures** with your in-house team. It
  is one of those pesky procedural things that are often overlooked in the race to bring software to market. Setting up
  an outsourced project often highlights the lack of internal
  procedures for protecting your IP. Do your employees know

what a trade secret is? Do they understand the value of your patent-pending software code and business processes? Do you have rules for who has access to key information and who shares what information with whom?

- **You are careless with employee nondisclosure agreements (NDAs).** Among all the other priorities in the rush of software development, NDAs are often forgotten or may even be considered an insult by core team members. Having employees sign an NDA not only provides legal protection for the idea, it reminds them that the secret information of your company, belongs to your company.
- **You have an outsourcing vendor that uses** computers with removable media that could be used to create unauthorized copies of your software and IP.
- **You use an outsourcing vendor that transmits your source code** in clear text over the Internet.
- **You have no** written agreement with your outsourcing vendor. No nondisclosure agreements. No copyright assignments. No document that clearly states who does what and when payments should be made. This puts your IP at severe risk. If you are creating a software product and you ever want to sell your company, there will be no trail of ownership, no clear title to the software that is the basis of your company value.
- **You have an agreement, but** you don't know if your vendor has the proper agreements with its employees. An employee who created your source could potentially leave and legally take your source code as his or her own creation!
- **You have critical IP in your source code,** but you don't divide or architect your software to isolate the most sensitive IP.
- **You use open-source software in your software without understanding license restrictions** both for use and geography. This may cause future legal problems with the ownership and sublicensing of your code and may impede your ability to reach global markets.
- **You assume your IP is safe** because your outsourcing vendor is in a particular country. Assuming that a vendor is honest, without proper reference checks, can lead to disaster.

Risk-Free Strategy #3:
Protect Your Intellectual Property

- **Hire an outsourced team** that is proactive about protecting your IP. They must be committed to fierce protection of your IP as a normal part of their service offering. Review their established procedures for the protection of client IP.
- **Make sure you have physical protection.** You probably have some sort of physical security for your computers, servers, and source code. Make sure your outsourced vendor has the same. The computers should be in a locked room, with card-key access.
- **Make sure you have electronic protection.** Basic firewall, VPN, and encryption technology is widely available to protect electronic assets like source code and electronic documents. Make sure both you and the outsourced vendor use them.
- **Architect your software for outsourcing.** When you outsource, keeping your sensitive IP isolated is key to ensuring your right to market your creative ideas worldwide. Dividing development of critical components between your in-house and outsourced team (or among multiple outsourced teams) allows you to accelerate your development safely.
- **Make sure you have secure legal protection**—patents, trademarks, and copyrights—at least in the U.S. and the country of your vendor. For full protection, you should register for IP protection in all the countries you intend to sell into, as the EU and other countries all have their own rules and requirements. No one entering into a business relationship ever wants a dispute to go to court. Having a clearly stated agreement helps avoid disagreements later and helps you avoid the expense of legal resolution of disputes.
- **Use a prime contractor,** based in the U.S., to follow through on every step of your outsourcing process and to ensure that your IP is protected to the maximum extent possible.
- **Make sure you have the proper licenses** for any IP the outsourced vendor incorporates into your software. Software products are available now to automatically examine your source code and report on open-source elements being used.

- **Sign an agreement with your outsourcing vendor** that covers the important points of IP ownership, copyright assignment, and nondisclosure of your source code and IP.
- **Get frequent updates** of your source code, or place the source code repository in your control so that your software cannot be held hostage if there is a dispute.

⚠ Danger # 4: You Don't Know What Your Software Should Do

You lack specifications for the software, making it impossible to predict when it will be completed. Programmers hate to write specifications. Yet having good requirements and specifications are key to successful software development, whether you outsource or not.

And don't forget about your hardware and performance requirements. Don't get caught by the old "Didn't I tell you it has to run on a Macintosh?" problem.

- **You code a detailed prototype instead of writing a specification.** This rarely results in robust software that solves your users' problems, because you get caught up in the minutia of making the software work. You lose the bigger picture, in which you understand what your software should do to solve the problems of your users.
- **You believe software cannot be specified ahead of time,** because writing software is a creative and innovative process. Then you hire an outsourced team anyway and hope for the best.
- **You believe every detail of your software must be specified before outsourcing can be used.** You think you must hand off a completely defined and encapsulated project to the outsourced team. While this removes the risk of implementation delays, it delays the start of coding. It also does nothing to accommodate changes.
- **You believe outsourced engineers are drones** who cannot make any creative contributions to your software development. You ignore the valuable design and development advice available from experienced outsourced software development teams.

- **You don't think through what should be developed in-house** and what should be outsourced. Your software should be architected for outsourcing, so that core development can be completed internally and the rest can be safely outsourced.
- **You don't specify performance requirements or provide software use information.** Do you know how many users your software needs to support? Or how long users should have to wait to complete important operations? Do you provide details of low-level algorithms but forget to explain how your customers will use your software? If so, there is not enough information to support outsourcing.
- **You don't specify all the hardware and systems** that must be supported. Expecting the outsourcing firm to guess what you're thinking sets the project up to fail.

Risk-Free Strategy #4:
Be Clear about What Your Software Should Do

- **Move from idea to software** with a reasonable specification that captures the correct level of detail needed to develop the software effectively. Otherwise you get lost in low-level coding issues instead of focusing on the needs of the customer. A clear software development plan is essential for successful outsourced software development. A complete plan specifying features, functions, and performance allows any qualified software engineering team to create your software.
- **Clearly define your hardware platform requirements** to use outsourcing effectively.
- **Focus on defining the major use cases of your software.** Define how exceptions will be handled in situations when you can anticipate what the exceptions will be. It is important for your software to respond gracefully with incorrect inputs and when errors occur.
- **Provide a high-level description** of the classes and objects you think are needed to implement your software. The additional details do not need to be specified initially, as they will become known as development proceeds.
- **Don't waste time by over-specifying your software** to levels of detail showing how it should be implemented. Stay

at the higher level of defining how your software will be used. The right outsourcing team will have expertise in your technology and/or market area and will provide outstanding contributions to enhance your software.

- **Provide as much definition of the user interfaces as you can.** Be prepared to edit the wording and grammar in user interface elements created by an offshore team, if English is their second language.
- **Many firms use** outsourced teams with an agile approach where just enough requirements are provided to get coding started. This is described further in Risk-Free Strategy #6.
- **Use a prime contractor,** and expert at designing software to help you prepare the proper level of specification required to make effective use of outsourcing.

Time and Money Spent Onshore and Offshore, with and without a Specification: A Comparison

Some people think it is a waste of time to write a specification. They would rather just use an in-house programming team and start coding to create the product as quickly as possible. The theory is that a specification is not necessary because informal and direct communication should be sufficient when programmers work in close proximity with customers or a product manager. Here is an analysis that shows how this approach not only takes longer but is also more expensive, whether you outsource or not.

Let's look at four scenarios, all using a single in-house product manager and five programmers that are either in-house or offshore. The first scenario produces a software release in 3 months of pure programming effort without a specification. The cost of the product manager and each programmer is $10,500 per month, which includes salary, benefits, and overhead.

The second scenario uses outsourcing with five programmers working offshore, also without a specification. This scenario is estimated to take an extra half month because of increased communication required. But each programmer costs only $5,500 per month, reducing the overall cost by 30 percent from development done in-house.

The third and fourth scenarios have a U.S.-based product manager spending a month gathering requirements and writing a specification before programming begins. Because there is a clear specification,

Table C-1. Cost of Software Development
With and Without Specifications

	Spec Months	Coding Months	Product Manager	Engineers	Total Cost	Savings
In-house no spec	0	3	$31,500	$157,500	$189,500	—
Outsource no spec	0	3.5	$36,750	$ 96,250	$133,000	30%
In-house with spec	1	2	$31,500	$105,000	$136,500	28%
Outsource with spec	1	2.5	$36,750	$ 68,750	$105,500	44%

coding is estimated to take only 2 months with in-house programmers. An extra half month is allocated for additional communication
when the offshore programmers are used in the fourth scenario.

Clearly, using a specification to direct your programming efforts
will reduce the overall cost of creating your software. Offshore outsourcing is an additional cost saver, even when extra time is added
and a U.S.-based product manager is used to guide the process to
success.

⚠ Danger # 5: You Use Meager Engineering Management

Unfortunately, you cannot completely rely on an offshore team to
manage your software development. You can outsource the development but not the responsibility. After all, it is *your* software. They
will do their best to meet commitments to schedules and to provide
a high level of quality. But in the end, it will be *your* users trying
to use the software. Here are how some companies go astray with
outsourcing management.

- **You hire a programmer to manage software development.** This is a disservice to the programmer and to the team
  being managed. Management and programming are entirely
  different disciplines, requiring different training and expertise. Being good at one has no relationship to being good
  at another. The net result is an unhappy programmer and a
  frustrated outsourced development team.

- **You leverage a scientist or CTO to manage software development.** This is worse than hiring a programmer for the role. The programmer may actually contribute to the release of the software. Scientists and CTOs often have a "timeless" quality about them, which can lead to delays or even to a lack of schedules to begin with.
- **You use an incompetent manager to manage development,** which delays the project and frustrates the team. It is critical that the project manager be able to make and keep commitments and ensure that others keep theirs.
- **You assign a person with limited technical knowledge** to manage software development. This leads to serious misunderstandings. The manager may be easily fooled by engineers, if he or she is unqualified to evaluate technical issues that arise.
- **You don't give engineering management the appropriate authority** to manage and approve work done by the outsourced vendor. This will lead to delays in completing the project.

Risk-Free Strategy #5: Use Effective Engineering Management

- **If a scientist or subject matter expert is required** to provide innovations for your software, have someone work with that person to translate the innovation into software specifications that can then be implemented.
- **Your engineering manager must be goal driven** and focused on releasing the software on time, rather than being focused on the technology.
- **Use a core technical team** with enough people to manage the various areas of technical detail of your software. They take responsibility for proper functionality and timely release of your software
- **Provide effective supervision** to track scheduled milestones and releases.
- **Have a member of the offshore team** work from your offices. This can be at the beginning, for short durations, or for the entire length of your project.

- **Outsource your project management to local resources** that are experienced with outsourcing. They work closely with you on-site when needed.
- **Use a prime contractor,** to monitor the performance of your outsourced team and keep your outsourced software development on track.

⚠ Danger # 6: You Use a Mediocre Software Development Methodology

How do you go about the process of developing software? Do you create an excruciatingly detailed spec and then micromanage? Do you pile up the features for a single stupendous major release? And do you insist that the offshore team cram all those features into the software by next Tuesday? If so, you have a mediocre software development methodology.

Do you assume that "no news is good news" if you have not heard from your offshore team? Do you strictly adhere to the strategy "You code, I'll design"? Do you not bother with QA until later? Do you not have a standard software release procedure or source code control system? If so, you have a mediocre software development methodology. Here are the dangerous details.

- **You outsource without a schedule of software release milestones,** leading to confusion and delays.
- **You dictate a schedule of software release milestones** to your outsourced team. Even if they cannot meet the schedule, they will probably say yes anyway. If the outsourced team's commitment seems too good to be true, it probably is. It is just a commitment to say what you want to hear.
- **You have just one major software release,** containing all the features. This creates a huge risk that keeps you holding your breath until the final release. It also keeps you from making the inevitable improvements and changes to requirements that come up during your software development.
- **You communicate only infrequently with the outsourced team,** because you assume things are going okay. As with your in-house team, if you don't ask, they're likely not to tell.
- **You make a strong (and artificial) distinction** between the people who specify the software and those who develop

it. This leads to a lack of teamwork and a breakdown in communication.

- **You rely on the heroic efforts of individuals to release your software on time.** This could create a disaster if a critical hero is unavailable or unwilling to deliver the extra effort required.
- **You don't require unit testing of software modules** by your outsourced team, and delays in your software release occur because changes to imperfect modules affect subsequent modules.
- **You don't have a source code control system,** and you have more than one programmer, leading to confusion, errors, and delays.
- **You don't use coding standards** or require engineers to document their source code. This creates issues for both in-house and outsourced developers.

Risk-Free Strategy #6: Implement an Effective Software Development Methodology

- **Employ tools like UML and "use cases"** to define the structure and behavior of your software. These time-tested tools are a good way to describe what your software will do and help define the milestones of functionality to be reached during development.
- **Involve the outsourced team in the design of your software.** You don't have time to completely design and specify the software. Sketch out the basic requirements and take advantage of the experience and skill of your outsourced team. They can help you get to a final design much more quickly and cheaply than you could on your own. And they learn the details of your software in the process.
- **Let the outsourced team make an estimate** of the development effort. If the estimate is reasonable, have them commit to achieving it. Hold them accountable if the release date is not met. Accountability may take the form of a scolding and possibly withholding payment until the release is complete. Continued poor performance should lead to replacing the ineffective outsourced team.

- **Have an acceptance test** that your software must pass before new code can be released as part of your software.
- **Use appropriate standards** and require documentation of your source code as it is written to facilitate a quick ramp-up by new engineers and employees. This is essential in a dynamic world where code development is frequently collaborative and shared.
- **To monitor progress, have frequent software builds** and release milestones, with a clear definition of the features and fixes targeted for each. It is better to have an intermediate release with new functionality that will not be shipped to customers than it is to wait twice as long for complete functionality that is incorrectly implemented or too complex to test effectively.
- **Communicate frequently.** This is essential to keep your development programs on track. Use a regularly scheduled online or phone conference to review status, or require written status reports at least weekly.
- **Consider using agile development methods** to help get your software development started quickly, and keep your development on track with frequent builds and releases. Use a prime contractor that is expert in agile development methods to help guide your outsourced software development.

⚠ Danger # 7: Your Quality Assurance Is an Afterthought

QA is a critical part of the software development process. It is also a major concern when you outsource to programmers that are far away. Here are some dangerous mistakes companies make when they outsource that lead to poor quality.

- **You use no bug tracking system** to keep track of defects, issues, and enhancement requests. You are constantly tripping over bugs, and known bugs are reported repeatedly. A lack of process for fixing the bugs affects your overall software quality.
- **You don't specify the release criteria for your software** and create unclear expectations for the final release. The lack of these criteria may lead to misunderstandings of contract requirements and ultimately unsatisfactory releases of your software.

- **You wait to start testing until just before you release your software** and rush an unacceptable product out the door. You let your customers or users find the bugs. These user experiences create negative word of mouth and press coverage that can doom a project, product, and company.
- **You think QA is what happens when users get your beta release.** This does not create goodwill. User expectations for quality "out of the box" are increasing over time. Your reputation is damaged by bad betas.
- **You think unit testing by your outsourced team is sufficient.** No integration testing lets bugs and unusable software get shipped, causing bad user experiences.
- **You wait until automated testing can be implemented** to test your software. Then you find a huge number of bugs, causing extensive rework and delays in the release of your software.
- **You don't invest in enough computers to create a sufficient test and QA environment,** which has a negative impact on overall quality and the performance of your software.
- **You don't test to verify load and performance requirements,** and as a result your software does not meet the performance and capacity specifications required to honor user expectations. Customers may like your features and functions, but they may find that your software does not work in "real world" situations.

Risk-Free Strategy #7: Build in Quality Assurance

- **Specify your defect tracking system,** your bug prioritization process, and the release metrics you plan to use with your outsourcing team.
- **Confirm that your outsourced team** will do unit testing to find low-level defects during development.
- **Create an acceptance test** that your outsourced developers must run and pass before releasing software to you.
- **Use automated testing tools to create regression tests and test for performance and load-dependent bugs.** Use some amount of manual testing until your user interface becomes stable. The earlier a problem is caught, the less impact

it will have on the remaining code being developed. A strong foundation is essential for high-quality software.

- **Consider outsourcing to a second team** to provide QA expertise and low-cost manual testing resources if needed.
- **Use alpha and beta tests of your software** with customers and prospects to verify useful and beneficial functionality (not as a way of finding bugs). This keeps your customers in the loop and shows them you are responsive to their needs.
- **Use QA engineers to test your code on a variety of machines,** in a mix of scenarios and workloads, to ensure a good customer experience.
- **Use a prime contractor** that is expert in software development and QA to coordinate the overall software development process. A prime contractor can help you use a second outsourced team dedicated to QA.

Bibliography

References are ordered by chapter in which they were cited or used. All references in the bibliography are available as links on the book web site, www.SoftwareWithoutBordersBook.com.

Introduction

Deloitte Consulting. "Calling a Change in the Outsourcing Market: The Realities for the World's Largest Organizations." April 2005.
http://www.deloitte.com/dtt/cda/doc/content/us_outsourcing_callingachange.pdf.

Chapter 1 Deciding to Outsource

Hagel, John, III, and John Seeley Brown. *The Only Sustainable Edge: Why Business Strategy Depends on Productive Friction and Dynamic Specialization*. Boston: Harvard Business School Press, 2005.

Malone, Thomas W. *The Future of Work: How the New Order of Business Will Shape Your Organization, Your Management Style, and Your Life*. Boston: Harvard Business School Press, 2004.

Moore, Geoffrey A. *Crossing the Chasm: Marketing and Selling High-Tech Products to Mainstream Customers*. New York: HarperBusiness, 1999.

Reuters. "Survey: Outsourcing Saves Less Than Claimed." April 13, 2006, *ZDNet*.
http://news.zdnet.com/2100-9597_22-6060771.html.

Chapter 2 Where to Outsource

Aon. "2006 Political & Economic Risk Map."
http://www.aon.com/about/publications/issues/political_risk_map.jsp.

A.T. Kearney. "United States Among Top Locations for 'Offshore' Work, According to A.T. Kearney's Annual Global Services Location Index." News release, November 22, 2005.
http://www.atkearney.com/main.taf?p=1,5,1,168.

Baker & McKenzie Webinars, "Global Sourcing—Destination the World" series. Baker & McKenzie.
http://www.bakernet.com/BakerNet/Resources/Webinars/default.htm.

Bennett, James C. *The Anglosphere Challenge: Why the English-Speaking Nations Will Lead the Way in the Twenty-First Century.* Lanham, MD: Rowman & Littlefield, 2004.

BRASSCOM. Brazilian Association of Software and Services Export Companies.
http://www.brasscom.com.br.

Bulgarian Foreign Investment Agency (BFIA). "Bulgaria: Country Profile."
http://www.priv.government.bg/ap/bg/05/pic/2000/country_profile2.pdf.

Clissold, Tim. *Mr. China: A Memoir.* New York: HarperBusiness, 2005.

Czech ICT Alliance. Czech Trade.
www.czechict.cz.

CzechTrade, National Trade Promotion Agency of the Ministry of Industry and Trade of the Czech Republic.
http://www.czechtradeoffices.com/Global.

Deloitte Consulting. "Calling a Change in the Outsourcing Market: The Realities for the World's Largest Organizations." April 2005.
http://www.deloitte.com/dtt/cda/doc/content/us_outsourcing_callingachange.pdf.

Fishman, Ted C. *China, Inc.: How the Rise of the Next Superpower Challenges America and the World.* New York: Scribner, 2005.

Gryga, Vitalii. "Legislation Background of Technoparks Activity in Ukraine." Paper presented at 4S & EASST Conference, Paris, August 2004.
http://www.csi.ensmp.fr/WebCSI/4S/search/search_P/search_P.php.

Horowitz, Alan. "Brazil: It's a Sleeping Giant with a Tradition of High-Quality Software." September 15, 2003. Computerworld, Inc.
http://www.computerworld.com/managementtopics/outsourcing/story/0,10801,84869,00.html.

Hungarian Investment and Trade Development Agency. ITD Hungary.
www.itdh.hu.

International Intellectual Property Alliance (IIPA).
http://www.iipa.com/.

Mangi, Naween A. "Pakistan: Better Late Than Never In Outsourcing." *Business Week online*. May 9, 2005.
http://www.businessweek.com/magazine/content/05_19/b3932079.htm.

Mantcheva, Gergana. "MENSA Stance on Bulgarian IQ." Radio Bulgaria, April 7, 2006.
http://www.bnr.bg/RadioBulgaria/Emission_English/Theme_Bulgaria_And_The_World/Material/mensa.htm.

Merriam-Webster. *Geography, Merriam-Webster's Atlas*.
http://www.m-w.com/maps/moremapsnyt.html.

Minevich, Mark, and Frank-Jürgen Richter. Global Outsourcing Report 2005, March 2005.
www.globalequations.com/global%20Outsourcing%20Report.pdf.

National Association of Software and Service Companies (NASSCOM). "Knowledge Professionals."
http://www.nasscom.org/artdisplay.asp?cat_id=952.

Pakistan Software Export Board (PSEB).
http://www.pseb.org.pk/.

Pakistan Software Houses Association (P@SHA).
http://www.pasha.org.pk/.

Polish Information and Foreign Investment Agency.
www.paiz.gov.pl.

Radkevitch, Ulad, and Natasha Starkell. "Ukraine: Will the Orange Revolution Boost the IT Outsourcing Industry?" *Outsourcing Journal,* October 2005.
http://www.outsourcing-journal.com/oct2005-ukraine.html.

Robins, Bill. "Bulgaria: Eastern Europe's Newest Hot Spot?" *Outsourcing Journal,* August 2005.
http://www.outsourcing-journal.com/aug2005-bulgaria.html.

Rosenthal, Beth Ellyn. "Nicaragua Wants to Become A Nearshore Hot Spot." *Outsourcing Journal, April 2005.*
http://www.outsourcing-journal.com/apr2005-nicaragua.html.

Silva, Marcio. "Brazil as an Outsourcing Destination." *Sourcingmag.com.*
http://www.sourcingmag.com/content/c060201a.asp.

Stephenson, Neal. *The Diamond Age*. New York: Bantam Books, 1995.

TechBA. Mexico–Silicon Valley Technology Business Accelerator.
http://www.techbasv.com/sv_eng/.

Thomas, Jeffrey. "United States Reinstates Trade Benefits for Ukraine." U.S.
Department of State, USINFO.
http://usinfo.state.gov/ei/Archive/2006/Jan/24-662230.html.

United States Department of State. "Consular Information Sheets." Bureau of
Consular Affairs.
http://travel.state.gov/travel/cis_pa_tw/cis/cis_1765.html.

United States Department of State. "Current Travel Warnings." Bureau of
Consular Affairs.
http://travel.state.gov/travel/cis_pa_tw/tw/tw_1764.html.

United States Department of State. "Travel Warning: Pakistan." April 7, 2006.
Bureau of Consular Affairs.
http://travel.state.gov/travel/cis_pa_tw/tw/tw_930.html.

United States Trade Representative (USTR). "2005 Special 301 Report." Office
of the United States Trade Representative.
http://www.ustr.gov/assets/Document_Library/Reports_
Publications/2005/2005_Special_301/asset_upload_file195_7636.pdf.

United States Trade Representative (USTR). "USTR Announces Continued
Review of Brazil GSP Benefits." April 4, 2005. Office of the United
States Trade Representative.
http://www.ustr.gov/Document_Library/Press_Releases/2005/March/USTR_
Announces_Continued_Review_of_Brazil_GSP_Benefits.html.

United States Trade Representative (USTR). "USTR Ends Review of Pakistan's
Protection of Intellectual Property Rights." January 24, 2006. Office of
the United States Trade Representative.
http://www.ustr.gov/Document_Library/Press_Releases/2006/January/USTR_
Ends_Review_of_Pakistans_Protection_of_Intellectual_Property_Rights.html.

USINFO. "Protecting Intellectual Property Rights." U.S. Department of State.
http://usinfo.state.gov/ei/economic_issues/intellectual_property.html.

Veillette, Connie. "Costa Rica: Background and U.S. Relations." CRS Report
for Congress. Federation of American Scientists.
http://www.fas.org/sgp/crs/row/RS21943.pdf.

Wilson, Dominic, and Roopa Purushothaman. "Dreaming with BRICs: The
Path to 2050." Goldman Sachs Global Economics Paper No. 99. The
Goldman Sachs Group.
http://www.gs.com/insight/research/reports/99.pdf.

World Information Technology and Services Alliance (WITSA).
    http://www.witsa.org/.

Chapter 3 How to Select Your Outsourcing Vendor

Armstrong, Thomas. *Seven Kinds of Smart: Identifying and Developing Your Multiple Intelligences*. Rev. ed. New York: Plume, 1999.

Corbett, Michael F. *The Outsourcing Revolution: Why It Makes Sense and How to Do It Right*. Chicago: Dearborn Trade, 2004.

Fischer, Tom, John Slater, Pete Stromquist, and Chaur G. Wu. *Professional Design Patterns in VB .NET: Building Adaptable Applications*. Berkeley, CA: Apress, 2003.

Freeman, Elisabeth, Eric Freeman, Bert Bates, and Kathy Sierra. *Head First Design Patterns*. Cambridge, MA: O'Reilly Media, 2004.

Gamma, Erich, Richard Helm, Ralph Johnson, and John Vlissides (a.k.a. the Gang of Four). *Design Patterns: Elements of Reusable Object-Oriented Software*. Boston: Addison-Wesley Professional, 1995.

Goleman, Daniel. Emotional Intelligence: *Why It Can Matter More Than IQ*. Reprint, New York: Bantam, 1997.

Kerry, John. Speech at Temple University, Philadelphia, Pennsylvania, September 24, 2004.
    http://www.nytimes.com/2004/09/24/politics/campaign/25TEXT-KERRY.html;
    http://www.vote-smart.org/speech_detail.php?speech_id=65417.

Metsker, Steven John. *Design Patterns C#*. Boston: Addison-Wesley Professional, 2004.

Chapter 4 Offshoring, or Creating Your Own Offshore Subsidiary

ACM International Collegiate Programming Contest.
    http://icpc.baylor.edu/past/default.htm.

Greguras, Fred M., and Liza Morgan. "2006 Update to Granting Stock Options in China." May 2, 2006. Fenwick and West LLC.
    http://www.fenwick.com/docstore/Publications/Corporate/Stock_Option_
    Grants_China.pdf.

Greguras, Fred M., S.R. Gopalan, and Steven S. Levine. "An Updated Guide to Establishing a Subsidiary in India." November 22, 2004. Fenwick and West LLC.
    http://www.fenwick.com/docstore/Publications/Corporate/Establishing_
    Subsidiary_in_India.pdf.

Kozaczuk,Wladyslaw, and Jerzy Straszak. *Enigma: How the Poles Broke the Nazi Code*. New York: Hippocrene Books, 2004.

Thurm, Scott. "Lesson in India: Not Every Job Translates Overseas." *Wall Street Journal*, March 3, 2004.

TopCoder.
http://www.topcoder.com/tc.

Chapter 5 Describing Your Software for Outsourcing

Beck, Kent. Extreme *Programming Explained: Embrace Change*. Boston: Addison-Wesley Professional, 1999.

Boehm, Barry W., Ellis Horowitz, Ray Madachy, Donald Reifer, Bradford K. Clark, Bert Steece, A. Winsor Brown, Sunita Chulani, and Chris Abts. *Software Cost Estimation with COCOMO II* (with CD-ROM). Upper Saddle River, NJ: Prentice Hall PTR, 2000.

Booch, Grady, James Rumbaugh, and Ivar Jacobson. *The Unified Modeling Language User Guide*, 2nd Edition. Boston: Addison-Wesley Professional, 2005.

Cockburn, Alistair. *Writing Effective Use Cases*. Boston: Addison-Wesley Professional, 2000.

Cohn, Mike. *User Stories Applied: For Agile Software Development*. Boston: Addison-Wesley Professional, 2004.

Hohmann, Luke. *Beyond Software Architecture: Creating and Sustaining Winning Solutions*. Boston: Addison-Wesley Professional, 2003.

Kovitz, Benjamin L. *Practical Software Requirements: A Manual of Content and Style*. Greenwich, CT: Manning Publications, 1998.

Robertson, Suzanne, and James Robertson. *Mastering the Requirements Process*. 2nd ed. Boston: Addison-Wesley Professional, 2006.

Royce, Winston W., "Managing the Development of Large Software Systems." *Proceedings of the 9th International Conference on Software Engineering*. Monterey, CA. Los Alamitos, CA: IEEE Computer Society Press, 1987. Reprinted from Proceedings, IEEE WESCON, August, 1970. http://www.cs.umd.edu/class/spring2003/cmsc838p/Process/waterfall.pdf.

Watson, Mark. *Understanding UML: The Developer's Guide*. San Francisco: Morgan Kaufmann, 1997.

Wiegers, Karl. E. Software Requirements. 2nd ed. Redmond, WA: Microsoft Press, 2003.

Wikipedia. "Waterfall Model." http://en.wikipedia.org/wiki/Waterfall_model.

Chapter 6 Controlling Your Outsourced Software Development

Ambler, Scott W. *Agile Modeling: Effective Practices for Extreme Programming and the Unified Process.* New York: Wiley, 2002.

Carnegie Mellon University, Software Engineering Institute. "Capability Maturity Model® for Software (SW-CMM®)." CMU.
http://www.sei.cmu.edu/cmm/.

Carnegie Mellon University, Software Engineering Institute. "Getting Started with CMMI® Adoption." CMU.
http://www.sei.cmu.edu/cmmi/adoption/cmmi-start.html.

Martin, Robert C. *Agile Software Development: Principles, Patterns, and Practices.* Upper Saddle River, NJ: Prentice Hall, 2002.

Object Mentor, Inc., and Advanced Development Methods. "Best Practices in Scrum Management and XP Agile Software Development." Control Chaos.
http://www.controlchaos.com/download/Primavera%20White%20Paper.pdf.

Paulk, M., B. Curtis, M. Chrissis, and C. Weber. "Capability Maturity Model for Software (Version 1.1)." Carnegie Mellon University, Software Engineering Institute.
http://www.sei.cmu.edu/publications/documents/93.reports/93.tr.024.html.

Poppendieck, Mary, and Tom Poppendieck. *Lean Software Development: An Agile Toolkit for Software Development Managers.* Boston: Addison-Wesley Professional, 2003.

Schuh, Peter. *Integrating Agile Development in the Real World.* Hingham, MA: Charles River Media, 2004.

Schwaber, Ken, and Mike Beedle. *Agile Software Development with Scrum.* Upper Saddle River, NJ: Prentice Hall, 2001.

Simons, Matthew. *Distributed Agile Development and the Death of Distance.* Cutter Consortium Executive Report, Vol. 5, No. 4, April 2004.

Sutherland, Jeff, Anton Victorov, and Jack Blount. "Distributed Scrum: Agile Project Management with Outsourced Development." Scrum Alliance.
http://scrumalliance.org/index.
php/scrum_alliance/for_everyone/resources/scrum_articles.

Chapter 7 Software Outsourcing Metrics

Arveson, Paul. "What is the Balanced Scorecard?" Balanced Scorecard Institute.
http://www.balancedscorecard.org/basics/bsc1.html.

Barnett, Liz. *Metrics for Application Development*. Forrester Research, Inc., May 2, 2005.

Card David N., and Cheryl L. Jones. "Status Report: Practical Software Measurement." November 2003. Practical Software and Systems Management. http://www.psmsc.com/Downloads/Other/StatusReportPracticalSoftwareMeasurement.pdf.

Card, David, and Robert MacIver. "Applying PSM To Enterprise Measurement." March 2003. Practical Software and Systems Management. http://www.psmsc.com/Downloads/Other/ApplyingPSMtoEnterpriseMeasurement-byDaveCard.pdf.

Kaplan, Robert S., and David P. Norton. *The Balanced Scorecard: Translating Strategy into Action*. Boston: Harvard Business School Press, 1996.

McGarry, John, David Card, Cheryl Jones, Beth Layman, Elizabeth Clark, Joseph Dean, and Fred Hall. *Practical Software Measurement: Objective Information for Decision Makers*. Boston: Addison-Wesley Professional, 2001.

Niven Paul R. *Balanced Scorecard Step-by-Step: Maximizing Performance and Maintaining Results*. Hoboken, NJ: Wiley, 2002.

Putnam, Lawrence H, and Ware Myers. *Five Core Metrics: The Intelligence Behind Successful Software Management*. New York: Dorset House, 2003.

Chapter 8 Protecting Your Intellectual Property

Black Duck Software, Inc.
http://www.blackducksoftware.com/.

Creative Commons.
http://creativecommons.org/.

Free Software Foundation (FSF).
http://www.fsf.org/.

Golden, Bernard. *Succeeding with Open Source*. Boston: Addison-Wesley Professional, 2004.

Open Source Initiative (OSI).
http://www.opensource.org/.

Palamida, Inc.
http://www.palamida.com/.

Raymond, Eric S. *The Cathedral and the Bazaar: Musings on Linux and Open Source by an Accidental Revolutionary*. Cambridge, MA: O'Reilly Media, 2001.

St. Laurent, Andrew M. *Understanding Open Source and Free Software Licensing*. Cambridge, MA: O'Reilly Media, 2004.

United States Copyright Office. "Copyright Registration for Computer Programs." Circular 61, revised December 2004.
http://www.copyright.gov/circs/circ61.html.

United States Copyright Office. "Information Circulars and Fact Sheets."
http://www.copyright.gov/circs/index.html.

United States Copyright Office. "Works Made for Hire Under the 1976 Copyright Act." Circular 9.
http://www.copyright.gov/circs/circ09.pdf.

Chapter 9 Outsourcing Your Quality Assurance

Cockburn, Alistair. *Agile Software Development*. Boston: Addison-Wesley Professional, 2001.

Cohen, Frank. *Java Testing and Design: From Unit Testing to Automated Web Tests*. Upper Saddle River, NJ: Prentice Hall PTR, 2004.

Chapter 10 Five Situations Right for Outsourcing

Blank, Steven Gary. *The Four Steps to the Epiphany: Successful Strategies for Products That Win*. Foster City, CA: Cafepress.com, 2005.

Ganssle, Jack. "The Trouble with the Embedded Tools Business." *Embedded.com*, April 15, 2004.
http://www.embedded.com/showArticle.jhtml?articleID=18901700.

Garrett, Jesse James. "Ajax: A New Approach to Web Applications." February 18, 2005. Adaptive Path, LLC.
http://www.adaptivepath.com/publications/essays/archives/000385.php.

Noergaard, Tammy. *Embedded Systems Architecture: A Comprehensive Guide for Engineers and Programmers*. Boston: Elsevier/Newnes, 2005.

O'Reilly, Tim. "What Is Web 2.0?: Design Patterns and Business Models for the Next Generation of Software." September 30, 2005. O'Reilly Media, Inc.
http://www.oreillynet.com/pub/a/oreilly/tim/news/2005/09/30/what-is-web-20.html.

Smith, Preston G., and Donald G. Reinertsen. *Developing Products in Half the Time: New Rules, New Tools*. 2nd ed. New York: John Wiley and Sons, 1997.

Chapter 11 The Future of Global Software Development

Abbott, Edwin A. *Flatland: A Romance of Many Dimensions.* New York: Dover, 1992.

Bhagwati, Jagdish. *In Defense of Globalization.* New York: Oxford University, 2004.

Friedman, Thomas. "For Workers 'The World is Flat': Interview with Thomas Friedman." By Terry Gross. *Fresh Air,* National Public Radio, April 14, 2005.
http://www.npr.org/templates/story/story.php?storyId=4600258.

Friedman, Thomas L. *The World Is Flat: A Brief History of the Twenty-First Century.* New York: Farrar, Straus and Giroux, 2005.

Mahajan, Vijay, and Kamini Banga. The 86 Percent Solution: How to Succeed in the Biggest Market Opportunity of the Next 50 Years. Upper Saddle River, NJ: Wharton School, 2005.

McKinsey Global Institute. *The Emerging Global Labor Market.* June 2005. McKinsey & Co.
http://www.mckinsey.com/mgi/publications/emerginggloballabormarket/.

Index

Page numbers followed by "t" indicate tables; those followed by "f" indicate figures; and those followed by "n" indicate footnotes.

A

I

IBM, 54, 55, 67, 108, 143
IDEs, *See* interactive development
  environments
IEEE Standard for Application and
  Management of the Systems
  Engineering Process (IEEE Std
  1220-1998), 137
IEEE/ANSI Guide to Software
  Requirements Specifications
  (ANSI/IEEE Std 830-1984), 137
In Search of Excellence (Peters), viii
independent contractors, 94
independent verification and
  validation (IVV), 203
India
  Bangalore, 34, 107
  in BRIC, 63
  cultural considerations, 36–37,
    100
  future trends, 221
  Hyderabad, 107
  number of suitable engineers,
    225t
  overview, 33–37, 107
  as Tier 1 market, 229
information technology (IT)
    services
  Belarus, 53
  Bulgaria, 54
  Canada, 44
  Chile, 65
  China, 38
  Czech Republic, 52
  Eastern Europe, 108
  governance and portfolio
    management, 147, 152–153
  India, 33
  Malaysia, 50
  outsourcing along with business
    processes, 10, 33

Pakistan, 66
Philippines, 46
problem-solving contests, 108
Romania, 55
Russia, 41, 42
selecting vendors, 226–227
Singapore, 50
supply of engineers, 226
Turkey, 69
Ukraine, 56
Vietnam, 48
Infosys, 232
in-house software development
  blending with offshore options,
    22–23, 235t
  cost comparisons, 251, 251f,
    259–260, 260t
  description, 19–21, 235t
  intellectual property risk and,
    181, 182t
  pros and cons, 20t
  quality assurance, 204
  sample decision matrix, 18t
innovation
  completing prior to outsourcing,
    12
  difficulty assessing, 171, 178
  difficulty finding vendors for,
    35–36, 47, 49, 60, 107
  Eastern European engineers, 57
  formal versus informal processes,
    157
  innovators and early adopters, 4,
    8, 101
  open-source projects and, 192
  risk taking and, 234
  Russian engineers, 42
  translating into software
    specifications, 261
instruction set architecture (ISA),
    214
integration testing, 13, 265